Janet McCabe is Research Associate (TV Drama) at Manchester Metropolitan University; and Kim Akass, along with McCabe, has co-edited and contributed to *Reading* Sex and the City (2004), *Reading* Six Feet Under: *TV to Die For* (2005) and *Reading* The L Word: *Outing Contemporary Television* (2006), all published by I.B.Tauris. Both are series editors of Tauris's Reading Contemporary Television series.

Reading Contemporary Television

Series Editors: Kim Akass and Janet McCabe
janetandkim@hotmail.com

The *Reading Contemporary Television* series aims to offer a varied, intellectually groundbreaking and often polemical response to what is happening in television today. This series is distinct in that it sets out to immediately comment upon the TV *Zeitgeist* while providing an intellectual and creative platform for thinking differently and ingeniously writing about contemporary television culture. The books in the series seek to establish a critical space where new voices are heard and fresh perspectives offered. Innovation is encouraged and intellectual curiosity demanded.

Published and Forthcoming:
Contemporary Quality TV: American Television and Beyond
edited by Janet McCabe and Kim Akass
Reading **CSI**: *Crime TV Under the Microscope* edited by Mike Allen
Reading **Deadwood**: *A Western to Swear by* edited by David Lavery
Reading **Desperate Housewives**: *Beyond the White Picket Fence*
edited by Janet McCabe and Kim Akass
Makeover Television: Realities Remodelled edited by Dana Heller
Reading **Nip/Tuck** edited by Roz Kaveney and Jennifer Stoy
Reading **Sex and the City** edited by Kim Akass and Janet McCabe
Reading **Six Feet Under**: *TV to Die for*
edited by Kim Akass and Janet McCabe
Reading **The L Word**: *Lesbians on TV*
edited by Kim Akass and Janet McCabe
with an Introduction by Sarah Warn
Reading **The Sopranos**: *Hit TV from HBO* edited by David Lavery
Reading **24**: *Television Against the Clock* edited by Steven Peacock
Third Wave Feminism and Television: Jane Puts it in a Box
edited by Merri Lisa Johnson

Reading *Desperate Housewives*

We dedicate this book to desperate housewives everywhere.

Reading
Desperate Housewives

Beyond the White Picket Fence

Edited by
Janet McCabe & **Kim Akass**

I.B. TAURIS

LONDON · NEW YORK

Published in 2006 by I.B.Tauris & Co Ltd
6 Salem Road, London W2 4BU
175 Fifth Avenue, New York NY 10010
www.ibtauris.com

In the United States and Canada distributed by Palgrave Macmillan, a
division of St. Martin's Press, 175 Fifth Avenue, New York NY 10010

ISBN 10: 1 84511 220 2
ISBN 13: 978 1 84511 220 2

A full CIP record for this book is available from the British Library
A full CIP record for this book is available from the Library of Congress
Library of Congress catalog card: available

Typeset in Caslon by Dexter Haven Associates Ltd, London
Printed and bound in Great Britain by TJ International Ltd, Padstow,
Cornwall

CONTENTS

ACKNOWLEDGEMENTS

The editors would first like to thank the contributors to this collection – David Lavery, Rosalind Coward, Ashley Sayeau, Samuel A. Chambers, Niall Richardson, Kristian T. Kahn, Brian Singleton, Sharon Sharp, Judith Lancioni, Sherryl Wilson, Anna Marie Bautista, Deborah Jermyn, Sherianne Shuler, M. Chad McBride, Erika L. Kirby, Stacy Gillis, Melanie Waters, Jennifer L. Pozner and Jessica Seigel. Their wonderful, thought-provoking and fascinating work, and their ability to adhere to the tight deadlines with grace, humour and a real generosity of spirit, are very much appreciated by both of us. Additional thanks to Pozner and Seigel for allowing us to reprint their dialogue.

Special thanks go, as usual, to Philippa Brewster, for a relationship that is creative, endlessly supportive and inspirational in ways difficult to articulate. Thanks also to Isabella Steer, who continues to liaise so efficiently between Tauris and Palgrave/ St. Martins, as well as all those at I.B.Tauris such as Deborah Susman and Andrea Lobo, who have helped this project on its way to completion. Thanks to ABC for providing the cover image, Coral Pettreti for clearing copyright, and Scarlet Scardanelli for the apple design. And we thank Gretchen Ladish and Robert Hastings at Dexter Haven for project-managing so efficiently.

We would like to acknowledge the Billy Rose Theater Collection at the New York Public Library for Performing Arts. Special thanks go to Eydie Wiggins, as ever.

Janet McCabe would like to thank the British Academy for awarding her a grant to travel and research in New York.

Deep gratitude also goes to our husbands – Mike Allen and Jon Akass – for their ceaseless support and endless patience so that we could disappear for weeks on end to think harder and write better together. Thanks also to Daryl and Caitlin, with love; and to Olivia, who gestated along with this anthology.

CONTRIBUTORS

KIM AKASS has co-edited and contributed to *Reading Sex and the City* (I.B. Tauris, 2004), *Reading Six Feet Under: TV to Die For* (I.B. Tauris, 2005) and *Reading The L Word: Outing Contemporary Television* (I.B. Tauris, 2006). She is currently researching representations of motherhood on American TV and is a founding editor of the new television journal *Critical Studies in Television* (MUP) as well as (with McCabe) series editor of Reading Contemporary Television for I.B. Tauris.

ANNA MARIE BAUTISTA is Lecturer in Media, Communications and Cultural Studies at the School of Professional and Continuing Education at the University of Hong Kong. Her teaching and research interests include various aspects of film and popular culture studies, particularly in representations of gender.

SAMUEL A. CHAMBERS is Lecturer in Politics at Swansea University. Along with his book *Untimely Politics* (Edinburgh University Press, 2003) he has published more than a dozen journal articles on a wide range of topics. He is currently working on two books on the political theory of Judith Butler, and a third book titled *The Queer Politics of Television*.

ROSALIND COWARD is Professor of Journalism at Roehampton University. She has worked for many years as a journalist, writing regular columns for *The Guardian*, *The Observer* and *The Ecologist* magazine as well as writing features for numerous other papers and magazines, including the *Evening Standard* and *Cosmopolitan*. She is the author of several books, including *Language and Materialism: Development in Semiology and the Theory of the Subject* (with John

Ellis) (Routledge, 1977), *The Whole Truth: The Myth of Alternative Health* (Faber and Faber, 1990), *Our Treacherous Hearts: Why Women Let Men Get Their Way* (Faber and Faber, 1993), *Female Desire: Women's Sexuality Today* (HarperCollins, 1996) and *Sacred Cows: Is Feminism Relevant to the New Millennium?* (HarperCollins, 1999), and has held several academic posts.

STACY GILLIS is Lecturer in Modern and Contemporary Literature at the University of Newcastle. The co-editor of *Third Wave Feminism* (Palgrave, 2004) and editor of *The Matrix Trilogy* (Wallflower, 2005), she has published widely on third-wave feminism, (post-)feminism and cyber theory. Current work includes a monograph on early British detective fiction and work with Rebecca Munford on feminism and contemporary popular culture.

DEBORAH JERMYN is Senior Lecturer in Film and TV at Roehampton University. She has co-edited *The Audience Studies Reader* (with Will Brooker) (Routledge, 2002), *The Cinema of Kathryn Bigelow: Hollywood Transgressor* (with Sean Redmond) (Wallflower, 2002) and *Understanding Reality TV* (with Su Holmes) (Routledge, 2003). She has published widely on women, feminism and popular culture, and is the author of *Crime Watching: Investigating Real Crime TV* (I.B. Tauris, 2006).

KRISTIAN T. KAHN is a doctoral research student in English and Comparative Literary Studies at the University of Warwick. His research focus is on psychoanalysis, cultural productions of homosexuality and queer theory. He has published on feminist revisionary mythology in the poetics of Plath, Bogan and Sarton; in addition he is the author of three poetry chapbooks, with work having appeared in *The Cortland Review, The Pedestal Magazine, Rattle* and many others.

ERIKA L. KIRBY is Associate Professor and Chair of Communication Studies and Director of Women's and Gender Studies at Creighton University. Her teaching and research interests include organisational, applied and work–family/life communication and discourses as well as their intersections with gender and feminism. She has published articles in outlets such as the *Journal of Applied Communication Research*, *Management Communication Quarterly* and *Communication Yearbook*. She lives in Omaha, Nebraska, with husband Bob and daughters Meredith and Samantha.

JUDITH LANCIONI is Associate Professor in the Department of Radio, Television and Film at Rowan University in Glassboro, New Jersey. She teaches film and television theory and criticism, feminist film criticism and television scriptwriting. She has published articles on the ideological implications of Ken Burns's framing of archival photographs in *The Civil War*, the ethics of reality television, especially *Survivor*, and adaptation of the Cinderella myth in *Billy Elliot*. Currently she is extending her research on reality television, especially dating and makeover shows.

DAVID LAVERY holds a chair in Film and Television at Brunel University, London. He is the author of over one hundred published essays and reviews, and author/editor/co-editor of eleven books, including *Reading Deadwood: A Western to Swear By* (I.B. Tauris, 2006) and *Reading The Sopranos: Hit TV from HBO* (I.B. Tauris, 2006) in the Reading Contemporary Television series. He co-edits the e-journal *Slayage: The Online International Journal of Buffy Studies*, and is a founding editor of the new journal *Critical Studies in Television* (MUP).

M. CHAD MCBRIDE is Assistant Professor in the Department of Communication Studies at Creighton University. He studies communication and identity management within personal relationships and social networks (including families) as well as mediated communication about relationships, and teaches courses in inter-personal, family, small group and gender communication. He has published in outlets such as *Journal of Social and Personal Relationships*, *Journal of Family Communication*, *Communication Studies*, *Communication Reports* and *Handbook of Conflict Communication*.

JANET MCCABE is Research Associate (TV Drama) at Manchester Metropolitan University. She is author of *Feminist Film Studies: Writing the Woman into Cinema* (Wallflower, 2004), and is co-editor and contributor to *Reading Sex and the City* (I.B. Tauris, 2004), *Reading Six Feet Under: TV To Die For* (I.B. Tauris, 2005) and *Reading The L Word: Outing Contemporary Television* (I.B. Tauris, 2006). She is managing editor of the new television journal *Critical Studies in Television* (MUP) as well as (with Akass) series editor of Reading Contemporary Television for I.B. Tauris.

JENNIFER L. POZNER is media critic and journalist, and founder and director of Women In Media & News, a women's media analysis, education and advocacy organisation. Through WIMN, she lectures regularly on representations of women in news and entertainment media, facilitates media training to give women the skills and strategies they need to challenge media bias and improve content, and works with journalists to help them connect with a diverse national network of women experts through the POWER (Perspectives Of Women Expand Reporting) Sources Project. Her work has appeared in *Ms.*, *Newsday*, *Chicago Tribune*, *Bitch: Feminist Response to Pop Culture*, AlterNet.org, and a variety of anthologies about women, media, politics and popular culture. She has offered commentary on *ABC News Now*, Comedy Central's *Daily Show with Jon Stewart*, *Fox News*, *The O'Reilly Factor*, National Public Radio, Pacifica Radio and numerous documentary projects. Learn more, and read a women's media monitoring group blog with fifty writers, at www.WIMNonline.org.

NIALL RICHARDSON teaches media and cultural studies at the University of Sunderland. His research interests include queer theory and the representation of gender and sexuality in film and popular culture. He has published academic articles in the journals *Paragraph*, *Social Semiotics*, *Scope: International Journal of Film Studies*, *Sexualities*, *Journal of Popular Culture* and *Feminist Media Studies*.

ASHLEY SAYEAU has written on popular culture, politics and women's issues for a variety of publications, including *The Nation*, *Salon*, *Dissent*, *The Boston Globe* and *The Philadelphia Inquirer*. Her work has also been included in multiple anthologies, including *Reading Sex and the*

City (I.B. Tauris, 2004) and *Reading Six Feet Under: TV to Die For* (I.B. Tauris, 2005), both edited by Akass and McCabe, as well as *The W Effect: Bush's War on Women*, edited by Laura Flanders (The Feminist Press, 2004). She is currently working on a 'cultural autobiography'. Visit her website at: www.ashleysayeau.com.

JESSICA SEIGEL regularly contributes to the *New York Times* and National Public Radio, and her articles have appeared in the *Los Angeles Times*, *Salon*, *Time Out New York*, *The Village Voice* and the *Washington Post*. Featured on *Good Morning America* and Fox TV, her hard-hitting coverage of women's issues has been recognised with the prestigious Front Page Award for a *Lifetime Magazine* investigation of the fashion industry. She also won the National Society of Journalists and Authors 'Outstanding Article' prize for a *Los Angeles Magazine* exposé of diet fraud. Working from Los Angeles and New York, she also covered media and celebrity as a *Buzz Magazine* contributing editor and *Brill's Content* senior writer. An editor and consultant for magazines ranging from *Folio* to *Archaeology*, she teaches graduate and undergraduate journalism at New York University. She also serves New York as an auxiliary mounted NYC Parks Department officer, patrolling Central Park on horseback.

SHARON SHARP is a doctoral research student in the Department of Film, Television and Digital Media at the University of California, Los Angeles. She is currently completing a dissertation entitled 'Yesterday Now: Television, Nostalgia, and the Mediation of the American Past'.

SHERIANNE SHULER is Assistant Professor in the Department of Communication Studies at Creighton University. She studies communication and gender within organisational contexts, with a special interest in emotion in the workplace and mediated representations of working women. Her research has been published in several book chapters and in journals such as *American Communication Journal*, *Management Communication Quarterly* and *Review of Communication*. She also teaches courses related to organisational communication and gender. She and her husband, Nathan, are both hoping to avoid desperate housewife status as they prepare for the arrival of their first baby, Lucy.

BRIAN SINGLETON is Head of the School of Drama at Trinity College Dublin. He is Vice-President for Publications of the International Federation for Theatre Research and co-editor of the Palgrave series Studies in International Performance. He has written two books on the life and work of Antonin Artaud and a monograph on Orientalism and British Musical Comedy, and is a contributor to *Reading Six Feet Under: TV to Die For* (I.B. Tauris, 2005).

MELANIE WATERS is a doctoral research student based in the School of English at the University of Newcastle. Her thesis aims to resituate the writing of Anne Sexton in relation to American political history and recent critical theory. Among her major research interests are feminist, poststructuralist and psychoanalytic theory, contemporary American women's poetry and popular culture. Aside from her PhD, she is currently preparing articles on the (feminist) politics of contemporary pornography, and the representation of domestic space in *Buffy the Vampire Slayer*.

SHERRYL WILSON is Senior Lecturer in Media Theory at the University of Gloucestershire. Her interests include the cult of celebrity, reality TV and popular culture. She is author of *Oprah, Celebrity and Formations of Self* (Palgrave Macmillan, 2003), and has published on *Trisha* and *Six Feet Under*.

CAST LIST

Betty Applewhite	Alfre Woodard
Caleb Applewhite	Page Kennedy
Matthew Applewhite	Mehcad Brooks
Edie Britt	Nicollette Sheridan
Mike Delfino	James Denton
Martha Huber	Christine Estabrook
Julie Mayer	Andrea Bowen
Karl Mayer	Richard Burgi
Susan Mayer	Teri Hatcher
John Rowland	Jesse Metcalfe
Lynette Scavo	Felicity Huffman
Parker Scavo	Zane Huett
Penny Scavo	Dylan and Jordan Cline
Porter Scavo	Shane Kinsman

Preston Scavo	Brent Kinsman
Tom Scavo	Doug Savant
Carlos Solis	Ricardo Antonio Chavira
Gabrielle Solis	Eva Longoria
Juanita ('Mama') Solis	Lupé Ontiveros
Felicia Tilman	Harriet Sansom Harris
Andrew Van de Kamp	Shawn Pyfrom
Bree Van de Kamp	Marcia Cross
Danielle Van de Kamp	Joy Lauren
Rex Van de Kamp	Steven Culp
George Williams	Roger Bart
Mary Alice Young	Brenda Strong
Paul Young	Mark Moses
Zach Young	Cody Kasch

Introduction

Airing the dirty laundry

Janet McCabe and Kim Akass

Desperately seeking... housewives

Before *Desperate Housewives* first aired in the UK, audiences were already anticipating a series pitched 'as desperate viewing for... women seeking a new *Sex and the City*' (Wittstock 2004: 7). Months had passed since Carrie Bradshaw had taken off her Manolos for the last time, and we were indeed the desperate viewers described in Melinda Wittstock's feature. The anticipation for ABC's new series about four women living in an affluent suburban cul-de-sac gathered momentum amidst reports of a backlash from sections of right-wing America and descriptions of the show as being too racy for prime-time television. We just couldn't wait. But when the series arrived on British screens in January 2004 we soon realised that *Sex and the City* it was not. It was a confusing experience. Social satire or trashy soap opera, ironic camp or damning indictment; beguiling and reactionary, peculiarly compelling and absolutely horrifying. The retro-cool, Lynchian overtones, bleakly comedic, anti-, pre- or post-feminist feel to it; we could not be sure what to make of this new American import. But nonetheless we were hooked.

This collection grew out of a need to make sense of initial reactions to *Desperate Housewives*, and to understand why a seemingly harmless, darkly comedic soap opera should prove an instant ratings winner – and immediately stir up controversy. Only on air for a few weeks and it was already a pop culture phenomenon. Critics initially struggled to understand why this show had caught the public imagination in quite the way it did. Some pondered why a show that was so trashy and sudsy was so delicious (Wittstock 2004: 7), why a show that is at root 'a soap opera, more like the daytime variety than the usual prime-time type', should be so compelling (Holston 2004: C22). Daring to be different from the average hour-long network drama (Blum 2004a: 19) and an inventive script format (Martel 2005: E7) were cited as other reasons for its success. Others thought that at a time when 'unscripted, though heavily manipulated, "reality" shows appeared to be on the verge of taking over prime time' (Holston 2004: C22) was the reason why *Desperate Housewives* stood out. As show's creator and executive producer Marc Cherry says, 'The audience is really thirsting for something new' (Weinraub 2004: B7).

This diverting hour of entertainment clocked up an American audience of 22.3 million when it first aired on 3 October 2004, and went on to average 21.6 million, according to the Nielsen Media Research. First Lady Laura Bush confessed to being a huge fan, and the *Oprah* show did a special called 'Wisteria Hysteria' featuring a 10-minute spoof starring Oprah Winfrey, playing new neighbour Karen Stouffer, alongside regular cast members (Weintraub 2005). The series was sold to most major international television markets and created a cottage industry of websites. It made instant stars out of the little-known cast (the exception being Teri Hatcher, already known for her eponymous role in *Lois & Clark: The New Adventures of Superman* – but it did rejuvenate her flagging career). The ladies of Wisteria Lane were the focus of scandal and an incessant rumour mill, featured on the cover of glossy magazines, fodder for newspaper column inches, fronting high-profile advertising campaigns, and guest-starring on daytime TV and radio talk shows. When the awards season came around Hatcher picked up a Golden Globe for Best Actress, and the show won The People's Choice Award and the Golden Globe for Best TV Series. *Desperate Housewives* without doubt became one of the watercooler shows of the 2004–2005 season.

The quirky premise is the sudden death of a seemingly happy suburban housewife, Mary Alice Young, who commits suicide after 'quietly polishing the routine of [her] life until it gleamed to perfection' (1: 1). Thereafter she becomes the show's omniscient narrator, commenting in dulcet tones each week on the trials and tribulations of her neighbours on Wisteria Lane. Focus of her posthumous attention is her small circle of girlfriends: Susan Mayer, a single-parent divorcee still looking for love; Lynette Scavo, a woman who gave up a high-profile career to raise her three unruly boys and baby girl; Bree Van de Kamp, a domestic goddess devoted to making a perfect home while driving her husband and teenage children demented in the process; and Gabrielle Solis, an ex-model who left the catwalk to marry money and enjoys an illicit affair with her teenage gardener, John Rowland. New to the area is Mike Delfino, a plumber by trade who is recently widowed – or so he says. Vying for his attention alongside Susan is Edie Britt, serial divorcee, real estate agent, who men find attractive and women suspicious. Husbands, children and various neighbours complete the cast of a series where nothing is ever quite as it seems.

The show was the brainchild of Marc Cherry and inspired by something his mother Martha said. Watching the news coverage of the 2002 trial of Andrea Yates, the Texan woman found guilty of drowning her five children in a bathtub, with his mom, he was shocked by her reaction. Turning to her, he said: 'Gosh, can you imagine a woman so desperate that she would hurt her own children?' Removing the cigarette from her mouth she said, 'I've been there.' Cherry was taken aback. He had always seen his mom as the ideal wife and mother, who had wanted nothing more than to be a homemaker.

> That's what she wanted and that was her life. And it was shocking to find out that she indeed had moments of great desperation when my sisters and I were little and my dad was off getting a master's degree in Oklahoma and she was alone with three kids, 5, 4 and 3, who were just bouncing off the walls, and she was starting to lose it. She started telling me these stories. And I realized if my mother had moments like this, every woman who is in the suburban jungle has. And that's where I got the idea to write about four housewives (quoted in Weinraub 2004: B12).

And the concept was born for a series about women making the choice to live in the suburbs but finding the reality not as imagined.

Involvement in female-centred television shows has long been a feature of Cherry's career. He began as personal assistant to Dixie

Carter, the actress playing Julia Sugarbaker on *Designing Women*, and started writing for television in the late 1980s. Signed up as a writer for the final two seasons of *The Golden Girls*, he would later serve as creator and executive producer on the 1994 comedy series *The Five Mrs Buchanans* about a formidable mother and her four daughters-in-law.

However, by the time he came to write the *Desperate Housewives* script Cherry's career was already in the doldrums. He initially found it quite difficult to find a home for the project. Originally touted as a black comedy, it was sent out to every broadcast and cable network, and was unanimously declined. Cable channel HBO passed on the project because, while they liked the writing, they felt it was 'not gritty enough' (Weinraub 2004: B7). Conversely, the Fox network rejected it because they did not like the writing but liked the idea. Having to find new representation, as his agent had been jailed for embezzlement, Cherry went to Paradigm, who read the script, loved it and decided to change the focus to soap. Within days Susan Lyne and Lloyd Braun of ABC snapped it up. According to Steve McPherson, President of ABC Entertainment, the reason the channel commissioned it was because it was 'a point of view that [was] not on the air. It [was] incredibly fresh writing' (ibid.). *Desperate Housewives*, along with the other breakout hit the plane-crash survivor drama *Lost*, gave ABC 'something it [had] not experienced in half a decade: a ratings surge' (Carter 2004: C1).

Desperately seeking... ratings; aka moments of quiet desperation for ABC

The year 2004 appeared to herald a shift in power in American television. The increase of multichannel television – cable, satellite and digital channels – splintered even further an already fragmented audience; and the dominance of the networks seemed in decline. Spring, and ABC remained at the bottom of the network ratings chart. Mismanaging the early success of *Who Wants to be a Millionaire?* proved that 'the network... could do no right' (Goldsmith 2005). ABC had nothing to lose and decided to take a risk with the launch of *Desperate Housewives*. The gamble paid off and found the network increasing its market share by 17 per cent in the key 18–49-year-old demographic (Goldsmith 2005), '(about 11.3 million viewers)' (Carter 2004: C3). In a twist of fate but perfectly illustrative of the pressure to deliver hit programmes, the executive team, Lyne and Braun, who commissioned and initially developed the show (as well as *Lost*) had long departed, sacked by the Disney-ABC Television Group for not being able to save the network fast enough. Putting substantial funds into launching *Desperate Housewives* helped create a strong initial buzz among viewers. Credit for this went to McPherson and 'his ability to identify the shows that needed special marketing and scheduling them to advantage' (Carter 2004: C3).

Network television is notorious for playing it safe. Reliant on advertising dollars means that it must deliver the mass audience to sponsors and alienate the fewest people possible. Once a network has found a reliable hit the formula tends to get repeated. But no one could have predicted the phenomenal success of *Desperate Housewives*. At a time when networks were commissioning procedural dramas to cash in on the immense popularity of *CSI* and *Law and Order*, 'drama execs [have] made a U-turn and added a few more quirky female dramas' into the mix, 'hoping to capture some of what made [*Desperate*] *Housewives* so appealing' (Schneider 2004: 17). It is not too surprising then, as Kate Arthur reports, that among the pilots for the 2006 season are 'a host of new shows set in suspiciously similar alternative universes' (2005: 4). For example, at the time of writing, in pre-production is ABC's new series *Soccer Moms*, about two suburban housewives teaming up as private investigators; and this is to say nothing of the recent cable channel Showtime's hit with *Weeds*, a black comedy focusing on a suburban mother turned marijuana dealer.

With *Desperate Housewives* and *Lost*, ABC dominated the 2004–2005 Sunday night schedules in the prestigious 9–11pm prime-time slots. It took over from the premium pay-for-view cable channel HBO, which, by the late 1990s, had the reputation as the 'must-have channel for anyone who appreciated good television' (Blum 2004b: 18). But in recent times HBO has conceded ground, the reason being that it lost its big hitters. *Sex and the City* bowed out in March 2004, *Six Feet Under* was finally laid to rest in 2005, and *The Sopranos*, returned in spring 2006, will have no encore after January 2007, when the bonus eight episodes of the mob drama air. ABC took advantage of the gap left by these shows. But, as is always the case, other networks and broadcast companies learn the lessons from those who buck convention and find the lucrative audience.

Desperately seeking...the moral high ground

Network television may seem to be taking more creative risks. But can it really push the envelope in quite the same way as the cable companies? Programmes like *Desperate Housewives* are increasingly subject to charges of indecency at a time when the issue of values has insidiously seeped into the popular culture of a polarised America divided by religious and moral principles. George W. Bush's re-election in November 2004 politicised the cultural wars as never before. Galvanised by his victory, conservative watchdogs have stepped up their policing of the airwaves. Parents Television Council, for example, runs a website containing a pro forma easily filled out in seconds. Submitting the complaint to the PTC it is passed onto the Federal Communications Commission (FCC). Indecency complaints rose from 350 in 2001 to more than a million in 2004, illustrating how the 'values warriors' (Harris 2004: 25) have seized the agenda. Especially given that the PTC were responsible for 99.8 per cent of the complaints in 2003, with an even higher proportion in 2004: 'It means that a really tiny minority with a really focused political agenda is trying to censor American television and radio', claims Jonathan Rintels, President for Creative Voices in the Media (quoted in Glaister 2005).

Sex is the familiar battleground. And with its libidinous secrets it was not long before *Desperate Housewives* enraged family values campaigners. Jessica Anderson of Concerned Women for America describes the show as 'treating infidelity as comedy and sex as gratuitous' (2005). She adds that women are 'allowing themselves to be "attacked" by the toxic immorality *Desperate Housewives* glorifies' (ibid.). President of the PTC, Brent Bozell, condemns further the assault of the series on American morality. '*Desperate Housewives* really should have an even more obvious title, like Cynical Suburban Sluts. It's just the latest in a long series of shows that aims to pulverize the cartoonish 1950s black-and-white stereotype of *Leave It To Beaver*, creating in its ancient wake a catty, snarky, amoral cesspool' (2004). Fighting talk indeed. The PTC rallied tens of thousands of its supporters to target the show's sponsors with letters and emails requesting they withdraw their advertising from the show. Companies including Kelloggs, Yum! Brands (the corporation behind Pizza Hut, KFC and Taco Bell), Lowe's Home Improvement and Tyson Foods kowtowed to the pressure; Tyson, issuing the following statement, said the show was 'not consistent with our core values' (Logan 2004: 8). But ABC had little difficulty in replacing lost advertisers. Other companies quickly lined up to buy the recently vacated spots, and prices leapt from $160,000 to $300,000 for 30 seconds (Guthrie 2004).

Controversy continues to plague the show. No better example can be found than with the now infamous opening skit on ABC's *Monday Night Football*. The scripted introduction featured Edie Britt, clad only in a towel, flirting with Philadelphia Eagles receiver Terrell Owens in an empty locker room. Asking Owens to forgo the game, Edie gets no response until she drops her towel. Broadly smiling, Owens says, 'Ah hell, the team's going to have to win this one without me.' Edie leaps into his arms. Reports that angry viewers jammed ABC's switchboard were soon revealed as an exaggeration when it became clear that 112 viewers complained among an audience of 10 million (Kitman 2004: C19). However, the damage was done. The National Football League (NFL) immediately issued a statement distancing themselves from the stunt; the Philadelphia Eagles released a statement saying that they wished it had never been aired; and ABC apologised to its viewers, saying its promotion was 'inappropriate and unsuitable for our *Monday Night Football* audience' (Flint 2004: B1). Given the brouhaha surrounding Janet Jackson's 'wardrobe malfunction' at the 2004 NFL Super Bowl, when the FCC fined the 'CBS division of Viacom $550,000 or $27,500 against each of the stations owned and operated by CBS' (Battista 2004: D4), networks are understandably nervous.

What the controversy reveals is a tussle over values and who has the right to police the airwaves. Any struggle for domination, as Michel Foucault has said, can be both systematic and hidden. Reading the controversy there is an unceasing interaction between moral guardians, cultural commentators, broadcast companies, regulatory bodies and audiences, seeking to dominate and weaken each other. Contestation is not arbitrary but is instead a struggle of values involved, one that entails the right to intervene and justifies the right to do so. Family values campaigners may demand punitive action against transgressors, but the liberal press coverage is not so much about engaging with what the public moralists have to say as exposing attempts to hijack the debate. Frank Rich, reporting on the controversy kicked off by the *Monday Night Football* stunt, explains: 'There's another, more insidious game being played as well. The FCC and the family values crusaders alike are cooking their numbers' (2004: 17). The struggle over morals and values operates with a compelling sense of the right and obligation to set an agenda at a time when 'television watching habits [are being] politicised as never before' (Harris 2004: 25).

Notions of contradiction and contestation are key to this compilation about an American network series that has created more than its fair share of public hullabaloo. Contributors read *Desperate Housewives* from diverse critical and theoretical perspectives; and it is our aim to understand what this seemingly standard night-time soap opera with its glossy production values has to tell us about the American culture wars and the politics of television viewing, the current state of feminism and ideas of femininity, attitudes towards family and sexual politics as well as contemporary television culture in terms of generic conventions, and narrative and aesthetic forms. Each chapter will give reasons for why a particular critical approach has been taken, and no doubt readers will feel that there are omissions. But it is our desire to initiate discussion and stimulate debate. Our hope is that the dialogue generated here will begin to address the question of what exactly 'is *the risk* of creating a show chock-full of gorgeous actresses and sexual innuendo' (Blum 2004a: 19) (emphasis added).

Desperately seeking... a political (a)gender

David Lavery's contribution immediately situates *Desperate Housewives* within the American culture wars and a nation divided over values. His tele-parody focuses on a fictional transcript of a recording discovered some 25-years in the future in the Presidential Library of the 43rd President of the United States, George W. Bush. In his imagined commentary on a single episode, 'Pretty Little Picture', (1: 3) Bush gives his reaction to the women of Wisteria Lane. But the question posed by Lavery's imagined commentator is: why should Bush undertake such an enterprise? In the wake of 9/11 the actions of the Republican administration split further an already divided America. Unease over the continuing conflict in Iraq, Hurricane Katrina bringing to light racial schism and social injustice, and the divisive Harriet Miers nomination to the US Supreme Court revealed the state of play in American culture in 2005. *Desperate Housewives*, the only new series in that year to centre on women, comes out of this contested political landscape.

At a time when women are allegedly more empowered, more liberated than at any other time in our history, we seem as desperate as ever. Perception has it that second wave feminism achieved its goals and a feminist politics is no longer necessary. Such a view (however misguided) has been fed by a conservative media backlash since the 1980s (Faludi 1991; Douglas 1995; Williams 2000; Douglas and Michaels 2004). Writes Susan Faludi, a reactionary media has 'neutralised' feminism and 'powerfully [shaped] the way people … think and talk about the feminist legacy' (1991: 76, 77). In addition, and witnessed since the early 1990s, is the emergence of a generation 'taking for granted the feminist victories … and thus for whom feminism exists at the level of popular common sense' (Moseley and Read 2002: 238). These post-feminist ideas, popularised by Naomi Wolf (1993), Christina Hoff Sommers (1994) and Katie Roiphe (1995), contribute to individualistic and depoliticised portrayals of female power and victimisation. Being mired in political contradiction and mixed media messages, and told that the feminist project is over but still experiencing depoliticisation and the violence of the cultural backlash mark the current state of play. Marc Cherry's reasoning on *Desperate Housewives* as a 'post-post-feminist take' captures the deep ambivalence of the post-feminist age: 'The women's movement said "Let's get the gals out working." Next the women realised you can't have it all. Most of the time you have to make a choice. What I'm doing is having women make the choice to live in the suburbs, but that things aren't going well at all' (Weinraub 2004: B12).

'*Desperate Housewives* has prompted the latest round of hand-wringing talk about "what women really want"', says Melinda Wittstock

(2004: 7). Critics in the popular media are divided over what to make of the show's feminist credentials. Alessandra Stanley is perturbed at what she sees as a turning back of the clock to a 'pre-Betty Friedan America' (2004: E1). Discerning a distinctly anti-feminist mood pervading contemporary television she laments how strong and feisty characters like Murphy Brown and Roseanne have given way to the 'cute, flirty and married woman [doing] housework' (E24).

> Mary Tyler Moore and *All In the Family* notwithstanding, the backlash against the women's movement has lasted far longer than feminism did. Why it has resurfaced so sharply this season is hard to fathom; it surely cannot be just political correctness fatigue or the fallout from Hillary Rodham Clinton's ascendancy and Martha Stewart's disgrace (ibid.).

Bonnie Dow (1996) was one of the first to chart the representational changes in the post-feminist age, where she describes an obsession with female identities and lifestyle choice, and a gradual reduction in engagement with feminist politics. More recently, scholars such as Joanne Hollows (2000), and Rachel Moseley and Jacinda Read (2002) have understood post-feminist contradiction not only as about the competing discourses that define a 'have-it-all' feminism, but also use it as a strategy to analyse seemingly contradictory texts.

Desperately seeking... representation

Contradictory definitions of what we mean by contemporary feminism and femininity, profoundly shaped by 'struggles between various feminisms as well as by cultural backlash against feminism and activism' (Heywood and Drake 2003: 2), constitute a dilemma that Rosalind Coward, Ashley Sayeau and Kim Akass grapple with in their contributions in Part 1. Coward investigates how *Desperate Housewives* serves as another example of Zeitgeist television, charting the vicissitudes of the women's movement and its impact on women's lives, and how it has been represented on our television screens. Sayeau picks up on the disappointment of critics like Stanley in her discussion of what she calls the show's faux feminism. Her discomfort reflects a broader cultural ambivalence about the show's artistic pretensions and political stance.

Focusing on motherhood in America and its relation to *Desperate Housewives*, Akass argues for the impossibility of combining motherhood and career in corporate America. Despite feminist gains, old prejudices remain.

The contributors in Part 2 tackle the ideologies behind the sexual politics, to investigate what lurks beneath the glossy surface representation. Samuel A. Chambers argues that there is more to this seemingly straight heterosexual series than meets the eye. He suggests that *Desperate Housewives* mobilises a crucial subversion of mainstream sexual politics and heterosexual norms *from within*, to call into question mainstream American family values. Finding herself obsessed with Bree Van de Kamp, Janet McCabe develops similar ideas to muse on why such a character that appears to betray the feminist promise should fascinate in quite the way she does. Investigating Bree as living *mise en scène* within and beyond the text, she argues for the ways in which privileged images of feminine normalcy are disguised to *not* look oppressive, when in fact they perpetuate the regulatory fiction and practices disciplining femininity and the female body within our contemporary culture. Niall Richardson, too, is captivated with Bree, but takes an alternative approach to sexual politics and representation. He argues that the camp representation of Bree offers more than a moment of light comic relief and instead re-evaluates the politics of camp and its aesthetics to reclaim it for a post-feminist agenda.

Hardly anyone failed to mention that creator Marc Cherry is a gay Republican. This incredulity of someone whose sexuality is not approved of by many of the party that he supports has not gone unremarked. Kristian T. Kahn takes this paradox as the starting point for his analysis of the ways in which a cultural agenda defined by the Bush administration and conservative values provide the ideological framework behind *Desperate Housewives*. Focusing on how this impacts on the representation of homosexuality, Kahn argues that the issue is continually repressed in and by the text. In so doing *Desperate Housewives* reinforces and re*enforces* the conservative (heterosexist) ideology of the American right through the 'seemingly liberal' (sexual) transgressions acted out in the series.

Like *Sex and the City*, *Desperate Housewives* enacts a role reversal with women as subject and men left to foreground their own 'to-be-looked-at-ness'. Brian Singleton develops such a notion to argue that male to-be-looked-at-ness is caught in a perpetual cycle of female desire and disappointment. Hegemonic heterosexual masculinity is determined in the gaze of the women; and, while the ladies living on Wisteria Lane are continually disappointed in the men, they nevertheless persist in their desire of heterosexual masculinity only to perpetuate the fantasy promised by the spectacle of the male body.

Part 3 deals with genre, gender and cultural myths. Cherry claims he is 'taking soap opera back to its roots' (Weinraub 2004: B12). "'It's like the old days of women sitting around the kitchen table with a cup of coffee listening to the radio'" but "'we've put ... a new tonality, a new twist to the genre, a little dark, a little funny, all mixed together'" (ibid.). Contributors in this section come to terms with the show's blending of various generic forms and conventions – romantic comedy, suspense thriller, murder mystery, family drama, magic realism, soap opera – to understand how these features impact upon representational forms and sexual politics. Sharon Sharp leads with her study of television's latest fixation with the housewife and domesticity. Comparing domestic reality TV shows with *Desperate Housewives*, focusing in particular on Lynette Scavo and Bree, Sharp argues that the reality TV shows subvert the cardinal television rule that women should never express dissatisfaction with housewifery and motherhood. Even over-investment in the domestic space is seen as dysfunctional behaviour. What *Desperate Housewives* exposes, she argues, is what these shows desperately try to keep hidden, namely our culture's deep ambivalence and contradictory attitudes towards housewifery and the homemaker. Extending Jason Mittel's textual approach to genre analysis, Judith Lancioni contends that *Desperate Housewives* fuses the generic conventions of comedy and drama to convey the paradoxical relationship of feminism and patriarchy, and how this impacts upon the experience of modern American womanhood in the new millennium.

'We wanted a heightened reality with this series,' said Cherry. 'We said, if we're going to do it on the back lot let's create a certain look that matches the tone of the proceedings' (Sloane 2005: 91). The final two chapters of this section look beneath the glossy production surface only to reveal familiar cultural myths and traditional patriarchal fictions. Sherryl Wilson identifies narrative containment and spatial confinement as a means of understanding how comedy and post-modern nostalgia do not allow for new forms of female subjectivity but, instead, close down these possibilities. She contests that, while the series may critique patriarchal ideals of love and romance, the opportunity of breaking free from such narratives is curtailed by the female protagonists. Concluding this section is Anna Marie Bautista and her discussion of how *Desperate Housewives* subverts notions of domestic bliss exemplified by past media representations and cultural myths of the 'happy housewife'. She interrogates contemporary discourses on motherhood and domesticity, to argue for the subversive potential of Bree's embodiment of the happy housewife.

Part 4 of this collection deals with television narrative convention, female confession and modes of intimacy. Opening this section is Deborah Jermyn's examination of the female voiceover in *Desperate Housewives*. While the omniscient female narrator has in recent time become a staple of series like *Sex and the City*, shaping audience perception, Jermyn locates *Desperate Housewives'* omniscient narrator, Mary Alice Young, within a much longer (media) history of women's struggle with language, where their voices have too often been marginalised, discredited or silenced.

The *Desperate Housewives* women 'don't trust one another', argues Matthew Gilbert (2004). It is a bold statement but one that Sherianne Shuler, M. Chad McBride and Erika L. Kirby would agree with. Taking their own friendship as a starting point, the authors use communication theory to explore the intimacy between the female characters. Responding to a show touted as about the *Sex and the City* girls grown up and moved to the suburbs, they find the female friendships wanting – more reminiscent of the bitchiness of *Mean Girls* than the celebratory intimacy of Carrie Bradshaw and her friends. Developing further ideas about women's talk are Stacy Gillis and Melanie Waters, with their contribution on female confession as a commodity with an exchange value. Situating their argument within the convergent Cold War ideologies of containment and conformity, as well as the social and cultural anxieties emergent in the wake of 9/11, they discuss how nostalgia and confession are used to construct gender primarily in relation to motherhood. Bringing this section and the collection to a close is a reprint of the feminist dialogue between Jennifer L. Pozner and Jessica Seigel, which originally appeared in *Ms.* magazine in September 2005. Is the intimate girl talk the latest version of the feminist idea of the personal as political, or is *Desperate Housewives* just another example of feminist backlash and cultural sexism? The polemics of their discussion tap into broader cultural debates related to the contemporary state of feminism and women's liberation in the new millennium. Together, the pieces in the final section make a persuasive case for finding new ways of talking and writing about women's culture as a powerful site of activism.

How best to understand what has been labelled 'a prime-time soap bubbling with devilishly dark humour' (Malcolm 2004: 32) remains enthralling and puzzling, mesmerising and frustrating, in equal measure. No easy answers emerge. Only contradiction and ambiguity remain. Each chapter pursues new avenues for talking about the 'lived messiness' of *Desperate Housewives'* modern sensibilities and pre-feminist nostalgia, guilty pleasures and critical distance, nuanced characters and stagey stereotypes, frothy comedy and dark secrets. This collection offers a vibrant and diverse conversation as it struggles over meaning and the complications of contradiction in a provocative series that has cleaned up in the American ratings while continuing to divide (often polemically) its audience and the critics.

Part 1:

CULTURE

I

'W' stands for women, or is it Wisteria?: Watching
Desperate Housewives with Bush 43

David Lavery

My first week in college and I went to a meeting of the Young
Republicans where Rex gave a speech, and I went up to him
afterwards and introduced myself and told him that I agreed with
his stance on the death penalty, and he took me out to a diner and
we stayed up till two in the morning talking about big government,
gun control, and illegal immigration. It was such a magical night,
and I knew by the time he got me back to my dorm that one day I
was going to be Mrs Rex Van de Kamp.

Bree Van de Kamp (1: 11)

'Brie and cheese'.

George W. Bush, taunting a reporter who recently spent time
on the West Coast, Crawford, Texas, 23 August 2001

Introduction (November 2030)

– Michael Bianculli, media historian

The text you are about to read is a transcription of a recording only
recently discovered, 25-years after it was made, in the Presidential
Library of the 43rd President of the United States. While researching
a book on President Bush's largely adversarial relationship with the
media during his time in office (2001–2009), I came upon a recordable

17

DVD apparently being used as a bookmark (between pages 10 and 11) in a hardcover edition of a novel (Tom Wolfe's 2004 *I Am Charlotte Simmons*) left among President Bush's papers.[1] The recording, made sometime in October of 2005, is Bush's voiceover commentary on a single episode, 'Pretty Little Picture' (1: 3), of the television series *Desperate Housewives*, which ran on ABC from 2004 to 2009.

Desperate Housewives first aired in the United States in October 2004, towards the end of Bush's first term and one month before he would defeat John Kerry and be re-elected President of the United States. A breakout hit for then television doormat ABC, *Desperate Housewives* quickly became embroiled in the culture wars of the Bush presidency. A few advertisers were troubled by the series' sexy subject matter, and some viewers complained about the 15 November 2004 *Monday Night Football* cross-branding promo, in which the Philadelphia Eagles' African-American star receiver Terrell Owens chooses to abandon the upcoming game in order to pursue *Desperate Housewives'* towel-dropping (white) siren Nicollette Sheridan (Edie Britt on the show).

It is not possible to say definitively why President Bush would use his valuable time on such a seemingly frivolous endeavour, but several contemporary developments in 2005 may help us to understand his underlying motives.

•   Why was the President watching DVDs of *Desperate Housewives*? Nearly five months before the recording was made, at the White House Correspondents Dinner (held on 30 April 2005), an annual event which politicians routinely used as an occasion to be humorous, or at least as funny as their scripted speeches would allow, First Lady Laura Bush had given an intentionally tongue-in-cheek speech.[2] In one of its most infamous moments Mrs Bush would make a surprising reference to *Desperate Housewives*, one of the most popular and talked-about shows of the television season.

> I am married to the President of the United States, and here's our typical evening: Nine o'clock, Mr. Excitement here is sound asleep, and I'm watching *Desperate Housewives* – with Lynne Cheney.[3] Ladies and gentlemen, I am a desperate housewife. I mean, if those women on that show think they're desperate, they oughta be with George.[4]

Created by the openly gay, down-on-his-luck, career-seemingly-over writer Marc Cherry, *Desperate Housewives* was a satiric black comedy with an anything but conservative agenda, a series unlikely to be considered even a guilty pleasure by Republican women (or men).

Not everyone loved *Desperate Housewives*. Early in its first season *Salon.com* television critic Heather Havrilesky would pen the following rant against the show:

> Despite high ratings, this dark exploration of the lives of women has not only slid quickly into clichés, but the acting feels forced and overplayed, the stories are wildly unrealistic, the direction is stuck in some awkward nowhereland between campy and leaden, and the voice-over is so grating and so peskily imitative of *Sex and the City* that the whole package is almost unwatchable.
>
> What the hell? I'd rather watch inanimate objects sit on their shelves than see Teri Hatcher do another absurdly overacted scene, from the 'Oh dear, I've lost my towel and now I'm on the street naked!' to the 'Oh dear! My new imaginary boyfriend's dog just ate my earring!' Plus, who buys that Bree switches from mannequin to soul-searching human being and back, or that the nosey neighbor found a measuring cup in the ruins of one woman's house, and *knew that it was a clue to how the house burned down*? And what could possibly be interesting about that trunk the dead narrator's husband tried to dump in the lake? (2004)

Writing in *Slate* at the end of season one, Matt Feeney, dubious from the start of the series about both *Desperate Housewives'* tone (he finds Mary Alice Young's beyond-the-grave narration 'like listening to someone who is either really dull-witted or thinks you're really dull-witted... rarely illuminating and always delivered in the deliberate cadence of a junior-high book report') and subject matter, would conclude that his worst fear had been realised: 'Cherry and his writers really do think they're telling us something important about suburban life, which means they really are that far behind the curve they think they're out in front of' (2005).

13-years earlier, Bush's father's Vice-President, Dan Quayle, had attacked a contemporary television comedy, *Murphy Brown*, for its liberalism and supposed mockery of family values.[5] In 2005, however, the Bushes, darlings of the religious right, were seemingly comfortable making light of themselves by incongruously evoking a far more subversive series. On *Desperate Housewives* a woman who has 'committed suicide...[becomes] the narrator of a television show' (Feeney 2005). Gabrielle Solis sleeps with her high-school teenage gardener. Mary Alice (the narrator) kills a young mother after she tries to reclaim her own child and, after dismembering her body, buries it in a toy chest under the family swimming pool. Rex Van de Kamp, a prominent physician and former Young Republican, seeks fulfilment of his sadomasochistic needs with a local housewife/prostitute/dominatrix (and he is not the only man on Wisteria Lane, the location of the series' seemingly idyllic suburb, to do so). Lynette Scavo becomes addicted to her children's Attention Deficit Disorder medication because it alone gives her the energy necessary to succeed as a housewife. A pharmacist alters the heart medication of a man married to the woman he covets and in so doing kills him. Carlos Solis doctors his wife's birth control pills in order to bring about a pregnancy against her wishes. A young son, Andrew Van de Kamp, a self-declared atheist, puts a woman in the hospital (where she will eventually die) in a hit-and-run accident for which he is never blamed, relishes his own homosexuality because, as he explains to his minister, it causes his mother pain, and later – in season two – makes fun of the 'sound my mother makes when she climaxes' to the pharmacist who has designs on his mother (2: 4). Edie Britt, Wisteria Lane's serial divorcee, sleeps with nearly every available male, even men she judges to be not in her league.

Whereas *Murphy Brown* had given America a title character having a baby out of wedlock, *Desperate Housewives* depicted a suburbia the dark and disturbed film director David Lynch might recognise, and yet it was not judged too unseemly a referent for a First Lady laugh line. If we assume that Laura Bush did enjoy the show, guilty or not, with or without the Second Lady, her notoriously early-to-bed spouse might well have been tempted to see what all the fuss was about when, in the fall of 2005, the first season of the series was released on DVD. But why would Bush have recorded a DVD commentary?

• It would be foolish not to consider the historical context of Bush's *Desperate Housewives* commentary as well. On 29 August 2005, Katrina, a category 5 hurricane, decimated the central Gulf Coast of Mississippi, Alabama and Louisiana, leaving the city of New Orleans 80 per cent flooded. On a six-week vacation at his 'ranch' in Crawford, Texas, at the time, Bush, who set records for the most days on vacation of any POTUS in the fifth year of his two-term presidency, was reluctant to return from Texas (and side trips to Arizona and California) to take a leadership role in Katrina's aftermath. Both Bush and FEMA (Federal Emergency Management Agency – the government entity charged with responding to disasters), run by his hopelessly unqualified political crony Mike Brown, seemed clueless in the days after Katrina had decimated the region, oblivious to the actual suffering of hundreds of thousands of survivors. The President's approval ratings, already low thanks to the escalating cost of gasoline and the situation in Iraq – labelled by the contemporary satire of *The Daily Show* as 'Mess-O-Potamia' – dropped even further.

•   In October 2005, for the second time in four months, Bush would make an appointment to fill a vacancy on the United States Supreme Court. (In July Bush's nomination of John Roberts to fill Sandra Day O'Connor's seat was met with wide acclaim, as was his later elevation of Roberts to Chief Justice upon the death of William Rehnquist). His naming of his own legal counsel, Harriet Miers, to now fill O'Connor's seat met with widespread scepticism. The religious right was dubious about whether she would prove to be the jurist they had long sought: one ready to overturn Roe v. Wade, and critics in both political parties wondered if this woman, who had never been a judge and had no background in constitutional law, was even qualified for the position. Most importantly, charges of cronyism were again levelled against a President who had sought to put his personal lawyer on the bench.[6] Bush's poll numbers declined still more.

It certainly seems likely that Bush might seek to take his mind off his and the nation's troubles by sitting down with the *Desperate Housewives* DVDs, released a month after Katrina's assault. The tabloids at the time were reporting that Bush, who until the age of 40 was known to have a serious problem with alcohol, was drinking again. Could Katrina, Harriet Miers and a return to booze have led to the DVD commentary transcribed below?

•   In 2003 a small press in San Francisco would publish Jeff Alexander and Tom Bissell's ingenious *Speak, Commentary: The Big*

Little Book of Fake DVD Commentaries, Wherein Well-Known Pundits Make Impassioned Remarks About Classic Science Fiction Films. Speak Commentary offers such make-believe commentaries as Noam Chomsky and Howard Zinn (both ultra-left voices at the turn of the century) on Peter Jackson's *The Fellowship of the Ring* (2001), Ann Coulter and Dinesh D'Souza (both strident contemporary liberal bashers) on James Cameron's *Aliens* (1986), Bill Bennett (former Secretary of Education) and Dick Cheney (Bush's VP) on George Lucas's *The Phantom Menace* (1999), and Jerry Falwell and Pat Robertson (both infamous televangelists) on Charlton Heston's *Planet of the Apes* (1968).

That the notoriously anti-intellectual Bush 43 would have read such an obscure book (indeed, no copy can be found in the library) appears unlikely. It seems at once strangely coincidental and highly improbable that 'W' would set out to really do what Alexander and Bissell would only imagine. Still, the authenticity of his *Desperate Housewives* commentary, one of the oddest, most implausible documents in the history of the American presidency, seems beyond dispute. (A comparison of the sound waves on the recording compared to known recordings of Bush's voice shows it to be genuine).

Before you begin to read the transcript of Bush's commentary that follows, permit me to comment on the perhaps surprising language you will find here. Though a born-again, evangelical Christian, Bush's language was known in his day to be frequently laced with four-letter words. Before he became President, the conservative journalist Tucker Carlson reported in a piece that angered the then candidate that Bush was frequently profane.[7]

'Pretty Little Picture' | *Original Air Date: 10/17/04* | *Written by Oliver Goldstick* | *Directed by Arlene Sanford*

Chapter. Scene. Summary	*Bush's Comments*
Chapter 1. Previously on *Desperate Housewives*...We hear Mary Alice in voiceover say: 'It's	I'm not sure I can do this as good as Cheney, Bennett and all. I'm not much good at being witty at

the age-old question, isn't it: how much do we really want to know about our neighbours?'

the whim of a hat. I'm hopefuller I can find something interesting to say. Stay tuned.

Chapter 2. Teaser: Mary Alice (hereafter MA) narrates: 'When travelling through eternity, it helps to travel lightly,' we are told. Only her memories remain. As we watch her casket being cremated, we see a flashback to a Van de Kamp dinner party and the 'look of fear' in Bree's eyes. In the present, Bree harasses Rex about keeping up appearances even if they are separated and later twists the springs in the sofa bed to make it more uncomfortable. Bree was afraid of many things, MA explains, but not of a challenge.

I don't get how a dead woman can tell a story after they're dead. And since she's a suicider, she's got to be in hell, right?

What a bitch this redhead is! I feel sorry for the doc, having to sleep on the sofa. Many a time back in my boozing days when I was sofaed too.

Chapter 3. Credit sequence.

I don't get this at all. Who are these cartoon people? What the fuck's up with the apple? Is this some kind of fancy symbolism?

Chapter 4, Scene 1. Morning – all the desperate housewives (hereafter DHs) are reading different sections of the paper; flashback to a month earlier, when MA announced her plans to host a dinner party.

This is confusing. How come the braless wonder is alive now?[8] Wasn't she pre-deceased? Did we go back in time or something?

Chapter 4, Scene 2. The surviving DHs meet to talk of the dinner and decide to go through with it, with three couples and Susan attending.

Where in hell is this Wisteria Lane anyway? These gals don't seem to be from Texas. Must be in a blue state.

Chapter 4, Scene 3. Gabrielle tells Carlos about the dinner party; he encourages her to find ways to relax. She calls her lover, John.

Or maybe it's Florida... aren't these guys Cubans? Did they vote for Jeb?[9]

Chapter 4, Scene 4. Tom, back from a business trip, is reluctant to attend the dinner party with Lynette.

Not sure I resignate with any of these people. This one's way too bossy. Always manipulating her guy, even if she's a stay-at-home.

Chapter 4, Scene 5. Bree and Rex talk about the dinner party. She warns him not to drink because he'll become 'chatty' and reveal they are in marriage counselling (they are using tennis lessons as a cover).

Been there too. Booze does make me chatty. Like now.

Chapter 4, Scene 6. Karl, Susan's ex, stops by to pick up Julie, and Susan becomes 'petulant' when new girlfriend Brandy (Anne Dudek) throws a soda can at (but not in) the garbage can.

Susan's another bitch, but they're real and spectacular,[10] so I'm willing to forgive.

Chapter 4, Scene 7. Paul Young and son Zach share a very tense meal. Zach wants to know why the paper carried no obituary for his mother.

Something's definitely up with these two. Imagine a boy rebelling against his seemingly perfect dad! Never happen.

Chapter 4, Scene 8. John arrives at the Solis house for a session of lovemaking with Gabrielle, but they are spotted by Ashley Bukowski (Emily Christine), a neighbour's little girl.

So much for family values.

Chapter 5, Scene 1. Susan and Lynette talk about the upcoming dinner party.

I'll take Susan. Don't like these too-smart-for-their-own-good women.

Chapter 5, Scene 2. After finding a photo of Tom having fun on a business trip, Lynette complains about his freedom. She vows to go to the dinner party without him while he watches the kids.

Busted! Always destroy the photographic evidence, Tom!

Chapter 5, Scene 3. Zach finds the gun his mother used to kill herself after searching the garage.

If there's a gun, somebody's going to get shot.

Chapter 5, Scene 4. Bree and Rex see their counsellor and agree to have individual sessions.

Thanks to Jesus, my therapist, I didn't have to go through such shit.

Chapter 5, Scene 5. Gabrielle tries to convince Ashley the kiss she gave John was merely 'a high five on the lips'. Ashley accepts her first blackmail down-payment and demands a new bicycle.

What a nice neighbourhood! A pre-teen blackmailer. Is anybody's children really like this?

Chapter 6, Scene 1. As Paul and Zach argue about why he kept the suicide weapon, Bree comes to the door to invite them to the dinner party. (Zach thanks her for remembering his mother).

Bree is such a stiff, even if she is a good Republican.

Chapter 6, Scene 2. Gabrielle gives Ashley a bike but laments that she doesn't know how to ride and now needs lessons.

What a fine piece of pussy this Langoria is![11]

Chapter 6, Scene 3. Susan looks at old photo albums and calls Karl, asking him to stop by.

Now she realises divorce is a bitch.

Chapter 6, Scene 4. Lynette gives the kids cookies before dinner to make them extra-hyper in order to get back at Tom.

Now this is exactly why the Baptists have required that woman be subservient to their men.

Chapter 6, Scene 5. Gabrielle gives Ashley bike riding lessons.

A girl like this are appalling.

Chapter 6, Scene 6. Karl appears unannounced at Susan's door and finds her in a towel, just out of the shower. She demands an apology, and he refuses. When the argument continues out to his car, Susan loses her towel when it gets caught in the door.

I watched this in slow motion. Lots of skin but nothin' to see.

Chapter 7, Scene 1. Naked Susan tries to get back into her house but falls into the bushes, where Mike Delfino discovers her.

More slow motion and freeze-frame.

Chapter 7, Scene 2. At the dinner party Rex immediately confesses that he and Bree are in counselling and not taking tennis lessons.

I knew Rex couldn't keep his trap shut. I really commensurate with the guy.

Chapter 7, Scene 3. Paul, watching TV, learns the chest he had dumped in a lake has been found.

Classic mistake. Not enough weight.

Chapter 7, Scene 4. At the dinner table, Susan breaks the ice by

What the fuck? Call the FCC![12] This is worse than Jackson's tit.

confessing about her naked adventures. Other confessions follow: Lynette admits she and Tom were once thrown out of Disneyland; Gabrielle and Carlos tell of breaking a waterbed in Cancun; Bree announces that Rex cries after he ejaculates. Rex flees the room.

You can't say that on television! Really funny, though. But why would he cry?

Chapter 8, Scene 1. Walking home from the party, Mike characterises Susan and Karl's relationship as a 'starter marriage'. When she thanks him for being a perfect gentleman when she was naked, he confesses that he peeked and exclaimed 'Wow'.

Lucky son of a bitch.

Chapter 8, Scene 2. Lynette and Tom talk about their 'little terrorists'. Tom insists he never thought Bree and Rex were happy.

Maybe I should alert DHS![13]

Chapter 8, Scene 3. Carlos insists to Gabrielle that he would never allow a woman to humiliate him as Bree did Rex.

Amen, brother.

Chapter 8, Scene 4. Bree packs for a departing Rex and, when she demands to know why he's leaving, he replies that one reason is she will not even let him pack his own suitcase.

Try being married to a librarian.[14]

Chapter 8, Scene 5. Susan apologises to Brandy, who insists

Women!

she thought the marriage was over
or she never would have slept
with Karl.

Chapter 8, Scene 6. Tom, in a
sombrero (as in 5.2), sets aside
45 minutes for sex with Lynette,
but they soon realise the kids
are watching.

More than enough time.

Chapter 8, Scene 7. Bree visits
Dr Goldfine and demands
inside knowledge about Rex.
When he leaves the room she finds
Mary Alice's audiotape.

Perhaps I've misunderestimated
Bree. A one woman Patriot Act!
Has she no conscious?

Chapter 8, Scene 8. Over a
montage of the DHs, MA
explains that 'to live in fear is not
to live at all'. Susan looks out
the window to see Paul Young
put up a 'For Sale' sign.

'To live in fear...' – sounds like a
perfect motto for the Bush era.
Better shut up now. Thanks for
listening.

Chapter 9. Credits.

Notes

1   *Time* magazine (Dickerson 2005: 45) and other sources had reported in
    January 2005 that Bush was reading the 676-page novel by his fellow
    conservative Wolfe.
2   Some on the right, especially conservative bloggers, were displeased with
    the First Lady's talk that evening, finding some of it crude and offensive,
    especially the following clearly off-colour joke:

    I saw my in-laws down the ranch over Easter. We like it down there. George
    didn't know much about ranches when we bought the place. Andover and Yale
    don't have a real strong ranching program. But I'm proud of George. He's learned

a lot about ranching since that first year, when he tried to milk that horse. What's worse, it was a male horse.

3 Formerly a college professor and writer, and the controversial chairwoman of the National Endowment for the Humanities (1986–1992), Lynne Cheney was the conservative wife of Vice-President Dick Cheney.

4 For a full transcript, see http://politicalhumor.about.com/od/laurabush/a/laurabushcomedy.htm.

5 In August 1992 Dan Quayle would say:

> It doesn't help matters when prime time TV has Murphy Brown – a character who supposedly epitomises today's intelligent, highly paid, professional woman – mocking the importance of a father, by bearing a child alone, and calling it just another 'lifestyle choice'.
>
> I know it is not fashionable to talk about moral values, but we need to do it. Even though our cultural leaders in Hollywood, network TV, the national newspapers routinely jeer at them, I think that most of us in this room know that some things are good, and other things are wrong. Now it's time to make the discussion public.

6 As a contemporary commentator (Noah) would observe, Bush's cronies included a steady sequence of individuals who might be labelled 'work wives', women who:

> would never ask you why you don't just put your dishes right into the dishwasher instead of leaving them in the sink – she doesn't know you do it! Also, she would never wedge your car between two others in the parking lot at Bradlees, sign you up to be the pie auctioneer at a church bazaar, or grab hold of your stomach and ask, 'What's this? Blubber?' She knows you only as you appear between nine and five: recently bathed, fully dressed, largely awake, and in control of your life (Owen 1987: 22).

7 Recall, too, that the release of President Richard Nixon's White House tapes back in the 1970s proved shocking, revealing as they did Nixon's vulgarity and racism.

8 'Braless wonder' appears to refer to the Mary Alice Young character (played by Brenda Strong), but it is not possible at this time to explain Bush's reference.

9 Bush's brother Jeb (1953–) was Governor of Florida from 1998 to 2008.

10 Another Bush reference I have not been able to identify.

11 Writing in *Salon* in 2000, Jake Tapper would note:

> Though he's done a decent job of hiding it in this election cycle, Bush has been known to use salty language. At the Republican National Convention in

1988, he was asked by a Hartford Courant reporter about what he and his father talked about when they weren't talking about politics. 'Pussy,' Bush replied (2000).

12 The Federal Communication Commission (FCC) regulates interstate and international communications by radio, television, wire, satellite and cable.

13 The Department of Homeland Security (DHS) was created after the 9/11 terrorist attacks in New York and Washington.

14 'Laura's known as a neat freak', John Powers would write, 'continually straightening things up; in one of their houses, she even arranged their books according to the Dewey decimal system' (2004: 19–20).

2

Still desperate: Popular television and the female Zeitgeist

Rosalind Coward

On first glance it is puzzling that *Desperate Housewives* has such appeal for contemporary audiences. Its title and visual rhetoric seem to conjure up visions of the pre-feminist 1950s. Surely anything that evokes such an outmoded idea as housewives, let alone desperate ones, is harking back to a different era with little relevance to contemporary lives? Yet all the signs are that *Desperate Housewives* has become what could be called a female Zeitgeist series, one of those key mainstream series, where characters and plots are discussed in the wider culture, where the next episode is eagerly awaited, especially by women who find the concerns of their own lives reflected back.

In this respect the series belongs to an honourable tradition. Since the 1970s there have been a number of key American TV series, aimed predominantly at women, which have achieved this status. Invariably these are just light entertainment – soaps or family melodramas. But their incredible popularity, the way the characters provoke identification or become icons, and the importance the series play in the audience's lives, all suggest the pleasures go deep. More than mere entertainment based on great characters, great stories and great production values, the pleasures of a truly unmissable series are meaningful ones which resonate with the fascinations, attractions and preoccupations of contemporary everyday life.

Having been involved both in feminist politics and media criticism over this period I have been struck by how often key popular series engage with critical social and emotional issues affecting women at the time. That might seem a platitude; after all, contemporary television necessarily reflects contemporary realities. But, more specifically, these key series often seem to have an organic connection to debates about women's position, which are being worked over in a different place and different discourse by politics or social theory. It is not a parallel place because, as I will show later in relation to *Desperate Housewives*, there is often a lag between when issues first arise and when they appear in popular representation. Yet it is striking how frequently there have been echoes (sometimes immediate, sometimes more distant) between the programmes that entertained me most and the social and personal issues that detained me most.

Dallas and *Dynasty* were the first mega-soap operas, and the narrative and characters of both were imbued with female pre-occupations of their moment. This is easier to see in retrospect but, even at the time, both were striking for the 'modernity' of their emotional and sexual worlds. This came through even though the glamorous world of the protagonists was impossibly remote from their audience's lives. *Dallas* was launched in 1978, *Dynasty* in 1981, and this was a period when changes in women's position and wider economic changes were transforming once and for all the old post-war lifestyles and outlooks. Feminism's first impact had been felt in the late 1960s, expressed in books like Betty Friedan's *The Feminine Mystique* (1965), Germaine Greer's *The Female Eunuch* (1971) and Kate Millet's *Sexual Politics* (1970). These ideas had a big impact among trendsetters and affected political and social discourse. But, as is always the case, it was later that the emotional revolution triggered by these ideas was felt in popular culture, as the public adopted the values without necessarily espousing the politics.

Dallas was in many ways a classic family melodrama, a story of a marriage between two rival oil dynasties and rivalry between good and bad siblings. For many, *Dallas* was synonymous with the larger-than-life, male character J.R. Ewing Jr. (Larry Hagman), but it was really female roles and storylines that were the series' emotional centre. The preoccupations were twofold. There was generational conflict between a traditional matriarch, Miss Ellie (Barbara Bel Geddes), and the younger generation of women. And there were the emotional dilemmas of the younger women struggling with male chauvinism, sexual infidelity, adultery and finding (usually sexual) fulfilment. In many ways, Sue Ellen (Linda Gray), J.R.'s wife – a glamorous trophy wife struggling to find identity and fulfilment in a ruthless marriage – could have strayed straight out of the pages of Friedan's defining feminist text. Sue Ellen's battles had the same distinctive flavour as those first types of feminism. The preoccupations were about 'liberation' – from oppressive marriages and as sexual beings – rather than economic equality.

Dynasty was a much more knowing, self-parodying, and somewhat more hysterical series than *Dallas*. But in many ways it occupied similar ground. Again the narrative structure was provided by bitter rivalry between two oil companies; but in *Dynasty* the rivalry was between a man and a woman – Blake Carrington (John Forsythe) and his ex-wife Alexis, played by Joan Collins. Alexis embodied fantasies of a new type of woman, sexually equal and financially powerful, challenging the old patriarchy head-on. The series was all shoulder pads and power dressing and, although American, evoked the 1980s ethos, which had its apotheosis in the figure of Margaret Thatcher, Britain's first female prime minister, who also embodied the ruthless new economic liberalism.

Like all melodramas, sexual and familial relations were at *Dynasty's* core, in particular, conflicts between different types of women. Krystle Carrington (Linda Evans) was the classic glamorous secretary-cum-new-wife set against a vengeful, financially powerful and independent ex. *Dynasty's* narrative was located in the complications of the divorce – conflicts between the old and new wife, old and new families. Children and stepchildren were set against each other by the machinations of sexual rivalry and failed marriages. In some ways *Dynasty*, like *Dallas*, was backward-looking, with an old-fashioned patriarch dominating the families. But like *Dallas* it was really preoccupied with women challenging male power for the first time, exposing their frustrations and exploring their newfound sexual freedoms – and the consequences for the family.

The next mainstream series to have the same significance in women's lives was *thirtysomething*, which ran between 1987 and 1991. A comparison with *Dallas* and *Dynasty* highlights how women's preoccupations were shifting, and also how exploring these shifts had been a critical element in really successful women's series since the 1970s. *thirtysomething* was a classic soap, with its sense of real parallel time and stronger, more realistic character development. But just as *Dallas* and *Dynasty* teased out, and entertained with, the core issues of women for the late 1970s and early 1980s, so *thirtysomething* worked over the conflicts and dilemmas faced by women as they moved forward from an initial preoccupation with sexual entitlement and sexual freedom into a new era of negotiating real emotional equality with men.

As the title suggests, *thirtysomething* was about a certain age group, embodied by the four principal characters. The issues were about women struggling to have careers, about combining work with a family, about negotiating equality not just at work but also in the bedroom, and about the effect of children on relationships. The series spoke directly to a new generation of women (and their partners), who defined themselves as career women but were now facing critical decisions: whether or not to marry, whether to have babies, what they could ask of men domestically. Like many viewers, I saw my own life reflected back in *thirtysomething*.[1] I was no longer preoccupied with 'freedoms' and 'self-expression' but with children and how to forge new relationships. In the 1980s feminism had moved on, no longer waving the flag of sexual freedom, but trying to forge deep equality at work and in the home. The term 'women's liberation' had been dropped in favour of 'feminism', a shift reflecting that the focus was no longer on self-expression but changing men and society to improve women's situation. These dilemmas were *thirtysomething*'s whole *raison d'être* and were handled in progressive ways. This is important. Many popular programmes use social concerns as story fodder, but series that achieved mega-popularity with women seem to be those which not only tapped into the massive changes in women's lives through this period but also empathised with women's desire to improve their lot.

If *thirtysomething* addressed the dilemmas and problems of women who tried to have it all, combining work with children and sexual equality with sexual interdependency, *Sex and the City* was about women who had taken a different path through the 1980s. The *Sex and the City* women had, to some extent, neglected relationships for their careers. Now as a group of high-flying, attractive single women whose relations with men are decidedly unsatisfactory, they are reviewing their choices critically. *Sex and the City* demanded a sceptical look at the 1980s ideals. Perhaps the ideal of a high-flying career and a good relationship with a man had always been an impossibility; perhaps, if women had power, they could not have men.

The success of *Sex and the City* and the affection many women had for it was surprising. Its starting premise was more divisive, never claiming to be about everywoman. Instead, these women, although materially successful, viewed themselves as rather marginal characters, cut off both from have-it-all women and those who settled for traditional roles as wives and mothers. Yet the series tapped into a wider cultural reservoir because it foregrounded recognisable general frustrations: the endless quest for a decent man; the real conflicts between work and sexual relationships; the longing for children among the childless; and the all-importance of female friendships to cope with these difficulties.

Some dislike the gender antagonism implicit in *Sex and the City*, with its occasional female chauvinism and representation of men as hopeless, disappointing, desired objects. But the exploration of female friendship as having its own life and significance clearly resonated with a wider public. As did the dilemmas that Carrie Bradshaw's (played by Sarah Jessica Parker) column raised explicitly – have we sacrificed too much for career? Are friendships as important as sexual relationships? Have men really changed? Are they ready to accept and love women who are more than their equal in the world of work? Again the ethos is progressive. The dilemmas are raised sympathetically from a woman's viewpoint, and the solutions are about female support and community rather than giving up hope of deep equality.

Can the same really be said for *Desperate Housewives*? Right from the start (titles included) there is a camp, retro feel, which seems to counteract unlikely claims that this series also taps into the female Zeitgeist and deals with it progressively. The name 'Wisteria Lane' hints at nostalgia, idyll, hysteria, connotations reinforced by the programme's aesthetic, which owes far more to Hollywood representations of the 1950s than to contemporary images. But, as Mary Alice Young might say in her voiceover, appearances can be very deceptive. Looking more closely at the themes and preoccupations, it is clear that *Desperate Housewives* is a worthy inheritor of that tradition.

Desperate Housewives opens with the classic tease of a thriller or melodrama, in this case the violent death of Mary Alice shattering the perfect surface of Wisteria Lane and opening up a mystery from which the narrative action will unfold (1: 1). Yet, in spite of this classic thriller 'come-on', what follows is a much more recognisable soap opera scenario with a cast of female characters, brought together by neighbourhood in a standard soap device, instantly recognisable to viewers.

Desperate Housewives is characterised by the way it mixes genres, most notably merging the thriller, with its opening enigma and strong linear narrative working towards a resolution, with the classic soap opera format, focused on families, friendship groups or neighbourhood, where just a sense of life going on moves the series forward. It also combines melodrama, which is usually serious and intense, with humour, even parody, like the kitsch segue between the graphic horror of Mary Alice's blood and the local busybody, Martha Huber, licking the ketchup from her finger (1: 1). Other genres are mixed in, like teen series *The O.C.*, where the teenagers' emotional dramas are as important as those of their parents. There are numerous other novelties: the story is narrated, in rather poor taste, by someone who committed suicide, and the mystery of Mary Alice's death is investigated by four female friends who together occupy the place of the solitary investigator in the Hollywood thriller.

Yet, overall, *Desperate Housewives* follows the episodic pattern of soap opera. One week the foremost storyline is Lynette Scavo's difficulties with her boys while the next is Rex Van de Kamp's sado-masochism. The skill of *Desperate Housewives* lies in exploiting the genre crossover to link the central mystery of Mary Alice with these more mundane dramas and secrets of suburbia. The subject quickly becomes what is going on behind closed doors in the lives of Lynette, Gabrielle Solis, Susan Mayer and Bree Van de Kamp (the hidden desires, dissatisfactions and hatreds festering underneath the wisteria) as much as it is the mystery of Mary Alice's suicide. As Mary Alice says at one point, 'Beneath the peaceful façade everyone has secrets and we need to think carefully before digging them up' (1: 6).

The secrets of the four main protagonists are not as immediately shocking as Mary Alice's. Materialistic Gabrielle is a 'drowning woman' and John, her teenage lover, is 'her life-raft'. Her secret is that, although she has everything she wants, she must 'have been wanting all the wrong things' (1: 1). For Lynette it is the façade of being the perfect stay-at-home mom. When she meets old colleague Natalie Kline (Nike Doukas), in the supermarket, who asks 'Don't you just love being a mom?' she responds 'as she always does', narrates Mary Alice, 'with the lie, "It's the best job I've ever had"' (1: 1). Under the immaculate surface of Bree's home, there is a disastrous marriage to a man secretly needing to express sexual dominance, and highly problematic relationships with her children. Behind Susan's door is emotional chaos, a messy divorce and an inappropriate dependency on her teenage daughter.

At different moments everybody has secrets from each other: Rex's sexuality, the Van de Kamp's marital therapy, Lynette's inability to cope. Everyone is presenting appearances and hiding things. 'What's visible to the dead could be visible to the living if only they looked,' says Mary Alice, and, as in her life, what gets repressed is dangerous (1: 6). The broodingly jealous Carlos Solis accidentally commits homophobic attacks, much to the bewilderment of his wife. His mother, Juanita, is killed when Bree's son Andrew steals the car to escape family conflict. Typically, these scenes are treated humorously, but the message is clear. Underneath the polished and perfect exterior, suburbia is a potentially dangerous place. There are malevolent neighbours, like Martha Huber, who watches for opportunities to blackmail and is rather gleefully murdered. There are the competitive soccer moms, like Maisy Gibbons (Sharon Lawrence), who turns out to be Rex's dominatrix. There is cruelty and violence between sexual partners and between parents and children.

As the title suggests, life in Wisteria Lane is one of quiet desperation. The women know this about their own lives but do not make it explicit. 'What could have made her so unhappy?' they ask each other at Mary Alice's funeral. After all, as Gabrielle says, 'She was healthy, had a great home, a nice family. Her life was...' Lynette interrupts: 'Our life.' They exchange significant looks (1: 1). What the women share is complicity about their condition, not overt criticism. It is evident again when they puzzle over how Mary Alice's life could have been so murky. Beneath the have-it-all façade is fear, loneliness and boredom. 'Do you know how bored I am?' shrieks Gabrielle at her husband. 'I came within an inch of doing the housework' (1: 2). It is

Mary Alice from beyond the grave who makes it explicit, articulating the unhappiness their polished lives is keeping at bay. 'Loneliness was something they knew all too well'. Of Bree she says, 'I remember the easy confidence of her smile, the gentle elegance of her hands, the refined warmth of her voice. But what I remember most about Bree was the look of fear in her eyes' (1: 3).

Marc Cherry, the series producer, says that Wisteria Lane reflects contemporary American society with incredible idealisation covering darkness. Behind the perfect façade, with immaculate houses, clean streets, perfectly tended lawns and apparently perfect families, there is obsession, malevolence, frustration and above all secrets – people hiding things from each other and themselves.[2] In this respect the series owes as much to Hollywood as it does its television forerunners. There are echoes of *American Beauty* (1999), where sexual frustration reaches out and destroys the family; of *Edward Scissorhands* (1990), where suburbia conceals and fails to contain the freakish; and of the recent Hollywood success *Far From Heaven* (2002), where the prejudices and restrictions of 1950s suburban America cripple love and female fulfilment.

The echo of these suburban dystopias might reinforce the idea that *Desperate Housewives* is a dated vision of suburbia and a version of male–female relationships that has long past. Yet the whole problematic of *Desperate Housewives* is resolutely rooted in modern dilemmas. The four main characters are extremely diverse, but what they have in common is affluence and post-feminist lifestyle choices. Neither hardship nor tradition forces any of them to take their particular path. Each has made different decisions. Gabrielle loathes housework and does not want to become a mother; Lynette is the ex-career woman who has unsuccessfully embraced life as full-time stay-at-home mom, or in season one at least. Susan is a single mother working from home. And Bree is the ultimate homemaker, the perfectionist whose whole life is devoted to her immaculate home, her perfect cooking. Yet, in spite of the fact that they have far more choices than women of previous generations, all are suffering from the gap between ideals and reality. No less than for earlier generations, their lives fail to live up to the brochure. Their relationships with men are unsatisfactory and their relationships with their children are difficult. The perfect exteriors add to their oppression.

In some ways there is a strong, almost old-fashioned feminist pulse beating in these scripts. Masculinity in *Desperate Housewives* is problematised. Lynette's boys are constantly fighting and undisciplined. Apart from Mike Delfino, male characters are pretty flawed, even sinister, like George Williams the pharmacist, or the policeman, Officer Rick Thompson (Steven Eckholdt), who dates Susan but turns vindictive when she rejects him: 'Why do I pick all the psychos?' he calls after her (1: 5). Carlos is an old-fashioned, neglectful chauvinist. Rex, who at first seems to have a case against his highly controlling wife, gradually emerges as emotionally and sexually inadequate. Lynette's husband, an erstwhile sexual equal, reveals himself as completely unable to understand the drudgery of domestic life. Susan's ex-husband Karl, has shirked family responsibility, and had an affair, which he defends with the statement 'The heart wants what it wants' (1: 3).

Yet, if an old-style feminism is present, it is equivocal. When explicitly feminist views erupt they tend to come from Bree, thereby linking them with a controlling personality. However, the scenes when it manifests are highly entertaining and tend to win sympathy for Bree rather than the male victim of her attack. On one occasion she seeks out her son at a strip club and delivers a devastating critique of sex worker victimisation, which emasculates the men around her (1: 4). Even more entertaining are her exchanges with the psychoanalyst, Dr Albert Goldfine (Sam Lloyd). Psychoanalysts in American film and TV, especially where the world portrayed is, like Wisteria Lane, ruled by the unconscious, tend to be patriarchal gods, the point of connection to the film's underlying preoccupations. Playfully, *Desperate Housewives* has Bree deliver a scathing attack on Freud's patriarchal attitudes: 'His mother must have felt so betrayed. Did he ever think to say thank you for all she did?' (1: 2). In the subsequent session the analyst chastises Rex for not thanking Bree enough for what she does.

Nor would it be true to say that representation of male–female relationships in *Desperate Housewives* is consistently anti-men or presents an image of men that belongs to another, more aggressive era of feminism. The four women are the emotional core of the series and are supportive of each other, a positive portrayal of female solidarity. But they are by no means perfect. There is a wonderful – and highly realistic – equivocation in some scenes between men and women. For instance, in several episodes sympathy vacillates between Bree and Rex. Meanwhile, Susan and her ex-husband are stuck in a circuit of mutual accusations in which Susan recognises her own complicity in the breakdown of the marriage. Significantly, too, the main narrative impulse of *Desperate Housewives* is a mystery centring on a father–son relationship, between Mike and Zach Young. In this, the series draws as heavily on male bonding movies as it does on suburban dystopias. The troubled son and the absent, wounded father, seeking out a relationship with his offspring, has been the staple of Hollywood movies for over a decade.

This relationship's centrality also points to other departures from dated versions of feminism. The relationship of the women with the men is as significant as that of the ones with their children. This is not as in *thirtysomething*, where small children served to focus the characters' dilemmas. In *Desperate Housewives* children are people in their own right, as in *The O.C.*, with their own dramas and dilemmas. What has moved to the forefront in *Desperate Housewives* is wider family relationships, with the teenagers' own lives, their insecurities and problems intersecting and contributing to the unfolding drama. Importantly, women's own role, perhaps even their complicity, in their children's problems is being recognised.

This is almost certainly the clue to the series' popularity. The complexity of wider families has come into view, not just male–female relationships. Even though the series is not conventionally realistic, often engaging in humour or parody, it is touching a core of reality. This is the reality of the contemporary family, with its broken relationships, difficult teenagers, repressed desires and disappointed hopes festering like Mary Alice's desperation for a child or Andrew's gayness. What is being exposed is the danger of forcing emotional life to reflect ideals. In particular it is touching on the illusion of post-feminism, the idea that, if women can choose how they live, they will be fulfilled. Instead, the retro exteriors link the modern wives of Wisteria Lane with 1950s suburbia. What is being articulated is a continuity of disappointment. The 1950s housewives railed against their circumscribed lives; in *Desperate Housewives* what is being exposed are false promises, the hypocrisy and unhappiness that coercive ideals, whether they are social or material, bring in their wake. This – the con of post-feminist consumerism – is very modern territory.

In this respect *Desperate Housewives* is a true inheritor of those other series, where the key gender issues of the moment are given expression. Like the other series discussed *Desperate Housewives* also feels as if it is articulating an emotional reality. As with those other series these issues have for some time been discussed and analysed by the politically or sociologically alert. I am very struck by how the lives of the women in Wisteria Lane evoke research I did a decade ago for a book called *Our Treacherous Hearts* (1993). The women I interviewed then, albeit in Britain and mainly with young children rather than teenagers, articulated very similar feelings. Many felt oppressed by the post-feminist ideals they were trying to live up to. Many found the have-it-all image to which they were aspiring was a source of oppression. In particular they felt emotional difficulties within families were hidden from view. The appearance of these issues in *Desperate Housewives* shows how these anxieties are filtering into the wider culture.

No one could accuse *Desperate Housewives* of hiding the emotional difficulties of so-called normal families, even if the mystery provided by them is buried and must be gradually unearthed. However 'unrealistic' and playful the programme appears, what it exposes is this emotional reality. Like the other series I have looked at in this chapter, its immense popularity comes from the way it taps into this Zeitgeist, and like those other series it does so in a way that is progressive, empathetic to the dilemmas and difficulties of contemporary women.

Notes

1 The series' director and writer, Joseph Dougherty, has talked about the way he aimed at achieving this recognition factor among their audience. He described *thirtysomething* as dealing with 'small moments examined closely showing the way people really talk, and dream, and even fantasise. Those seemingly random events that somehow add up to deep emotion. The kind of show that people might look at and say, "That's my life, I said that last night"'(www.thirdstory.com/thirtysomething/misc/interview2.htm).

2 Interview with director Marc Cherry. DVD *Desperate Housewives*. Season one, 2004–2005.

3

Having it all: *Desperate Housewives'* flimsy feminism

Ashley Sayeau

The problem with *Desperate Housewives* is that it is too much trouble. And I am all for getting my hands dirty, particularly when it comes to women's popular culture. I have spent sunny afternoons alone in dark, museum cubicles with Estelle Getty, Murphy Brown and middle-aged *Star Wars* types. I've defended Britney, or at least the idea of her. Read, underlined and highlighted articles on Rosanne Barr. And I have made some really hard calls – that waif Ally McBeal is no great wit like Carrie Bradshaw, never was, never will be.

But *Desperate Housewives* is another story. I do not know whether ex-executive Lynette Scavo is a saint or a sucker for staying home with her four children. I am glad she is not a diehard Donna Reed, I suppose, but as many a conservative has pointed out, she still embodies family values (more at least than she embraces family planning). And Bree, the gun-toting hair roller, is so camp (or Van de Kamp, in this case) that her 1950s lifestyle is almost endearing. When it is not – that is, when her peachiness borders on pathetic – I worry about a culture that still thinks making jokes at Joan Cleaver's expense is cutting-edge.

My uncertainty is a reflection of a wider cultural ambivalence about the show's artistic and political postures. The popular American media seems to be of distinctly two minds about *Desperate Housewives*, unsure of whether it is progressive programming or TV trash. *Entertainment Weekly* applauds Edie Britt for being so 'spectacularly liberated' she 'falls somewhere between feminist and hair-metal groupie' (Gopalan 2005: 26). Even the *Washington Post* is stumped. 'Is this *Twin*

Peaks or *Days of Our Lives*? (Booth 2004: N01). Of course 'quality' television has always walked the fine line between 'mindless' entertainment and social commentary. Alan Ball, creator of *Six Feet Under*, called his esoteric masterpiece '*Knot's Landing* in a funeral home' (quoted in Gamson 2001: 36). And everyone knows Tony Soprano (James Gandolfini) means one thing to warring dads duking it out over their sons' hockey games and another to critics battling the meaning of Adrianna La Cerva's (Drea de Matteo) acrylics. But *Desperate Housewives* takes this age-old conundrum to a new level, marketing itself as a little bit of everything that, in the end, makes for a puzzling blend of politics and so-called feminism. As emblematised in the quotes above, this has garnered the show plenty of attention but not especially poignant criticism. Gloria Steinem or Rod Stewart's hausfrau? Mother Theresa or Mother Jones? Who has the energy to figure it out anymore? And who really cares in the end?

This intellectually lazy approach befits our cultural and political times – when the Iraq war was begun without fact-checking the reasons and no viable counter-movement exists, despite a widespread lack of 'support' – but has specific consequences for women and feminism today. At a time when websites are coined 'Mothers Who Think' and domestic-diva-turned-cheating-CEO-turned-penitent prisoner Martha Stewart is hailed as a modern heroine, it seems no one knows, or increasingly cares, what constitutes feminism any more. It is just too complicated, hysterical, outdated. No other show represents – and inspires – this schizophrenic and politically suspect way of discussing women today quite like *Desperate Housewives*. Too over-whelmed by the mixed messages, those on the left have generally gone against their gut and called the show just a 'guilty pleasure', while Republican commentators like Myrna Blyth revel in the backwardness of it all. 'Who cares if it's shallow, retro, and anti-feminist?' she asks giddily in *The National Review Online*, before applauding the show for its progressive portrayal of female friendships (2004). Even Republicans cannot help being a little PC some of the time.

That everyone has politely agreed to agree on the show's flimsy sort of feminism is a marketer's dream. As Frank Rich pointed out in the *New York Times*, the series is 'even a bigger hit in Oklahoma City than it is in Los Angeles, bigger in Kansas City than it is in New York'

(2004: 1). Despite being so famously divided, Americans have been united by *Desperate Housewives* – a show that taps into our ambivalent relationship to modern women's lives, a dynamic that mirrors the love–hate relationship the show inspires in critics like myself. The series, after all, was born at a time when women were being increasingly cast as schizophrenic themselves – educated and savvy but nevertheless confused about their goals and priorities. More specifically, while the 1990s were preoccupied with the shoes, miniskirts and marriage prospects of single women, the new millennium gave way to psychological profiles of married women – not wild and sexy women, but mothers, both the crazy, speed-popping ones who worked, and the 'lonely and boring' ones who did not (Fels 2004: xv). 22 per cent of mothers who hold graduate or professional degrees pick up crushed Cheerios for a living, declared *Time* magazine in 2004 (Wallis 2004: 51–59). 'What happened when the Girls Who Had It All became mothers?' asked *Newsweek* a year later (Warner 2005: 42). Of course, we know the answer.

Desperate Housewives was the direct product of such a mother-gone-crazy tale. Moved by the 2002 story of Andrea Yates, a mother from Texas who suffered from post-partum depression so severely that she drowned her five children in the bathtub, creator Marc Cherry wanted to capture the 'moments of great desperation... [that] every woman who is in the suburban jungle has' (Weinraub 2004: B7). In and of itself, this is surely an admirable goal – as are attempts to reconcile breakfast cereal and female CEOs. And, on the surface at least, *Desperate Housewives* seems sincere in its representation of the trials and tribulations of stay-at-home moms. Lynette's daily nervous breakdown is refreshing, and perhaps even groundbreaking; and Bree does deserve a 'thank you' for all the buttons she has sewn on, the silver she has polished. But, in the end, as is the case with so much of American culture's preoccupation with mothers – working and not – the show's ambitions fall flat, and the women are left more helpless than ever.

Desperate Housewives represents the best of what we might call faux feminism – that subtle, yet increasingly pervasive brand of conservative thought that casts itself as deeply concerned with the frustrations of modern women, but can ultimately offer no alternatives except those of a traditional stripe. We find this in articles, like

44

those mentioned above, that appear sympathetic to the financial and intellectual strain suburbia (and all that goes with it) can have on women, only to argue that – while not ideal – mothers staying at home is best for everyone. Despite the economic hardship it brings, 'My daughter is better for it,' one stay-at-home mother is quoted as saying. 'I can tell it in her vocabulary' (Wallis 2004: 51). This sentiment is mirrored in television shows like *Trading Spouses* and *Wife Swap* that portray women as completely schizo 'This week: loony vegan meets alligator huntress!', but also the heart of the family; and 'family-friendly' legislation that allows companies to give people comp time in lieu of overtime pay, because what working mothers need is not extra money but extra time with their children.

These shows, articles and policies borrow from the language of feminism, though in the end it is feminism that they attack. Frequently, women's equality is dismissed as a nice, but impractical ideal. In a *Time* cover article on mothers staying home, a 'male perspective' bemoans that tradition is such a difficult nut to crack. 'In the early 1970s ... we were convinced that the world of stay-at-home moms and job-trapped dads had ended, oh sometime around 1969. We were wrong, of course' (Elliott 2004: 59). After explaining how technological advances have actually sent the work–life balance even more off-kilter – though never explaining why women should have to pick up the slack – he concludes (again): 'Thirty years ago, we dreamed of something different. Pity it didn't work out' (ibid.). Lia Macko and Kerry Rubin in their treatise *The Midlife Crisis at 30: How the Stakes Have Changed for a New Generation – and What to Do about It*, wherein they cite writers like Barbara 'Dan Quayle Was Right' Dafoe Whitehead and the moderate Peggy Orenstein as if they are interchangeable, also pay homage to feminism – sort of. 'Ironically, part of our generation's new and ambiguous but omnipresent dilemma stems from a shared sense of inadequacy for failing to live up to the dreams and expectations those inspiring women ["Betty Friedan and her contemporaries"] defined' (Macko and Rubin 2004: 14).

Similarly, all is not what it seems on *Desperate Housewives*. Despite all the silent tears lost in cake batter, Wisteria Lane is no secret feminist retreat. 'Satire sounds like you're making fun of something. And the truth is, I'm not making fun of the suburbs,' Cherry has said.

'I love the values the suburbs represent. Family, community, God' (quoted in Pozner and Seigel 2005). In fact, this gay Republican (the irony never ends!) seems highly sceptical of feminism – despite the superficial signs like Edie's sexual prowess and Lynette's evil twins. 'We've reached the point where we realize that no, you really can't have it all...Long ago, it used to be easier: Society laid down the rules for you. Now, there are a lot of choices, but sometimes choices can lead to chaos' (ibid.). At least in the mind of their creator, the women of Wisteria Lane suffer from too much freedom, it seems.

And, ultimately, they walk the line – as do the mothers in the *Time* exposé, as do the heroines of *Trading Spouses*. Lynette longs for intellectual stimulus in the midst of her children's school play but in the end cannot make the decision to work again. When she does – and in a classic faux feminist move – it is her husband who forces her hand when he declares (ever so heroically) that he has decided to stay at home. Gabrielle Solis suffers at the hands of her husband – a fairly uncommon sight on network television – but not so much she will sacrifice her shoe collection. And when they do make a stand, as Bree does with the cheating Rex (aka, the King), the women are often punished, as Bree is with the dead and thus suddenly sympathetic Rex. That these women are *desperate* – not courageous, not strong, not complicated – is fundamental to the series. According to *Vanity Fair*, when a colleague suggested the show's title be changed to *The Secret Lives of Housewives*, Cherry threatened to quit (Zeman 2005: 264). Women's despair is non-negotiable.

Of course, there are undoubtedly good arguments in favour of *Desperate Housewives*. Feminism, work–family issues, and even Cherry's idea of choice are more complicated than I am suggesting (and I should know, as I sit writing, praying that my lovely two-month-old will sleep just one more hour in her swing, so that I might write just one more paragraph). There are aspects of the series that warm the progressive heart. Bree's NRA membership is pitch-perfect, only rivalled by her daughter's membership in her school's abstinence club. But I am talking about the broad strokes here. Whether Cherry has suburban moms' best interests at heart is debatable, but the pandering the show does – at once shocking, licentious, and thus liberal and yet also down-home, heartfelt, Billy Bob – is not. It is a sign of our centrist and thoughtless times, when everything down to the weather is presented as a point–counterpoint. Not only does this make for a boring culture, it has drastic implications for women, because moving to the centre in this respect (and many others) means placating conservatives, thus whittling away gains in women's rights. Nearly every successful public female figure – whether Martha Stewart, Madonna or Hillary Clinton – must drape her successes in business, in entertainment, in politics in conservative garb or else risk alienating the right. Of course, women's rights have progressed well enough that false gestures are in order. Republicans praise female friendship, and Laura Bush, whose husband drifts off around 9pm, has proclaimed herself a 'desperate housewife'. But these are by and large illusions, masking truly dark secrets. When the First Lady made the declaration, she was stumping for her husband at the 2005 White House Correspondents Dinner, in a truly desperate attempt to take the heat off a man who had led so many others to die in war.

The spring 2005 cover of *Ms.* magazine, founded by Gloria Steinem and once a sort of beacon of feminist journalism, wondered not why America is nearly the only developed nation without paid maternity leave or a decent daycare system, but rather asked, '*Desperate Housewives*: Do We Hate It or Secretly Love It?' The piece pitted two female journalists against one another – one thought the show represented a positive step for women; the other, of course, did not. In the end, the forum sanctioned both positions and nothing was lost, but nothing was gained either. It is this zero-sum game that *Desperate Housewives* – and so many other cultural artefacts today – inspires, and that worries me as a feminist. I do not expect the series to centre around strictly political issues, for the girls' poker game to double as a good old consciousness-raising session. I am far more realistic – and fun – than that. But I miss the clarity of older shows like *Maude* and *Murphy Brown*, series that took on public policy and out-of-touch vice-presidents. I am tired of seeing feminism co-opted by the right, who borrow its language but denigrate its essence. I want debate to result in better lives for women, not just redundant and confusing rhetoric. I want to know feminism when I see it. And I want it desperately.

4

Still desperate after all these years: The post-feminist mystique and maternal dilemmas

Kim Akass

In the past sixty years we have come full circle and the American housewife is once again trapped in a squirrel cage. If the cage is now a modern plate-glass-and-broadloom ranch house or a convenient modern apartment, the situation is no less painful than when her grandmother sat over an embroidery hoop in her gilt-and-plush parlour and muttered angrily about women's rights.

Betty Friedan 1992: 25

'Happy to be Desperate' claims the headline of the news review section of *The Sunday Times* (2005: 4). A large photo shows the female stars of ABC's *Desperate Housewives* hemmed in by a white picket fence sporting the caption '*Desperate Housewives* caught the madness but also the strange satisfaction of domestic life for women'. The irony of this is not lost on India Knight, the article's author, as she argues that the series 'does not seem like a piece of twee fantasy to me, or like satire, but like a high-kicking piece of bang-on social realism. Well, apart from the murders, obviously' (ibid.). Why does she make this claim? Could it be Lynette Scavo's desperation to be a good mother, which 'brilliantly depict[s] competitive parenting'? Or maybe it is her empathy with Susan Mayer's terror at 'the idea of being left alone and unloved, and her relief when that possibility starts to recede'? Or is it Gabrielle Solis's 'archetypal bored housewife drowning in money and gasping for air, too desperate to behave decently and too frightened of financial loss to call it a day'? (Apparently resembling at least five women known by the writer.) Surely it is not Bree Van de Kamp's 'old-school house-wife extraordinaire, with her stay-put hair and her twinset and pearls', that makes *Desperate Housewives* smack of reality? Ponderings aside, for Knight, the fact that the 'middle-aged married women in *Desperate Housewives* should have become heroines to their viewers' is not surprising. Especially when you consider her claim that the popularity of the series is proof that 'women, more than ever, still want nothing more than the old-fashioned dream of stay-at-home domestic content-ment' (ibid.). Despite the fact that domestic contentment could not be further from what is represented in *Desperate Housewives*, Knight is undeterred in her final analysis: 'We're all either Desperate Housewives, or yearning to be one. It's time to wield that rolling pin with pride' (ibid.).

Fighting talk indeed. But can this really be true – especially in this post-feminist, postmodern, post-9/11 era? Surely women know better than to yearn to be a housewife, especially one living in the 'astonishingly true to life' Wisteria Lane (ibid.). It is not as if the series makes any attempt to hide the grim reality of this role. Indeed, the first few minutes of ABC's *Desperate Housewives* exposes just how desperate life as a housewife can get. Mary Alice Young makes breakfast, cleans and tidies her house before calmly shooting herself in the head (1: 1). Our only clue to this seemingly random act is the subsequent discovery of a note saying: 'I know what you did. It makes me sick. I'm going to tell'. Thus a narrative conundrum for the first season of *Desperate Housewives* is set: what would make an apparently happy housewife commit suicide in the middle of a sunny suburban utopia? Gathering at the wake her friends ask the same question; after all, according to Gabrielle 'she was healthy, had a great home, a nice family'. But, more shocking still, as Lynette points out, her life was their life. Ending in suicide, is it one that twenty-first-century women really yearn for? And, if it is, the question that has to be asked is: why would any sane woman swap a life of independence for one of quiet desperation like those lived on Wisteria Lane?

The post-feminist mystique

There can be few commentators who missed the connection between Betty Friedan's 1963 seminal text *The Feminine Mystique* (1992) and *Desperate Housewives*. It is hard to tell if the following is Mary Alice's voiceover or Friedan's observations written over 40 years ago:

> Millions of women lived their lives in the image of those pretty pictures of the American suburban housewife, kissing their husbands good-bye in front of the picture window, depositing their stationwagonsful of children at school, and smiling as they ran the new electric waxer over the spotless kitchen floor. They baked their own bread, sewed their own and their children's clothes, kept their new washing machines and dryers running all day. [...] They gloried in their role as women (1992: 16).

It is helpful to remember that the image that Friedan is referring to here is the 'mystique of feminine fulfilment [which] became the cherished and self-perpetuating core of contemporary American culture' (ibid.) in the 15-years after the Second World War. According to Susan Douglas and Meredith Michaels, while this may have been the privileged ideology of the time, it is undermined by the fact that 'by 1955, there were more women with jobs than at any point in the nation's previous history' (2004: 34). There is obviously a discrepancy here between the representation of the happy housewife and her reality. To push the point further, Miriam Peskowitz reports that in 1948 'nearly one-third of all women in America worked' (2005: 67), although it was not until 1976 that 'women's participation in the workforce inched near 50 percent' (68). Be that as it may, it is difficult to see how the prevailing ideology of domesticity as a goal has any currency with women when the facts of their lives seem to tell a different story.

Or do they? It may be that the facts and figures do not reflect what is at stake here. Joan Williams, a professor of the Gender, Work and Family programme at the American University Law School, suggests that despite the 'true story' told by the number crunching 'the ideology and the practice of domesticity retain their hold. A recent survey found that fully two-thirds of Americans believe it would be best for women to stay home and care for family and children' (2000: 2). Interestingly, there is nothing here to determine which gender (or class or ethnicity) thought this was the best way forward. And yet there seems to be at least some evidence for Knight's claim that women still yearn for that 'old-fashioned dream of stay-at-home domestic contentment' (2005: 4). And why not? Despite Friedan's call to arms in 1963 for women to live their lives in pursuit of more than 'feminine fulfilment' (1992: 24), it seems that once children come along women are more than happy to climb off the corporate ladder and settle for a life of motherhood and domesticity. And it would make sense if Williams is to be believed when she argues that the 'shift of women into the workforce has undermined neither domesticity's linkage of women with caregiving nor its association of men with breadwinning' (2000: 27).

So what is going on? Surely the twenty-first-century post-feminist woman has more to look forward to than Friedan's women, whose chief ambition was 'marriage and children' and included those 'in their forties and fifties who once had other dreams [but] gave them up and threw themselves joyously into life as housewives', or those who 'quit high school and college to marry, or marked time in some job in which they had no real interest until they married' (1992: 24). We have moved on since then, haven't we? Not according to Douglas and Michaels, who assert that 'what the feminine mystique exposed was that all women . . . were supposed to inhabit one and only one seamless subject position: that of the selfless, never complaining, always happy wife and mother who cheerfully eradicated whatever other identities she might have had and instead put her husband, her children, and the cleanliness of her house first' (2004: 34). What is most disconcerting about their thesis is that this is not a subject position that was left behind in the 1960s, but one that has risen 'pheonixlike, and burrowed its way once again into the media and into the hearts and minds of millions of mothers' (ibid.).

The rhetoric of choice

The much-repeated source story for *Desperate Housewives* tells of Marc Cherry's conversation with his mother about Andrea Yates's murder conviction for drowning her five children. Responding to his mother's assertion that 'we've all been there,' he says that 'if a perfectly sane, rational woman could have the life she wanted, being a wife and mother…and still have moments of insanity', then anyone could (September 2004). He claims that things are pretty much the same now as they were in the 1950s when his mother was at home, the only difference being that the post-feminist woman 'can decide for family over work but must accept responsibility for the outcome. Now it's "I've chosen it, I'm in control. Oh, I can't blame anyone for my own unhappiness, what do I do?"' (ibid.).

According to Williams and Peskowitz it is this idea of choice that is so completely disingenuous when describing women's attempt to combine motherhood with the workplace. As Peskowitz points out, we 'talk about the glass ceiling and the mommy track so regularly that these phrases seem passé, yesterday's news' (2005: 67), and yet they still hold much currency in twenty-first-century American life. She says:

> Scratch the surface and there's the glass ceiling. Peer into the company accounts and there's the persistent gender wage gap. Look at who's taking family leave, or why our public life seems so devoid of fortysomething women, and why it's still mostly men running for office or men running the TV news, and it's pretty clear that we aren't as postfeminist as we'd like to be (66).

Even more worrying for Peskowitz is the fact that the 'gap between men's and women's earnings is 10 to 15 percent larger for mothers than for women without children; in fact the wage gap between mothers and nonmothers is larger than that between men and women' (67). As she puts it, 'the gains for women in the past decades have not meant a similar gain for mothers…childraising remains mothers' work, and in many families it's the mother's salary that is balanced against daycare costs' (66–67). Hardly surprising when the shocking truth is revealed 'that mothers who work full-time earn only sixty cents for every dollar earned by full-time fathers' (2000: 2).

If this is the case, why does this wage gap persist, especially in our post-feminist society? Surely one of the most important feminist gains was that of equality in the workplace – and surely the days of a distinction between women's and men's work are long over? According to Williams the gendered wage gap exists because the workplace 'continues to be structured in ways that perpetuate the economic vulnerability of caregivers', with a preference for the ideal worker who 'works at least forty hours a week year round' (2) with an expectation to work overtime at any given moment. The result is that even when mothers do manage to work full-time they get forced onto the 'mommy-track' as they can only rarely work the amount of hours expected of them. She adds: 'A rarely recognized but extraordinarily important fact is that jobs requiring extensive overtime exclude *virtually all mothers* (93 percent)' (ibid.). She reluctantly comes to the conclusion that

> Domesticity's organisation of market and family work leaves women with two alternatives. They can perform as ideal workers without the flow of family work and other privileges male ideal workers enjoy. That is not equality. Or they can take dead-end mommy-track jobs or 'women's work.' That is not equality either. A system that allows only these two alternatives is one that discriminates against women (39).

If this is the case, and the evidence certainly supports this view, then where does the rhetoric of choice come from? According to Peskowitz the slight downturn in the amount of working mothers with infants since 1998 (when the figure stood at 58 per cent) to a steady 55 per cent has been accompanied by a series of newspaper and magazine articles that have claimed 'a new traditionalism, a resurgence of old-fashioned motherly feeling' (68). She claims that, before October 2003, 'well-educated mothers who left fancy professional jobs were merely quitting', but since an article in the *New York Times Magazine* suggested that 'these women were "opting-out"…the phrase really caught on. …and "opting-out" quickly became part of the national vocabulary to describe mothers who left full-time jobs' (87). Unfortunately, for Peskowitz at least, one of the main problems with the phrase 'opting-out' is that 'it forecloses any discussion about what "choice" means and about what kinds of options women have…"Opting-out" assumes that women have options' (99). Williams expands on this point and suggests that it is 'not surprising that women facing the constraints handed down by domesticity speak of having made a "choice"' (2000: 37), especially in the twenty-first century, when the idea of choice (however problematic) is embedded right into the very heart of American feminist ideology.

As much as it has been a phrase of feminist politics, choice itself is a fantasy, one that emerges from a classic American belief that we are independent, free, and autonomous; that we have choices and choose our options freely; and that as a result, we ourselves are solely responsible for the results (Peskowitz 2005: 99).

For Williams 'choice and discrimination are not mutually exclusive. Choice concerns the everyday process of making decisions within constraints' (2000: 37). The constraints that the workplace clearly places upon mothers are such that, when faced with working long hours, putting a large portion of their salary towards childcare costs and being too exhausted to enjoy their family, they will often surrender to domesticity. This does not mean that they have made a free choice, or one based on a need to spend 24 hours a day with their children, but rather a choice based on the ideal worker system versus domesticity. It is clear that any decision to 'opt out' is more often than not made within the constraints of a system that 'pulls fathers into the ideal worker role and mothers into lives framed around caregiving' (39), and furthermore it is one framed in a rhetoric that only partially describes the choices facing working mothers who 'don't get to choose the structures of the workplace ... This workplace predicament is not our choice. Let's be clear about that' (Peskowitz 2005: 98). For both Williams and Peskowitz this predicament affects all women and, rather than thinking about it as a personal decision, a 'choice' to 'opt out', it is more helpful to see it for what it is – a 'maternal wall' – a phrase that 'helps us see what we all face individually as something broader and more generally shared among women' (67).

Attempting to scale that 'maternal wall'

If the workplace predicament is one that affects all women with children, then Lynette's choice to opt out and be a stay-at-home mom should be indicative of how that decision is made. In flashback we see how her joy at discovering she is pregnant is quickly marred by her husband Tom's suggestion that she should quit her job as 'kids do better with stay-at-home moms', adding: 'It would be so much less stressful' (1: 1). So much for a choice, especially when the real stress of Lynette's life is now attempting to care for a baby and three unruly pre-school boys while her husband is free to work the extended hours of an ideal worker. Her spontaneous punch to his jaw when he attempts to have unprotected sex with her and risk another pregnancy shows just how disenchanted Lynette is with her role. And, as if that is not enough, during a fraught shopping expedition she lies to an ex-work colleague who asks her 'Don't you just love being a mom?'. Mary Alice's voiceover reveals that 'for those who asked it, only one answer was acceptable', and Lynette's answer confirms that she has much to share with Friedan's women, who found it impossible to talk about the real desperation of their lives (1: 1).

It is not until the beginning of season two that *Desperate Housewives* directly addresses the problem of what happens when mothers attempt to return to work. Again Lynette's 'choice' is pre-empted by Tom's resignation from his job. She may have interfered with his promotional prospects in an attempt to prevent him working even longer hours, but is taken aback at his insistence that it is now her turn to get a job and his to be a stay-at-home father (1: 23). Despite her protestations, Tom makes it clear whose choice it is when he tells her: 'I already made the decision. You're going back to work.'

Lynette's foray into the working world begins, somewhat uncomfortably, when confronted with another face of the maternal wall. Nina Fletcher (Joely Fisher) represents the harsh voice of power feminism, one that is well aware of the sacrifices that have to be made in order to succeed in a man's world. Looking aghast at Lynette's confession that she has four children, Nina tells her: 'I knew I could never do both jobs justice. That's why I chose not to have a family. I didn't want to be one of those kinds of women. You know, sloughing things off onto co-workers because of a paediatrician appointment or a dance recital' (2: 1). Nina clearly speaks for women who 'have been working long enough to know the possibilities of advancement, the struggles women face to achieve, and the subtle discriminations that persist' (Peskowitz 2005: 94). Using the rhetoric of choice to describe her decision *not* to have a family proves Williams's point that the twenty-first-century workplace allows only two options for women if they want to succeed within it. Nina may talk of choosing a career over family, but is this really a choice? In Peskowitz's opinion 'we should not confuse a bunch of decisions we make with real "choice" that we don't have as women or mothers' (2005: 107).

If Nina's attitude suggests that the odds are stacked against Lynette's successful integration into ideal worker status, then the following day will push the Scavo family's role reversal to the limit. It may be that the maternal wall prevents women from full access to the workplace, but it is soon clear that the other side of the coin is 'domesticity's peculiar structuring of market work and family work [which] hurts not only women but also men...' (Williams 2000: 3). It may have been Tom's choice to take a break from work but by day two he is confronted with the stark reality of life as a stay-at-home father. Williams confirms something that many working women already know: despite 'our self-image of gender equality, American women still do 80 percent of the child care and two-thirds of the housework' (2) and, according to one study, 'an average American father spends twelve minutes a day in solo child care' (3). If these figures are to be believed, then it is hardly surprising that Tom is flat on his back after only 24 hours of domesticity and childcare, and it is obvious that it is not only Lynette who will have to prove her worth. After all, being an ideal worker depends upon a primary caregiver providing 'immunity from family work' (20). Lynette may tell Nina that her children 'won't get in the way of the job because my husband's staying home with them from now on', but this very much depends on Tom's ability to prove himself a reliable caregiver. Untrained for the job, he is soon to find out that, in Lynette's words, 'being a mom is like being an E.R. doctor – there are no days off' (2: 1).

And in the real world...

Ellen Goodman writes in the *Washington Post* that she knows that she should not like *Desperate Housewives*, as it is 'either post-feminist or pre-feminist. It's too racy or too retro. It's either an example of the backlash or a product of the cultural collapse', but, despite all this, it had her from 'hello' (2004: A19). Unlike India Knight's take on the subject, it is not women's longing to be housewives that makes the show so compelling but Lynette's depiction of 'the power of the updated and eternal myth of momhood' (ibid.). What is refreshing about Goodman's article is that it pulls no punches when talking about the reality of working mothers' lives and, unlike Knight's homage to the fantasy of domesticity, recognises that the present tide of new American mothers are facing a fairly unusual workplace problem. Echoing Peskowitz's observations that the current trend for new mothers is 'part of an explosion into parenting by a certain class of women and men in their thirties and forties' (2005: 69), she says that these are the mothers who 'worked hard and had children later', adding that the 'postpartum choices they face include 60-hour jobs or none' (ibid.). What these women find, according to prominent sex discrimination attorney Judith Vladek, is that building a career first and having children later makes no difference to their prospects. She says:

> Women should be told the truth. Having a baby is used as an excuse not to give women opportunities. The assumption is that they have made a choice, that having children ends their commitment to their career...putting off motherhood doesn't help (quoted in 2000: 69).

Barbara P. Billauer, president of the Women's Trial Board, confirms this in her testimony to the ABA's Commission on Women:

> Every single woman that I have spoken to without exception, partner or associate, has experienced rampant hostility and prejudice upon her return [from maternity leave]. There is a sentiment that pregnancy and motherhood has softened her, that she is not going to work as hard (ibid.).

In the face of such damning evidence it is no surprise that the women of *Desperate Housewives* evoke Friedan's housewives – with one basic difference: as Goodman reminds us, 'Lynette's entire cohort grew up with the message that women can choose what they want' (2004: A19). This may be so but it should be clear that this rhetoric of choice is brought into play when describing a no-win situation. Choose motherhood or a career. Have-it-all or nothing, love it or leave it – in the face of this Hobson's choice most women are stymied. Asking if we have come 'full circle to a post-feminist mystique', Goodman wonders if American women 'have been so busy fighting the mommy wars that we've forgotten that shared pressure' (ibid.). Maybe the rhetoric of choice has lulled mothers into a false sense of security and led to a resurgence of Friedan's problem that has no name. The difference being that the women who are now suffering were born into a post-feminist world that gives them education, careers and the illusion of equality; only to have that illusion shattered when they attempt to combine motherhood and work. The ladies of Wisteria Lane may be desperate, but is it any surprise when we find that equality no longer extends to them?

Part 2:

SEXUAL POLITICS

5

Desperately straight: The subversive sexual politics of
Desperate Housewives

Samuel A. Chambers

Desperate Housewives. That truly is the title of the show, as I had to
reassure myself (repeatedly) when I saw the first advertisements for it
before the series premiere. 'Really'? I asked out loud to the television
set. (And I wasn't the only one asking: see Peterson 2004; KATC
2004). Then I backed up the TiVo to check again. Yes. Really. The first
commercials in the US ran back to back with announcements for *Wife
Swap.* 'Are they serious'? I queried, turning my exchange with the TV
into a full-fledged conversation. It turns out they were, indeed, quite
serious. This chapter poses the question of just how serious, and
answers: perhaps much more than we might at first imagine. *Desperate
Housewives* centres, as the title would clearly indicate, on the lives of
five suburban women – three married housewives, one divorced
housewife, and one, well, 'slut' – and their struggles with
being... housewives. There are no central gay characters (in the first
season at least). The entire show is set (and shot) in manicured,
whitewashed, sun-splashed California suburbia. Everyone is what
Americans call 'middle class' – which means quite rich. The one
exception to the all-white cast in season one comes in the form of
Carlos and Gabrielle Solis, the most materialistic, high-class members
of the group. In other words, the show appears to be about as straight
as one can humanly conceive.

Not despite all this, but rather because of it, I seek to argue here
that *Desperate Housewives* mobilises a crucial *subversion* of mainstream
sexual politics and heterosexual norms. While we often conceive

subversion as the overturning of a system from outside it, the concept can also be thought as the challenge to, or even erosion of, a set of norms *from within*. In this chapter I will both *reveal* the concept through a reading of the first season of *Desperate Housewives* precisely as I *employ* that concept in order to expose a certain (unexpectedly radical) politics in the show. Thus, I argue that, in what appears to be their very effort to maintain normalcy – within their straight, white, suburban world – the actions and choices of the characters on the show ultimately call mainstream American 'family values' into question. In the effort to shore up the heterosexual norm, *Desperate Housewives* reveals its operation, and, despite any and all intentions, this amounts to a subversion of heteronormativity.

The politics of subversion

To claim *Desperate Housewives* as a subversive show for its sexual politics sounds rather nonsensical on the surface. After all, to reverse the slogan: this is not HBO, it's TV. And *Desperate Housewives* certainly bears little resemblance to the latest path-breaking, cutting-edge, never-before-aired (or pick your own favourite television marketing cliché) product from Home Box Office. Even worse than the show's failure to create its own new genre is the status of the already existing genre into which TV critics typically place the show. As if being on network television were not bad enough, *Desperate Housewives* is a night-time soap opera. Thus, it simply cannot be the next *St Elsewhere*, *thirtysomething*, *Hill Street Blues* or *My So-Called Life*. Rather, for genre comparisons, readers/viewers of *Desperate Housewives* find themselves stuck with *Dallas*, *Dynasty* or *Melrose Place*. Perhaps more awkwardly, multiple members of the *Desperate Housewives* cast are veterans of multiple night-time soaps (Doug Savant and Marcia Cross both from *Melrose Place* and *Knots Landing*, and Nicollette Sheridan from *Knots Landing*).

Thus, if I am to make good on my claim for the show's subversiveness, evidence will have to come from somewhere other than the novelty, genius or heavy-handed seriousness of the show; on all these counts, *Desperate Housewives* will be unlikely to measure up.

The first step lies in a careful consideration of the concept of subversion. Following a particular reading of the works of Judith Butler, I seek to conceptualise subversion as a practice of *undermining from within*. Particularly when it comes to the idea of challenging norms, subversion is best thought of not as a radical overthrow or external transformation, but as a practice that works from *inside* the terms of the norms. This means that subversion must operate from *below*. Norms of gender and sexuality cannot easily be overthrown from the outside, but they can be overturned from the inside. Here we have a theory of subversion that remains fully within the terms of culture (norms are cultural artefacts), working with those terms so as to rework them (see Butler 1999: 119). On this account, we can never get outside the system that we wish to subvert; to claim that we could would be, instead, to undermine the possibility of subversion (Butler 1999: 185, cf.; Butler 1993; 1995; 1997, cf.; Butler 2000).

This particular theoretical articulation of subversion raises pointed questions for our reading of *Desperate Housewives*. Can a show working within (fully or partially – a debate I will leave for others) the soap opera genre serve to challenge certain norms of gender and sexuality? Can a show centred on the lives of (mostly white) suburban family housewives somehow wind up thwarting or eroding heteronormativity? Can a prime-time network soap prove subversive?

Wisteria Lane – a very straight road

The task of situating *Desperate Housewives* inside mainstream norms of gender and sexuality proves far less than daunting. All circuits of the show run through the five central female characters. Bree Van de Kamp, Gabrielle Solis and Lynette Scavo fill the role announced by the title of the show. Each of these characters takes up a different version of the traditional role of a wife who does not work outside the home. No television critic can stop from describing Bree as a 'Martha Stewart-like' character; she is a mother (to two teenagers), a wife, and, above all, a *homemaker*. While Bree lives the subject position of wife to its maximum, Lynette struggles with the constraints that the role places upon her: as a former high-powered business executive, she now wages war (to great comic effect) with her home and children as a mother of three young boys and a baby girl. Gabrielle deviates from the norm slightly; she is the only wife who is not yet a mother. But Gabrielle remains firmly within the role, serving as her husband's trophy and doing all she can to spend his money.

Neither Susan Mayer nor Edie Britt is married, but they round out the 'housewife' subject position by appearing just outside its contours. On one side we find Susan, a divorcee with a teenage daughter and a fragile heart of gold. She upholds the role of wife because her exclusion from it comes at the hands of a cheating husband. The viewer has little doubt that Susan wants nothing more than to marry again some day; she is the wife who was and the wife who would be. And, finally, on the other extreme we can locate Edie, the exception that proves the rule. She has been divorced multiple times, for reasons – unlike the case of Susan – never made clear to the viewers. But one has every reason to suspect that Edie often *chose* to leave her husband, just as she regularly chooses whom to sleep with. Edie is the slut, the abject other that clarifies and shores up the role of 'wife' played (or potentially played) by all the other women. Edie, the slut, forms the constitutive outside to the housewives: she is that which they reject and exclude in order to constitute the subject position of wife.

And the show upholds norms of binary gender, standards of femininity and presumptions of heterosexuality in other ways. First, one may note that all three husbands work in professional, high-status, suit-wearing environments, while none of the wives work at all. Susan works at home, allowing her daily life to mimic that of her housewife friends. Edie, of course, works as a professional (again, the exception that proves the rule). However, as a real estate agent, she holds a job that is today gendered very much female, one that has her relying heavily on her looks, and one that places her working in the neighbourhood (we never see her in the office). Mike Delfino, the central male character who is not a husband, pretends (as his cover) to be a plumber. In reality, we witness his involvement with guns and money and then with covert and illegal actions. Finally we discover Mike's past: conviction for murder and time spent in prison. How could anyone possibly be any more masculine than Mike?

Rounding out the straight attributes of Wisteria Lane certainly requires mentioning that none of the main characters on the show's first season are gay. This fact is perhaps not all that shocking in the context of network TV generally. However, one might expect that in 2004 a night-time soap opera would include at least one gay character; after all, most daytime soap operas now do. More significantly, the universe that *Desperate Housewives* creates proves significantly unqueer, since almost the entire show is shot on Wisteria Lane. That is, the show operates almost exclusively within suburban space, the one place in America today where one is, supposedly, least likely to find gay and lesbian citizens (Lynch 1992; Dunlap 1996; Peyser and Jefferson 2004).

Finally, the mainstream press has done an excellent job making sure that the show stays within traditional norms of femininity. No case better makes this point than the infamous flap over the perfectly timed *Vanity Fair* cover story on *Desperate Housewives'* amazing popularity. The caption to the *Vanity Fair* cover image reads 'You wouldn't believe what it took just to get this photo'. This caption, rather than the specific claims and the general mood of the article itself, provided the hermeneutic key to the dozens of press reports written on the *Vanity Fair* article. Almost all these 'reports' mislead terribly. They all gave the impression that the actresses on the show are all whiny, fighting, crying, hair-pulling little girls. A careful reading of the entire *Vanity Fair* article leads one to believe that the writer and/or the magazine's editors were engaging in a meta-political debate with, in general, publicists in their attempt to control access to 'talent' and, in particular, the ABC rep on this photo shoot who sought to micromanage all details. In contrast, the press reports written about the article detail the prissy nature of the actresses, their conflicts with one another and their emotional fragility. These reports play on, and play up, the idea that, given their essentially feminine nature, a group of five women cannot possibly work together as professionals.

If this account sounds at all overstated, I simply ask the reader to imagine the articles on the conflict being written about a group of five male actors. As Felicity Huffman herself states, 'The prurient interest is gender-specific' (Traister 2005). Just as 'gay-themed' shows such as *The L Word* are easily co-opted as sites of heterosexual fantasy

(Chambers 2006: 81–98), coverage of *Desperate Housewives* operates to reinforce both heterosexual and feminine norms. I conclude here that the mainstream press wants to read the show as just as straight as we might think it is. *Desperate Housewives*: a show about housewives in traditional roles, a show about suburbia, a show populated by thoroughly 'feminine' actresses. We will have to dig quite a bit deeper to find subversion here.

Out of the suburbs and into the studio: 'real-life' political subversion

I want to begin this process in, perhaps, a surprising place, by looking at the comments of two of the actors, particularly those made in response to so-called controversies that took place surrounding the show. Marcia Cross, Huffman and – in his own way – creator Marc Cherry all help to provide an alternative lens through which to view the text of *Desperate Housewives* in relation to dominant norms of gender and sexuality. I will show that their actions and arguments open a space for a more subversive reading of the series.

I start with the rather phobic 'scandal' surrounding Marcia Cross. In February 2005 media madness produced swirling rumours that Cross was gay and that she planned to come out by way of a cover story in *The Advocate* (Freydkin 2005; cf. Warn 2005b). The real shock comes from the source for the story: an anonymous post by an unregistered user on a gay gossip message board. Mainstream media outlets – including CNN and *USA Today* – ran with stories reporting on the 'rumour' and 'speculation' without making any attempt to verify the information. *The Advocate* was planning to put Cross on their cover, but she had no plans to come out in their pages, and yet *The Advocate* was the first to contact Carl Pritzkat, the president of the company that runs the message board, in an effort to verify the information. In his turn, Pritzkat simply declared his 'shock' that the media would point to the message boards as a source at all.

Nevertheless, by the time Marcia Cross co-hosted ABC's *The View* on 8 February 2005, the question of her sexuality had already become a full-blown news story. Still, Cross herself saw no need to address the issue, having had her publicist issue a statement the day before calling the rumours 'completely untrue' (Slan 2005). The hosts of *The View* saw things differently, raising the issue repeatedly. Barbara Walters went directly to the topic, giving Cross something explicitly to deny: 'There is a big rumor about you – that you are gay' (Giantis 2005). Cross instead took the opportunity to question the entire problematic: 'Well it was very odd. I just assume this is what comes of being 42 and single. I don't know if they just needed to find a reason why I wasn't married or – I mean, I'm not' (ibid.). One might wish to take this final 'I'm not' as an answer to the more than implicit question 'Are you gay?', as focused by Walters following the media frenzy. Indeed, a number of transcriptions of the interview that one finds online choose to write the quotation this way, 'I'm not (gay)', and this is not to mention the perverse manner in which a few sites report on Cross's 'angry denials' of the rumour, despite the fact that one can find (either cited in these articles or elsewhere) not one shred of evidence to suggest that Cross was either angry about the rumours or gravely intent on denying them ('TV News' 2005; 'Lesbian Slur' 2005). At this point in the conversation, a different host, Star Reynolds, offered to fix Cross up, confirming her point that folks just are not comfortable with the idea of a famous, beautiful, single 42-year-old.

Still, the 'I'm not' proved too ambiguous for the ladies of *The View*; thus Joy Behar followed up with this rather subtle question: 'So you are not a lesbian?' To this, Cross repeated the 'I'm not' (this time, given context, less ambiguously) before elaborating: 'I did think it was really weird, though, that there was all this curiosity about something like that, about sexuality. And I thought, what a world we live in that that's so important' (Giantis 2005). Again, hard to locate an angry denial here. What we find instead is not only – as would be expected from most heavily managed Hollywood personalities – an incredibly careful and diplomatic response from Cross to a series of questions that she should never have to answer in the first place, but also a rather significant elaboration and critique of the power of heteronormativity. Cross takes no offence at the idea that someone might think she is gay, but she does take the opportunity to question the notion that any of this should cause controversy and she challenges the idea that this question must even be definitively answered. Adam Vary puts it quite eloquently and accurately in the article in *The Advocate* – a piece that, in fully postmodern self-referentiality, wound up being *about* the controversy over the cover story itself. Vary claims that Cross 'handled herself [graciously] on *The View*, where she appeared more incredulous that anyone would care about her sexuality at all than that anyone would think she's gay' (2005). She directs her incredulity towards exactly the twin homophobic assumptions that a) being gay is bad or wrong, and b) that being straight is important or essential.

In her own way, then, and from within the particular constraints of the Hollywood context, Cross hereby challenges the power of heteronormativity by refusing the terms of the question. Even her dry and succinct publicist's statement achieves this goal. It states: 'In response to recent rumors about Marcia Cross, they are completely untrue. She is, however, very supportive of the gay and lesbian community' (Slan 2005). Once again, the last line of support for the gay and lesbian community might be expected as good PR (although, even at that, few would take the time to make the claim), but I would prefer to focus on what is not said in the first sentence. The statement calls the rumours 'untrue', but it refuses to say 'Marcia Cross is a straight woman' or that she is not gay. This did not stop the news reports from proclaiming just that, sometimes even from their headlines. *USA Today* ran this headline: 'I'm Single and Straight, Cross says,' despite the fact that she says no such thing, either on TV or in her official statement. *Entertainment Weekly* went with this headline, offering a similar, and similarly falsely attributed quote: 'Marcia Cross: I'm not gay!' Perhaps most amazing of all, *TV Guide* online ended their brief entry with this sentence: 'Just don't call her a lesbian!' (Freydkin 2005; Susman 2005, 'Plot Thickens' 2005). All these media misreports serve as efforts to reconstitute the power of heteronormativity in the face of Cross's small confrontation to that very power. Such a challenge proves politically significant, i.e. potentially subversive, even if it requires archaeological work to uncover.

Much less buried will be the political work of Felicity Huffman. The most critically acclaimed but perhaps least well-known actress on the show, Huffman is certainly one to participate in subversive on-screen work – including her recent award-winning role as a transgender person in *Transamerica* (2005). In an interview about *that* role,

Huffman stresses the path-breaking power of *Desperate Housewives*: all the lead roles have gone to actresses in their thirties and forties. When asked why such a show would emerge now when in the past there have been almost no good roles for women over 35-years old, Huffman gives a rich and significant answer: 'I think gay men appreciate women differently than straight guys do. ...we're not the objects of their sexual desires, but they always consider us sexual objects. ...I think gay men write women differently' (quoted in Traister 2005). Huffman's response calls on the logic of a long-standing feminist argument: women should be in positions of power not merely for fundamental egalitarian reasons, but also because many things will change in society (in ways we perhaps cannot foresee) when the powerful positions are no longer dominated by one, rather singular subject position (the straight white male). Yet the argument has been completely reworked and amplified, since Huffman suggests that it is creator/producer Marc Cherry's position as a gay man that provides the show with a different take on gender roles.

For his own sake, Cherry provides a name for this perspective, calling it 'post-post-post-feminist' (quoted in Vary 2005). I have no idea what Cherry means by that, and I am even less certain that he knows himself. But if feminism takes an oppositional stance to traditional gender roles in an effort to seek women's liberation, and if post-feminism wrongly assumes that no such change in gender roles, no such liberation, is necessary, since women are somehow already equal to men, then whatever lies beyond the second category would need to consider the case for resistance to those categories of gender and sexuality – resistance that can only come from within, a radical political praxis through subversion.

Normalisation and subversion; or, Wisteria Lane – not as straight as you think

To delineate this politics of subversion fully requires a clearer under-standing of normalisation. In both its narrative and dialogic structure *Desperate Housewives* makes a concerted effort to maintain the surface appearance of both heterosexual normality and traditional gender roles. However, on the reading offered here this is precisely the point: the show *tries so hard* to uphold straightness that it betrays itself. The reason that Wisteria Lane proves something less than straight lies in the very desperation to remain straight. Often the characters on the show work so hard to preserve normality that in the process they *reveal the workings* of gender and sex norms. Despite surface appearances, hidden queer moments and unknown queer spaces can be found up and down Wisteria Lane.

Certainly, Bree's family comes to mind in this regard. The most obvious case may appear in the unexpected form of Andrew Van de Kamp, Bree's son. Finding himself in the strictest, most uptight (read 'straightest') family on Wisteria Lane, Andrew is either the most likely or unlikely (depending on your perspective) character for the viewer to find making out with his male friend, Justin (Ryan Carnes), in the swimming pool. That is precisely where we locate Andrew in the episode 'Impossible' (1: 15). Andrew and Justin's on-screen kiss, some viewers and readers may be surprised to hear, turns out to be just the sixth male–male kiss in network television history – and the first one hardly even counts (Warn 2005a). Andrew himself turns out to be a very queer character to the extent that he actively refuses any particular sexual identity – first denying his homosexuality, then coming out to his parents as gay, and finally telling his pastor, Reverend Sikes (Dakin Matthews), that the coming out was itself a lie (1: 15; 1: 18; 1: 19).

As if this were not enough queerness to thoroughly trouble the heteronormativity of the nuclear Van de Kamp family, we later discover that Rex Van de Kamp, Bree's husband, has significantly non-normative sexual proclivities: he thoroughly enjoys S/M role-playing and has been paying a prostitute to fulfil his desires (1: 10). Even worse, the prostitute in question is another housewife just down the street on Wisteria Lane. When Bree discovers these 'unspeakable' (in her mind) transgressions, she is, needless to say, not amused. Bree denigrates Rex, stigmatises him for his actions, and upholds her normative vision of narrowly constrained sexual practices. And yet her very devotion to a vision of the nuclear family eventually leads her to agree to role-play with her husband. Thus, we find queerness at the very deepest heart of the heterosexual norm.

Bree herself remains so intent on preserving her vision of the perfectly mannered, brilliantly behaved, normal nuclear family that she will take her cheating husband back into their home and participate in S/M sexual scenarios with him. Clearly, her effort to uphold normality serves instead to undermine it. In general, to reveal the norm may be to subvert it, since norms work best when they are never exposed. In other words, the optimal operation of the norm is an invisible operation. Once norms reach the point that they require significant shoring up then they have already been significantly weakened. This means that reinforcing a norm can never bring it back to full strength, since the very act of reinforcement serves to expose it as weaker than it could be. Put another way, as David Halperin has argued, the best way to call one's heterosexuality into question is to declare it, since if one is really straight one need never say so (1995: 48; cf. Chambers 2005: 178). For viewers of the show, this argument will likely call up the scene in which Susan catches Andrew and Justin making out in the pool, and Andrew immediately and adamantly declares, 'I'm not gay' (1: 15).

By revealing the heterosexual norm and exposing its operation, *Desperate Housewives* proves successful (despite whatever its intentions might be) in undermining heteronormativity. The show subverts the norm from within, not by eroding it from the margins, but by undermining it from the centre. To capture this particular meaning of subversion (and its political significance) requires maintaining a clear distinction between 'what the majority do/are' on the one hand and *normalisation* on the other. This distinction entails not taking heteronormativity as a mere description of the fact that a supermajority of people in the world act/identify as heterosexual. The political concept heteronormativity offers not a bare description of fact (most people 'are heterosexual'). Rather, heteronormativity provides a political articulation of the *normativity* of heterosexuality. In other words, 'heteronormativity' tells us that heterosexual desire and identity are not merely assumed, they are expected. They are demanded. Thus, heteronormativity must not be reduced to the idea of an assumption in the heads of individuals that says, 'My guess is that you're straight'. Heteronormativity is written into law, encoded in the very structures of institutions (think restrooms, think locker rooms), built into an enormous variety of common practices – particularly since so much of society remains structured around dating and romance.

Thinking heteronormativity in this more expansive yet more precise manner serves to specify *Desperate Housewives'* specific form of subversion. The show does not subvert heteronormativity by emphasising the margins. Obviously, the women of Wisteria Lane are neither political radicals, nor gender/sexual deviants. If they were, they would not live on Wisteria Lane. Across their differences, Bree, Lynette, Susan, Gabrielle and Edie all find themselves relatively close to the median point on the normal curve. Yet, here we see a crucial point about normalisation: it produces its effects even on those it marks as ostensibly 'normal'. The power of the norm is felt in different ways (sometimes more violently) by those at the margins of the curve, but it is still felt by those towards the centre. The norm wields a terrible force against the women of Wisteria Lane and we witness their struggle with, through and sometimes against that norm. Obviously, resistance to norms can come from the margins, but resistance may arise at the centre as well. As the women of Wisteria Lane wage their struggle with normality, they often expose heteronormativity – and sometimes they undermine it.

Indeed, challenging the norm from the centre has the potential to wield a much greater force than questioning the norm from its margins. This logic can be illuminated with the following rhetorical question. Whose gender deviations prove more disturbing to the power of the norm: those abject others whose very difference consolidates the power of the norm, or the normal ones themselves? If gays, sexual radicals, even (occasionally) single people challenge norms of sex and gender, this behaviour is to be expected (even if it is not 'normal'). But to challenge sex and gender norms from inside the upper-class, white, nuclear family is potentially to do serious damage to heteronormativity. No wonder the American Family Association (AFA) was so upset about *Desperate Housewives* (Potts 2004).

If a politics of subversion sounds weak or somehow hollow, if it reads like a feeble attempt to praise a show that in the end one might wish to condemn as nothing more than a soap opera, then perhaps it will be worth reminding readers of what *Desperate Housewives* manages to carry off. Unlike a whole host of ostensibly more 'radical' shows on television, *Desperate Housewives* successfully (and, perhaps surprisingly, with little controversy) raises a number of controversial, complicated and important questions concerning the politics of gender and sexuality. *Desperate Housewives* aired one of the very few kisses between two males on network TV, but it seems worth adding that the *Desperate Housewives* kiss had an important context – the characters were both teenagers, and they were alone at night, ostensibly naked, and in the swimming pool. Beyond this, as is also well known, the show plots an affair between an older married woman and another teenage boy. And then we have Rex Van de Kamp's infamous sexual proclivities; unlike 'gay kisses' I am unsure if anyone has bothered to document serious characters with a taste for S/M, but I will run the risk of conjecture: if Rex is not the first, he finds himself on a very short list indeed.

All of this could be trivialised, and certainly the show's dark humour plays many of these examples as much for their comic effect as for any other more serious purposes. Nonetheless, one should not downplay the significance of the fact that *Desperate Housewives* has been able to raise issues such as these, ones that would never appear on shows such as *Will and Grace*. And while they may certainly crop up in other quarters, e.g. *Queer As Folk*, they are just as likely to be dismissed there. In other words, audience is always important, and *Desperate Housewives* speaks to a very different and much larger one. These factors all come together to produce the counter-intuitive but nevertheless powerful conclusion that *Desperate Housewives* motivates a significant cultural politics, subversive of heteronormativity.

6

What is it with that hair? Bree Van de Kamp and policing contemporary femininity

Janet McCabe

I have no reason to like Bree Van de Kamp. I could say my aversion relates – superficially, at least – to how she represents an image of feminine success, the white, middle-class, über-homemaker living comfortably in the suburbs, which exists as if to remind me feminism never happened. That's partly it. But not completely. I have a guilty secret that I feel I need to hush up. It has something to do with her svelte body and sartorial elegance – the impeccable tailoring, the classic cashmere twin-sets, the colour coordination. I cannot 'do' pastel. I know, I know. Call me shallow. Never have I worn a rose pink cardigan without looking anything less than tragic. I'm convinced that women like Bree are put on this TV earth to shame me. Judging me for not being brave enough with my knits, for not daring to take more risks with accessories, for never being quite good enough. Yet this is no reason to take against another woman. Or is it?

But as I gaze longingly at her gorgeous flaming-red locks – perfectly coiffured, beautifully lush – and wonder who in their right mind chose Eva Longoria over Bree to be the hair of L'Oréal I can't help wondering why, when Bree Van de Kamp stands for everything that troubles me about contemporary feminism (and even my own, come to think of it), I am so drawn to her.

Is there not another deeper secret here, darker even than the one lurking beneath the well-manicured lawns of Wisteria Lane? Is it not something to do with me silently accepting and even approving particular images of feminine beauty and success designated as the norm? Intoxicatingly presented as being about my personal choice, persuasively offered to me as about embodying female aspiration and satisfaction, Bree (or should I say my fascination/difficulties with her?) says much about my own ambivalent investment in dominant images of feminine success and normalcy. After all, it is easy to follow the rules; and there is contentment in being uncomplicated. I know where I am – I know what is expected of me, what I am supposed to want; and I know that wishing to embody such an image grants me privilege, making me feel good about making the 'right' choice, and social rewards will be mine for picking correctly.

But choosing such normalising images of femininity 'requires', contest Leslie Heywood and Jennifer Drake, 'silencing dissent' (2003: 41). 'Living up to images of success,' they argue, 'requires keeping secrets [and]... collusion with approved scripts' (ibid.). But is not this idea of women investing 'in the work of keeping silent, shoring up images and narratives that we *think* help us survive but that are actually killing (the other in) us' (ibid.), what I enjoy most about *Desperate Housewives*? And does not this breaking the silence help me unravel the ways in which these privileged images of feminine normalcy are disguised to *not* look oppressive, when in fact they perpetuate the regulatory fiction and practices disciplining femininity and the female body within our contemporary culture?

Keeping up appearances: living the feminine ideal and textual paradox

To be fair to Bree, she is more than aware of '*needing* to live the lie of the image' (ibid.). Heavily invested in her construction as an upper middle-class married woman with children living in the suburbs, she understands only too well the privilege bestowed on women prepared to wear the mask and *live* an ideal of feminine perfection applauded by dominant culture. What does it matter, she confesses to Dr Albert Goldfine (Sam Lloyd), if she settles for a life of 'repression and denial' so long as she can host 'civilised and elegant' dinner parties (1: 14)? Week after week Bree offers us lessons in the politics of appearance, instructing us in the tastes, behaviours and preferences that make visible certain privileged class, racial and gendered identities. But in her performing a certain version of American middle-class femininity that does not 'disturb Anglo-Saxon, heterosexual expectations and identifications' (Bordo 2003: 25) what gets exposed is how living that image requires endless self-monitoring and a ceaseless maintenance of a well-disciplined body.

Of course, none of the ladies violate our contemporary obsession with bodies obedient to the social norm, the toned, waxed, slender, youthful-looking female body. But, whereas we see the others 'letting go' – Edie Britt giving in to her erotic passions, Gabrielle Solis indulging in spending sprees and delighting in afternoon romps with her teenage lover, Susan Mayer literally losing control with those calamitous pratfalls, and Lynette Scavo struggling to marshal her young brood – Bree remains a model of self-composure and self-control despite the chaos encircling her life. Constant watchfulness over the self is necessary to ensure conformity to the ideal. It is what she does best. The other women (and so do we) may know all is not well in the Van de Kamp household but nonetheless recognise Bree as embodying the beguiling ideal of a well-managed feminine self. A conspiracy of silence shrouds her. She looks fabulous. She is perfect – too perfect, in fact. We may see Lynette as offering a more 'natural' depiction of the kinds of dilemmas faced by women told they can choose what they want (maybe too 'natural' that we must be suspicious), but we also understand that what Bree represents is no less 'real'. We may laugh and think ourselves terribly clever for seeing through the façade – but is not the joke on us? She may look plastic, like an anachronistic cliché, especially when played against Lynette, who can barely hold it together, but what might seem like a trivial, comical and innocuous representation exacts a powerful normalising hold over us. That body – willowy, poised, graceful, well-groomed – is shaped and 'inscribed' with the imprint of prevailing historical and political forms of discursive power that manage and animate our perception and experience of what the 'correct' female body should look like.

Bree more than any other woman seems to visibly confirm what Michel Foucault (1991; 1998) had in mind when he focused attention on the grip that culture has on our bodies, imposing on them – its movements, gestures, attitudes, behaviours – certain restrictions, rules and requirements. She is sensitive to any slight infringement of social norms and habituated to self-surveillance and self-disciplining in the service of those prevailing dominant ideals. When husband Rex asks her for a divorce in a lowly steakhouse, for pity's sake, saying: 'I just can't live in this detergent commercial anymore' (1: 1), I hooted less at his heavy-handed wink to us media-savvy viewers about the tyranny of living with a media-produced ideal as much as her (textual) retribution. Vigorously cutting into a small loaf, she retorts that she will not discuss the dissolution of her marriage in an establishment that has 'dudes' and 'chicks' on the restroom doors. She then proceeds to send him into anaphylactic shock after piling onions, to which he is allergic, on to his plate. You go, girl! Lurking beneath her gestures dutiful to family obligation is the literal silencing of Rex for his dissent. Okay, so she takes her performance as suburban housewife too far; overdoing things with always having to be so perfect. But does he have to be so mean about it? Disclosing what should not be said, to denounce that ideal of American womanhood the media works so hard to promote and on which our culture places such high premium as false, is just plain reckless. No wonder he has to die. So privileged is what Bree represents in the text as feminine body and female subject – and not least because Marcia Cross is one of the stars – that it comes as little surprise that Rex is inadvertently killed off at her hands. Just as she works hard to self-regulate her feminine self *in* and *through* the narrative – yes, she is a control freak – she also functions to police the text for any transgressions that challenge what she embodies as representation. She operates inside meticulous narrative, generic and cultural codes – and her considerable influence comes from acting out 'that [which] we no longer perceive ... as the effect of power that constrains us' (Foucault 1998: 60).

But the self-referential, self-reflexive *Desperate Housewives* text alerts us to the contradictions and inconsistencies inherent in living the ideal, between a critique of what it takes to sustain the ideal and female participation in colluding with, and self-policing, those same culturally privileged constructions. This is television for 'pop-culture babies' like me (Heywood and Drake 2003: 51), a postmodern, post-feminist media text where cultural critique and indulgent pleasures meet in an amusingly ironic play of textual disruption and surface delight. In its formal, generic and narrative properties, it acknowledges the powerful hold – both pleasurable and strongly normalising – that particular representations of the culturally inscribed female body have over us; and it understands only too well media-produced 'images and stories – representations of the "real" – *are* as "real" as it gets, because they make and are made by the social scripts that we live' (ibid.).

The highly stylised *mise en scène*, for example, leaves us in no doubt about representation as arising out of, (re)producing and functioning to police feminine ideals as performed by Bree. Superficially at least, as a glossy media image, she is 'simply another impossible contrivance of perfect womanhood' (Walker 1995: xxxiii). Immediately she is presented as a vision of feminine accomplishment and harmony polished to perfection. Introduced first through a light-hearted montage sequence narrated in dulcet tones by Mary Alice Young, she is seen 'making her own clothes', planting out a shrub and upholstering a winged-back armchair – images that suggest there is no reality for Bree Van de Kamp beyond her immaculate colonial-style home and orderly herbaceous borders (1: 1). The melodious and charming strains of classical chamber music accompany her going about her daily domestic routine, dressed appropriately for the task at hand. Brisk edits and the sweeping camera rationalise Bree's energetic labours to maximise efficiency. These features along with the sleek aesthetics give a distinct *mise en scène* to the modern cult of domesticity, the flawless, picture-perfect house and garden, and the middle-class housewife skilled in domestic chores and finding true happiness in her efforts. Breezy Bree makes it look so easy. So alluring, so rewarding. It is when she inhabits the representation that she is at her best. Sequences like this one in which representational strategies do not merely transform but *normalise* the feminine self reveal how prevailing norms defining and regulating the female – her body, her subjectivity – are inscribed right into the very form of the *mise en scène* as it is used. The function, furthermore, is not to ask questions about whether these norms are 'right' and worth pursuing in the first place, but to keep them more or less in place. It is a media-produced deception of what feminine normalcy should look like that has, in fact, assumed the status of 'truth'.

Glossy production values giving off a 'curious retro glow' (Press 2004) self-reference a filmic and television landscape, from *American*

Beauty to *Leave It To Beaver*, from *Six Feet Under* to *Melrose Place*, from *Twin Peaks* to *Blue Velvet*, that let slip nothing is ever quite as it seems. The heightened colour palette that makes Bree and her life look as if it has been lifted straight from the luscious pages of *Homes and Gardens*, and reminiscent of 1950s Sirkian melodrama, portrays a charming world crammed full of furniture, pastel shades and domestic accomplishment. The sheer artificiality of these lush images, the retro-textual cool, indulges in a pop-culture nostalgic yearning for a return to better days, seducing us with the utopian promise of simpler, better times when women knew who they were and life was less complicated. Of course, we know it is only a representation. Eclectic cultural references and textual traces produced by a sophisticated (televisual) media culture (Collins 1995). It is meant to be ironic, a pastiche. We get it.

But does not the tantalising postmodern strangeness give representation to the dilemmas of contemporary femininity obsessed with 'defining' identities – where we endlessly talk about ourselves, ceaselessly justify our lifestyle choices and incessantly police our bodies – at a time when we are told we have unlimited opportunities and no need for radical feminist politics? Here the surface shine where the lawns are a little too trim and the houses a little too pristine alerts us to what feminist psychologist Betty Friedan (1965) once described as a discrepancy between how women's lives are perceived and how they really are. Calling attention to the artifice does not necessarily mean to critique as much as to assign representational form to the paradox and uncertainties defining contemporary femininity, 'shaped by struggles between various feminisms as well as by cultural backlash against feminism and activism' (Heywood and Drake 2003: 2). As a post-feminist text, then, *Desperate Housewives* suffers from a mild case of textual hysteria – a quiet desperation, if you will – bubbling under the surface as it at the same time normalises dominant ideals of the feminine self, her body (slender, fashionable), her lifestyle choices (wife, mother), her aspirations (suburban family life).

Not too surprising that it falls to Bree, the most enticing ideal of a well-managed feminine self, to lift the lid on the inconsistencies and conspiracy lurking beneath, where a constantly shifting cultural power works to produce and normalise forms of female selfhood and subjectivity in the post-feminist age. As Edie says about Bree, 'The supermom is always the first to snap' (2: 5). Working in and through generic forms, like melodrama and comedy known for exposing hidden meanings, for lifting taboos and revealing cultural prohibitions, gives this most repressed of characters the tools to reveal discrepancy and discrimination. Required to talk incessantly by the demands of the televisual serial format, what she chooses to make known is what goes on behind the judging and regulating of feminine normalcy. Never questioning her choice to live that ideal, and speaking through a conservative rhetoric that makes what she has to say seem more palatable, more morally acceptable, even, she nonetheless is prescribed the narrative task of taking charge of, and tracking down, as it were, the paradoxes of the policing process – 'to allow it no obscurity, no respite' (Foucault 1998: 20).

Nowhere are these textual eruptions more evident, or funnier, than when she is defending other women against patriarchal injustice. It is she who tells Dr Goldfine that Sigmund Freud was wrong for 'peddling a theory' that traced back 'the problems of most adults ... to something awful their mother' did (1: 2). Did Freud not consider the sacrifices his mother had made for him – and at a time when domestic appliances were not available? Managing to re-stitch the loose button on Goldfine's jacket while giving Freud a stern ticking off shows that, as ever, she is a class act. Given the contemporary desire to blame women for the consequences of changes in the family, especially as they relate to men, her attack on one of the founding myths of patriarchal culture and her vindication of the mother is nothing less than an act of sedition. It is a confusing moment. Not least because she is the most unlikely advocate for women struggling against patriarchal opprobrium. Common sense replaces radical ideology; individual empowerment substitutes for collective action. Yet her sentiments have nonetheless a distinctive feminist tone.

But is not this paradox embedded right into the very cultural forms that give representation to contemporary femininity? Using Freud's theory of the tendentious joke (sorry, Bree) may help us unlock this paradox to pleasure. If, as Freud described, humour works in the interest of our unconscious desires to overcome what cannot be said – a mild form of anarchy for the psyche, lifting internal inhibitions and poking fun at cultural prohibitions and taboos – then could it not be argued that what Bree has to tell us about how Freud's mother must have felt lifts the lid on how patriarchy has long vilified the very ideal it celebrates? Where there is power, Foucault would later come to suggest, there is also resistance. Saying what the women's movement worked hard to reveal (taking apart patriarchal fictions) but packaged in a dutiful gesture strongly associated with a traditional feminine skill (sewing) disorients before making us laugh out loud. Matricide might be the original sin of *Desperate Housewives,* but, as Bree reminds us, women are driven to it in pursuit of needing to live the ideal feminine self defined as the norm.

Dressing like Bree: style images and the disciplined feminine body

I take *Desperate Housewives* as materialising the uneasy contemporary post-feminist struggle to make sense of the power of images as disciplining the feminine self – the body, behaviours, identities – and maintaining them as the prevailing norm. Yet while the series is far more ambivalent about Bree Van de Kamp's over-investment in images of feminine perfection that 'convince women who *fail* to embody [those] ideals...that they need to bring themselves into line' (Bordo 2003: 298), her image of retro-chic 1950s housewife with a modern twist celebrated in glossy magazines and the print media is quite another matter. Never mind that she holds membership of the National Rifle Association (NRA), and feels it necessary to make the bed before taking her ailing husband to the hospital (1: 22); she looks fabulous in vintage. What else matters? What I am suggesting is that, while we *know* that she is 'performing' a certain ideal of femininity, we understand what her representation is doing – I know I have my 'Bree' moments, as brief and as calamitous as they may be – we still compulsively *pursue* the aesthetic ideal of what she represents as something that counts. We are invited to scrutinise it, to take pleasure in the minutiae of it, to discerningly consume it, to desire the coherence it promises – and to understand it as the norm. Just as Bree delightfully reminds us when she climbs into Rex's coffin to swap her late husband's ghastly orange prep school tie for Tom Scavo's muted blue stripes (2: 1), appearance matters. Maybe it is because I am bedazzled by that hair, but I am reminded of what Susan Bordo said about how in our media-saturated age it is becoming increasingly 'difficult to discriminate between parodies and possibilities for the self' (2003: 174).

Women are constantly being invited to pore over and inspect Bree (rather than Marcia Cross) in the fashion pages of celebrity and lifestyle magazines, in the newspapers, and on the Internet and the show, as a way of instructing us on how to imitate, transform and 'improve' ourselves in that image. Scholars like Charlotte Herzog (1990) and Jackie Stacey (1994) have long explained to us how Hollywood taught the female spectator to put together elements of style and 'to transform themselves into a "look" by comparison with another woman who is "looked at"' (Herzog 1990: 159). Week after week fashion editors and stylists from magazines obsessed with celebrity body image are on hand to tutor us on how to look like our favourite housewife (*Heat* 2005: 73–74, 76; *Now* 2005: 52–53). Advice on haircare products and its management – 'simply blow-dry your hair straight but flip the bottom up with a round steel brush' – facial creams – Crème de la Mer – fashion combinations – cashmere twinsets teamed with a tweed pencil skirt – jewellery – pearls, of course – and shoes is given so that we too can look as immaculately groomed and as pristine as Bree. Nothing is left to chance. No opportunity is given for failure. These instructions (accompanied by head-to-toe glossy fashion plates) provide us with a prescribed lexicon of feminine beauty and style, and inform us of the everyday practices by which our experience and perception of the female body is organised. Extending Naomi Wolf's observation that '*the beauty myth is always actually prescribing behavior*' (1991: 14) leads me to consider how the Bree 'look' is privileged, perpetuating conventions, assumptions and attitudes of the contemporary female body in very particular ways.

Immediately her sartorial style evokes the 1950s, another time of perceived firm boundaries when strategies of containment were key to foreign policy, and Republican conservative values of family and Church profoundly shaped the domestic agenda. Glamorously reviving and parodying the 1950s housewife, the Bree style belongs to what feminist Gloria Steinem calls a 'generation of translation and backlash' (1995: xx). On-screen ice queen turns into postmodern ice maiden

– cool and detached, a decorative style to be borrowed and parodied, imitated and played with, a living *mise en scène*. Translation here is informed by nostalgia, which, like Bree, is about yearning for better days, for a kinder, gentler world where family values and common decency prevailed. Her style is a symbol of middle-class affluence and success, her body pastiching social identity and historic 'place'. Classic cuts and defined (political) borders in the new Republican age speak of a (feminine) body politics concerned with self-esteem, self-reliance, self-mastery and personal discipline, a female empowerment based not on political action and radical feminist ideology (especially as the style references pre-second-wave feminist times) but on taking control of, and incessantly policing, the image. Control over style, over (consumer) impulses, over the body translates into control and power over one's own life; or as Bordo astutely puts it: '...arising out of and reproducing normative feminine practices of our culture...train the female body in docility and obedience to cultural demands while at the same time being experienced in terms of power and control' (2003: 27).

Identifying a fashion style associated with a time that delighted in the curvaceous female form – one that accentuated breasts and hips with close-fitting bodices, nipped-in waists, long, full skirts and stiletto heels – implies a renewed celebration of woman as about intimacy, sex and reproductive destiny. But immediately apparent is how the more androgynous and sleek body form of Bree/Marcia Cross replaces this 1950s coercive ideal of the voluptuous feminine body shape. If the hourglass figure, emphasising breasts and hips, is, argue feminist scholars, a marker of reproductive femaleness (Bordo 2003: 208), then what are we to make of this slimmed-down version of the 'happy homemaker heroine' (Friedan 1965)? Bree's designer outfits and form-fitting sartorial elegance have everything to do with the quest for firm body margins and a complete self-mastery over the feminine self – style, lifestyle and body. Coherence is desired, wished for, in fact, where nothing is left to disrupt the regulatory fiction of female normalcy. If the fashion pages dissect the minutiae of the Bree style as about self-management and self-control, then the paparazzi shots of Cross leaving the local supermarket in dodgy old clothes remind us of what happens when we are not attendant to the care of the self.

Susan Bordo has argued the new slim-line look may in fact symbolise not so much the containment of female desires as its liberation from a domestic, reproductive destiny (2003: 206). Which leads me nicely to Marcia Cross. Interesting how the image of Bree is predicated upon the disavowal and often denigration of the actress. Pitting woman against woman in a misogynistic sleight of hand. Well, Cross only has herself to blame. A fortysomething-year-old woman who has never been married and has no children. What are we to make of such a creature? Cross made headlines in early 2005 when an anonymous Internet posting rumoured that the actress was planning to 'come out' in *The Advocate*. In the subsequent article Adam Vary concluded that 'the notion that beautiful, feminine, Stepford-worthy Bree might be embodied by a closet actress was, it seems, just too steamy to ignore' (2005: 49). The mainstream media gossip machine went into overdrive, and Cross felt compelled to issue a denial. The brouhaha has as much to tell us about our celebrity-crazed culture as it does about our culture's anxieties, unease and confliction when speaking about and representing women not adhering to convention. Such controversy has much, in fact, to tell us about the unwritten (and often unconscious) rules that define what can and cannot be said within any given discourse, and the discourse regulating femininity has distinct rules that function according to custom, expectation and assumption. Interviewed at the time by Barbara Walters, Cross seemed to anticipate how she disrupts the conventional wisdom: 'It's very odd and I assume this is what comes of being 42 and single. I don't know if they just needed to find a reason why I wasn't married...' Successful, single, childless and over 40: she must be gay. What other explanation can there be? Despite repeated denials, her fate seemed sealed. Ever since she has been plagued by rumours of diva-like behaviour (as with the *Vanity Fair* debacle [Zeman 2005: 197–205, 264–266]) and being a lesbian until she announced her engagement to financial adviser Tom Mahoney in August 2005. Illustrated here are the difficulties involved in doing different and creating new representations in a culture that is opposed to anything but the most restricted forms of meaning it regulates and polices.

No wonder feminists (Pozner and Seigel 2005) and conservative cultural watchdogs alike are divided over what to make of this show and what it has to say about contemporary womanhood. Calls from feminist theorists like Donna Haraway demand that feminism address these kinds of problems, and identify 'a politics that acknowledges the multiple and contradictory aspects of both individual and collective identities' (quoted in Siegel 1997: 53). So violent has the backlash against feminism been that women have been left confused and uncertain. Contradiction and paradox are clearly not only the preserve of theoretical inquiry, but on the evidence of series like *Desperate Housewives* are embedded right into the very forms representing contemporary femininity – our choices, our lifestyles, our bodies. But is there not resistance here? Struggle over meaning in and across media texts makes visible the struggle over the meaning of femininity at this particular historical moment.

Inhabiting what Heywood and Drake call 'that contradictory space' (2003: 51–52) I, like many other contemporary feminists, acknowledge that femininity is a scripted cultural performance and subject to strict regulation, but am at the same time entangled in that process; I understand how the representation of the ideal female body remains strongly normalising, preserving prescribed dominant structures of heterosexist power, while deliberately participating and consuming those images. Caught in this paradox is Bree – textual character, fashion icon.

It's the hair. It's definitely something to do with her flaming-red tresses. Can't get enough of it. Unable to restrain myself a moment longer I am lost in reverie.

7

As Kamp as Bree: Post-feminist camp in
Desperate Housewives

Niall Richardson

Despite camp's seemingly exclusive affiliation with gay men and misogynist tendencies, camp offers feminists a model for critiques of gender and sex roles. Camp has an affinity with feminist discussions of gender construction, performance, and enactment; we can thereby examine forms of camp as feminist practice.

Pamela Robertson 1996: 6

In 'Love Is In the Air' (1: 14), Bree Van de Kamp attends her weekly session with her marriage counsellor and remarks that she would be content with a loveless, hollow marriage provided she could always have *fabulous* dinner parties. Such campy remarks, in which style and appearance are valued over substance, have been characteristic of Bree throughout the series. Mrs Van de Kamp – the supreme Stepford Wife who, according to her husband, has hair that *never* moves – can simply be read as yet another example in popular culture's tradition of camp women, ranging from Mae West and Raquel Welch to Joan Collins. Whether for comic relief, or an attempt to pander to gay male spectatorship (see Farmer 2000), camp women have been a staple part of American popular media. However, in this chapter I argue that the camp representation of Bree is more than simply fun or comic relief. Instead, I reconsider the politics of camp and suggest that *Desperate Housewives* can be read as employing camp for a post-feminist agenda.

Desperate Housewives continues the current stream of 'quality' American television dramas that have focused on women's issues in a post-feminist era. Following *Ally McBeal, Sex and the City, Charmed, Family Law* and *Judging Amy, Desperate Housewives* represents 'feminist characters who are "new, new women"' (Lotz 2001: 106). Yet unlike *Sex and the City*, which represented a 'postpatriarchal world' (Thornham and Purvis 2005: 126), *Desperate Housewives* offers a darker image and is one of the first mainstream dramas to criticise, in a *very* savage fashion, the institutions of heterosexual monogamy. Focusing on the lives of four different housewives, the show represents the oppression of upper-middle-class, suburban life and the difficulties that these women encounter in their roles of housewife and mother. Despite appearing to have achieved the *Ally McBeal* dream, these women are *desperately* unhappy with their situation.

However, Amanda Lotz points out that in order to analyse contemporary representations, critics need to use post-feminism as a 'useful critical tool' to understand internal contestation within the text (2001: 115). I argue that, in the case of *Desperate Housewives*, one of its most interesting representations – Mrs Bree Van de Kamp – is best analysed by recourse to the sensibility known as 'camp'. This chapter will argue that *Desperate Housewives* is employing camp for a feminist political agenda, and will therefore firstly consider the debates about post-feminism and then explore its relationship with the politics of camp.

Post-feminism

Post-feminism is still a slippery term and, as Jane Gerhard points out (2005: 39), many critics are dubious that it has any validity at all. In its most generalised sense, post-feminism is read as arguing that 'the aims of feminism have been largely achieved, and that women can now accomplish whatever they want to, provided they are prepared to make sufficient effort' (MacDonald 1995: 226).

However, there are contradictions within post-feminist politics. Some critics, such as Rachel Moseley, see post-feminism as a re-evaluation of the tensions and bewilderment that is thought to exist 'between feminism (as female power) and femininity' (2002: 403). As Moseley suggests, a 'postfeminist identity,...while informed by second-wave feminism, rejects the feminist identities associated with it, instead celebrating and understanding conventional modes of femininity as *not necessarily* in conflict with female power' (2002: 419; see also Moseley and Read 2002). According to Moseley, post-feminism can be read as trying to put the 'traditional' performances of femininity (i.e. a touch of glamour) back into feminist politics.

Yet, on the other hand, some feminists dismiss post-feminism as a marketing ploy engineered by companies to sell more products to women (Greer 1999). Tania Modleski argues that post-feminism is discarding all the years of hard work by second wave feminists and is 'undermining the goals of feminism – in effect delivering us back to a prefeminist world' (1991: 3; see also McRobbie 2004). Far from building upon the achievements of second wave feminism, post-feminism returns women to the situation they were in before the work of Betty Friedan (1965) and Germaine Greer (1971). With such distinct contradictions within post-feminist politics (some critics argue that it develops second wave feminism while others argue that it discards it), claiming a post-feminist identification requires an awareness of the paradoxes within the movement's ideological stance and a sophisticated juggling of these inconsistencies.

Myra MacDonald makes an insightful point about post-feminist identifications, pointing out that they require a 'dash of self-conscious parody' and a 'twist of humour':

> Postfeminism takes the sting out of feminism. The subjectivities of femininity, presented seriously earlier in the century, are re-incarnated towards its end with a twist of humour and a *dash of self-conscious parody*. The outwardly caring woman willingly shares the lapses in her devotion, with *a wink in the direction of the audience*. The superwoman is so sophisticated that she looks poised to leave the planet and return as a *Blade Runner* replicant (1995: 100; emphasis added).

Although MacDonald is not using the term 'camp' in her description, she draws upon terminology usually associated with analyses of camp representations, especially the knowing 'wink in the direction of the audience'. In other words, post-feminism embraces the ironies of postmodernism, especially its play with signifiers, emphasis on style over substance, and collapse between representation and reality; as

Andy Medhurst famously argues, 'Postmodernism is only heterosexuals catching up with camp' (1991: 206). Therefore, it is hardly surprising that one of the most influential of the postmodern feminists – Judith Butler – should celebrate the potential of camp in her influential book *Gender Trouble* (1990).

Although Butler rarely uses the word 'camp' in her writing, critics have praised her for having 'done the most to revise the academic standing of camp and to suggest its politically subversive potential' (Bergman 1993: 11). In her innovative thesis, Butler contests that gender is a performative effect – in other words, a 'doing' which, within a recognised cultural regime, constitutes a 'being' (Butler 1999: 180; 1991). However, she stresses that, although gender performativity is not natural, nevertheless it is not optional. The subject does not just go to the wardrobe and decide what gender (s)he wishes to be for the day (Butler 1993: x). Instead, Butler argues that exposing the performativity of gender can only make political advancement, in other words in 'camping up' gender roles. Therefore, she praises examples of camp, notably drag, as politically important. (It is, of course, important to remember that 'drag' is not a synonym for 'camp' but merely 'one room in camp's mansion' [Medhurst 1997: 282]).

What is camp?

There have been many attempts to describe what camp is. But much of this writing has often resorted to giving long lists of 'things' that the author considers camp (Blachford 1981; Babuscio 1984; Dyer 2004). Susan Sontag, however, made a brave attempt at theorising camp in her now infamous 'Notes on Camp' (1982). According to Sontag, camp is a 'way of seeing the world ... in terms of the *degree of artifice*, of stylization' (Sontag 1982: 106; emphasis added). Yet, although this is a useful starting point, it does not really clarify how camp is different from parody, or even irony.

Therefore, Sontag's essay has been criticised by many theorists (Meyer 1994; Miller 1993 and Medhurst 1997). Arguably, one of the key areas missing from her analysis is the question of gender. Camp, if it is to maintain a specificity that distinguishes it from other forms of irony or parody, must be structured around gender. In other words, camp is an ironic performance of gender; it is gender which camp represents in terms of artifice or stylisation.

Historically, this has been important to gay men because homo-sexuality is perceived as a gender-based semiotic – being gay is thought signified by gender transitivity or effeminacy. Therefore, from as early as the school playground, everyone learns that being labelled 'gay' is dependent upon gender performance. In dealing with this, gay men either focus upon 'passing' for straight and concentrate on constructing a masculine performance, or they emulate a 'camp' performance and flaunt exaggerated feminine signifiers. Yet both the 'straight acting' gay or the effeminate queen do so because they are aware of the cultural perception of sexuality and gender as collapsible categories. Camp, therefore, has been one of gay men's most powerful weapons – a strategy of 'defensive offensiveness' (Medhurst 1997: 276). The camp queen is drawing attention to the stereotype of the 'gay-male-as-effeminate' by caricaturing gender signifiers.

However, one of the issues that often becomes blurred in debates about camp is the difference between the theory of camp (camp as the representation of gender in terms of artifice/stylisation) and the history of its usage. Simply because a minority group, such as gay men, have felt an affinity with camp and been its main ambassadors does not mean that it is their exclusive property. Just because gay men have found camp to be a survival strategy in times of oppression does not mean that the same sensibility cannot translate to representations structured around a feminist agenda.

Pamela Robertson argues as such, and points out that, 'for feminists, camp's appeal resides in its potential to function as a form of gender parody' (1996: 10). I argue that this is the case with Bree Van de Kamp in *Desperate Housewives*. Unlike the other three housewives, who are represented as unhappy and constricted by their social roles, Bree's campness continually draws attention to the gender roles as being nothing more than constructs or performances. Far from being mere comic relief, Bree's campness is a survivalist strategy in a post-feminist era.

Post-feminist camp and Bree

Bree first appears with camp exuberance at Mary Alice Young's wake. The director, as if tutored by Laura Mulvey (1975), shows Bree framed beautifully in the doorway and, unlike the fraught Lynette Scavo or pouting Gabrielle Solis of the previous scenes, represents Bree as utterly serene. Her Titian hair gleams in the afternoon sunlight, her alabaster skin would make even Snow White jealous and her Chanel-esque black suit and pearls are immaculate. However, like the opening shot of Wisteria Lane, there is a sense of irony about this image, heightened by its juxtaposition with the previous two wives. Where Lynette and Gabrielle were represented as quietly flustered, Bree looks too serene, too perfect. Indeed, the camera pans up from the two baskets of muffins, which she carries in her exquisitely manicured hands, to show her sighing gracefully before breaking into a 'Say-cheese' (her name is Bree, after all) type of smile. The impression is very much of a woman steeling herself to perform a social role at this occasion; a *noblesse oblige* sensibility; a woman who believes that she must engineer a performance of grace because it is the correct thing to do. Yet this performance draws attention to itself as actually being a performance, emphasised even further by the diegetic music which now breaks into Vivaldi-esque classical strings, the type of music often employed in bad films to connote upper-class elegance.

Mary Alice then narrates that Bree has brought baskets of muffins which 'she baked herself from scratch' and reveals that she is 'known' throughout the neighbourhood for her cooking and also 'known' for making her own clothes and for doing her own gardening and for re-upholstering her own furniture. Mary Alice concludes that most people 'think of' Bree as being the perfect wife and mother. Therefore, unlike Lynette and Gabrielle, Bree is represented in terms of what she *does* or what she is *known* for rather than how she herself feels. While the emphasis in the previous scenes was on Lynette's and Gabrielle's private difficulties, the representation of Bree shows only the public persona. Indeed, as the flashbacks reveal, most of the actions for which Bree is 'known' appear to be highly theatrical performances. The flashback represents Bree in a caricatured gardening outfit, complete with matching hat, as she replants a shrub, and then she is shown re-upholstering the furniture, which, of course, she does in the driveway of her house so that all the neighbours can have a clear view. Therefore, unlike Gabrielle and Lynette, the initial representation of Bree conveys no sense of this woman's unhappiness or discontent with her situation because the performance is so immaculately groomed. She does in every way appear to be perfect.

However, an appreciation of this image is dependent upon the spectator reading it as camp. Indeed, some spectators may not 'get' the irony at work in the representation and simply view Bree as an unsympathetic character. Secondly, even if the image is read as camp this raises the question of the politics of this representation. It would be very possible to read Bree simply as an element of comic relief, a dash of humour in the midst of the dark satire. Yet I would argue that this representation is a strategy of post-feminist critique. As Mary Alice narrates, Bree is 'known' for performing certain roles. Bree's identity – the Stepford Wife and mother – is a collection of acts that performatively constitute her gendered self. Yet, although the narrative makes it clear that 'Bree' is very much a construct or role, it affirms the necessity of this role for the woman's sense of 'being'. Peel back the surface that is 'Stepford Bree' and there will be nothing underneath – no essentialist identity waiting to break through.

Therefore, although Bree *appears* to represent the pre-feminist ideology that Betty Friedan critiqued in *The Feminine Mystique*, she is very different from Friedan's pre-feminist housewives, trapped in a culture in which they learned, through media images, that 'correct' femininity was domesticity (1965). The key difference in the representation of Bree is the post-feminist sense of irony, the knowing wink at the audience – in short, the campiness of the performance. Although Bree may be trapped in a 'comfortable concentration camp' (Friedan 1965: 245) she is *aware* of the role, the performance she is *supposed* to engineer. As such, Bree acknowledges that she is in a 'desperate' situation but that she will counteract it by 'playing' her allocated role to its very limit. Bree will be the ultimate Stepford Wife, thus showing, through the campiness of her performances, that she is playing a socially constructed role within an oppressive culture. In other words, camp Bree exposes that 'the style becomes the content' (Kleinhans 1994: 189) and, at times of crisis, her coping mechanism is to 'play' a particular domestic role. This camp representation of idealised femininity is represented beautifully by a sequence in a later episode where Bree's husband Rex Van de Kamp admits to the dinner party guests that he and Bree are in marriage counselling. Although Bree is horrified, even to the point of dropping her tray of hors d'oeuvres, she simply pauses, draws a deep breath, before smiling a cheesy smile and announcing: 'If the guests will kindly take their seats – dinner is served' (1: 3).

Similarly, in the pilot, Bree visits Rex in hospital and is distraught to learn that he wants a divorce. In true Bree fashion, her coping mechanism is to 'perform' idealised femininity, declaring that the bedside flowers need water and hurrying to the bathroom to fill the vase. However, what makes the sequence so chilling is that when Bree reaches the safe isolation of the bathroom, she sobs her heart out in front of the mirror. This image is disconcerting because it affirms both the constructed nature of Bree's Stepford femininity, but also its necessity for her daily survival. It is Bree's realisation that everything she considered important in her life – husband, house and family – can unravel as easily as her husband saying 'I want a divorce' that finds her sobbing quietly in the hospital bathroom. Even so, after composing herself for a few minutes, she emerges looking perfect yet again. Therefore, as opposed to Lynette and Gabrielle, who are represented as unhappy because of their role, Bree draws attention to how the role *itself* is a construct but also emphasises that there is no alternative beyond the performance. As Butler's politics call for, Bree camps up the idea of traditional femininity, embracing stereotypical roles but with the knowing 'wink at the audience'. Therefore, representing her as 'camp' is not simply comic relief. Instead, Bree shows that camp is very much a survivalist strategy. She may be trapped in an oppressive role, but it is only through demonstrating that this role is actually a performance that she can maintain her sanity. Therefore, far from displaying a post-feminist paradise or the *Ally McBeal* dream, *Desperate Housewives* asserts the difficulty contemporary women face in a post-feminist era.

In his delicious article on camp, Andy Medhurst argues that camp is a gay male preserve because it has been a strategy of 'survival' for many gay men (1997: 275). According to him, women *may enjoy* camp but, because they have never experienced the prejudice accorded to gay men, they do not recognise camp as a survivalist strategy. Yet, as *Desperate Housewives* demonstrates, camp is very much a survival strategy for Bree. In times of intense crisis she always pauses, takes a deep breath and then smiles as she breaks into another spectacular performance of idealised femininity. She may be 'desperate' but she can still ensure that everything looks good.

Therefore the beauty of *Desperate Housewives* lies in its pointed critique of feminine oppression exemplified by Bree's campiness that constantly draws attention to idealised femininity as being a theatrical performance. Far from being comic relief or an attempt to pander to gay male spectatorship, her campiness supports a feminist agenda. Like a heroine in Todd Haynes's films (Carol in *Safe*, 1995, or Cathy in *Far From Heaven*, 2002), Bree asserts the suffocating nature of traditional femininity yet also emphasises the necessity of this role for the character's survival. Therefore, unlike another post-feminist 'icon' – Ally McBeal – who, as L. S. Kim points out (2001: 324) is ignorant of her own performance of femininity, Bree asserts an ironic understanding of her performance, or what MacDonald terms the knowing 'wink at the audience'.

In 'Come Back to Me' (1: 10), Bree and Rex are dining at their country club when they realise that all the other diners are staring at them and gossiping about Rex's indiscretions with Maisy Gibbons (Sharon Lawrence). While Rex wants to flee, Bree insists that they stay and perform the image of the happily married couple. Taking a deep breath, she opens her menu, smiles a 'Bree smile' at the woman seated at the next table and remarks that 'the veal looks good'. And as long as it 'looks' good, it will surely be all right, won't it?

This chapter is an abridged version of an article published in *Feminist Media Studies* 6. 2. 2006.

8

Queer dilemmas: The 'right' ideology and homosexual
representation in *Desperate Housewives*

Kristian T. Kahn

Marc Cherry, *Desperate Housewives'* creator, is a self-proclaimed 'gay
Republican'. While such an identification may seem oxymoronic in the
light of the current right-wing American climate – an identification
that has been likened to being 'a Jewish Nazi' (Wright 2005) – its odd
balance of liberal sexuality and right-wing politics is crucial to an
examination of *Desperate Housewives*. My aim here is to analyse the
ways in which George W. Bush's America and the conservative values
associated with it provide the ideological framework behind *Desperate
Housewives* and, in addition, also inform representations of homosexuality in the television programme. In doing so, it will become
clear that – while the programme does have both a left- and a right-
wing audience – the conservative (heterosexist) ideology of the
American right is actually reinforced and re*enforced* through the
'seemingly liberal' (sexual) transgressions acted out in the series. The
ways in which American media depictions of homosexuality must
recuperate this transgression to restore heteronormative order will, as
this chapter will show, be exemplified here in the example of *Desperate
Housewives*. It is first imperative, however, to contextualise the show
within these political frameworks and to discuss the increasing
censorship of network television in the US.

Judith Butler aptly remarks in the opening pages of *Precarious Life*:

> Since the events of September 11, we have seen both a rise of anti-
> intellectualism and a growing acceptance of censorship within
> the media ... [It] seems crucial to note that a critical relation to

government has been severely, though not fully, suspended and that the 'criticism' or, indeed, independence of the media has been compromised in some unprecedented ways (2004: 1).

This rise in media censorship is directly relational to the stress on family values, tradition and religiosity which heteronormative American culture consistently emphasises.

As *Desperate Housewives* continues to soar in popularity, constant analogies are drawn between this network phenomenon and premium subscription channel HBO's *Sex and the City*. While it is true that both shows deal with the social and sexual predicaments of four heavily nuanced and unique women, such a comparison forgets a critical difference. *Sex and the City* was allowed to cross more boundaries due to its home on cable television; the series, therefore, could be more daring because it was not subject to the constraints of the Federal Communication Commission (FCC) to which *Desperate Housewives*, as a network prime-time show, is forced to adhere. *Desperate Housewives* thus must, on the surface at least, appeal to the broadest constituency possible and offend the least – both right and left. Its popularity with viewers of both political groups (even Laura Bush is a fan) and, conversely, its unpopularity with right- and left-wing viewers are indicative of the show's own inherent oxymoronic attitudes. Like Cherry, the gay Republican, *Desperate Housewives* speaks to both liberals and conservatives alike but, in the end, must exist within the constraints of an increasingly right-wing-mediated American media. 'Gay' is therefore usurped by the more weighty term 'Republican', just as I shall argue later 'homosexuality' is usurped in *Desperate Housewives* by a heteronormative, fundamentalist order.

That ABC – the *American* Broadcasting Corporation – airs the show in the US should make us immediately wary of who is 'filtering' or skewing the programme to fit in with conventional needs and desires in Bush's America. The America of George W. Bush is not just a Republican, right-wing country but a nation with the ever-growing influence of the religious fundamentalist right. It is a country on the brink of potential disaster with regard to rulings on private individuals, ranging from abortion legislation to gay rights, the former a looming but virtually real nightmare after Sandra Day O'Connor's resignation from the Supreme Court on 1 July 2005. At the time of writing, Bush recently nominated John Roberts to fill O'Connor's place, and NARAL Pro-Choice America, Planned Parenthood and Human Rights Campaign are all protesting the nomination on the grounds that Roe v. Wade could actually be overturned by the presence of Roberts, who could move the court further to the right. Traditional family values are stressed under this presidency: the threat of sexual education classes in junior high schools being replaced by programmes teaching 'abstinence only' without educating about safer sex at all; the denunciation of stem cell research as 'immoral' to a foetus, leading pro-life extremists to argue more vocally the immorality of abortion. Religious fundamentalist leaders, such as Jerry Falwell, are therefore not necessarily in the minority when they condemn any sex act (i.e. homosexuality) that does not yield progeny, further emphasising this religious-capitalist drive to make family values appear of the utmost importance to America's future.

Marc Cherry, a supporter of Republican values, but also as a homosexual, is caught up in the fervour of such homophobic right-wing values, whether or not he views himself as a victim of these ideologies. That the show is just as divided, in reception, as Cherry's purported sexual/political identity is hardly surprising. In the wake of the proposed Federal Marriage Amendment and the continuing struggle for a recognition of gays and lesbians as same-class citizens in America, Cherry's status as a 'gay Republican' makes one question rather critically just to whom such a programme is, in fact, speaking.

This is not to discount, however, the few glimpses we are allowed of homosexuality on Wisteria Lane. *Desperate Housewives'* appeal to right-wing viewers is obviously due to the show's seemingly restorative social order based on family and community; but left-wing viewers also enjoy the show for its transgressive nature and the satiric subversion of sexual and social norms. This is something, though, of which we should be wary. Similar to the Gothic literary genre, the show allows for an exploration of unconventional themes only, in the end, to restore traditional values in the eventual patching up of any given transgression. This becomes more problematic, for example, in *Desperate Housewives* with the depiction of homosexuality, for how can such an 'unspeakable' transgression ever be fixed? Speaking generally about sexuality in the Gothic and more specifically about *homo*sexuality, Eve Sedgwick observes that 'the veil that conceals and inhibits sexuality comes by the same gesture to represent it, both as a metonym of the thing covered and as a metaphor for the system of prohibitions by which sexual desire is enhanced and specified' (1986: 143). Thus, the *illusion* of reality is, in *Desperate Housewives*, a similar sociocultural veil that reveals and ultimately conceals as it restores and reaffirms heteronormative order. What will become apparent are the ways in which the American media is actually presenting a *tableau* of exactly what it wants viewers to believe is the reality of America today; it does this by enhancing, specifying and delineating the boundaries within which such subversions or transgressions (like homosexuality) must be contained.

The issue of homosexuality in *Desperate Housewives* is one worth isolating in a discussion of the capitalist-run, media-censored world of America from which, it must be remembered, the series comes to us. *CNN Money* reported, less than a month after the show premiered, that 'the American Family Association has rallied thousands of followers' – namely family-geared corporations and companies such as Lowe's and Tyson – to cease buying advertising space that sponsors *Desperate Housewives* (Crawford 2004). In an America obsessed with family and moral values, many conservatives understandably view a show depicting adultery, suicide and statutory rape as a threat – not to mention homosexuality, a transgression that can hardly be put so easily to rights.

But not all right-wing viewers see the show this way. We already know that First Lady Laura Bush is a big fan and, purportedly, will make 'a series of cameo appearances' on Wisteria Lane in the second season (D'Arby 2005). The debate over which interpretive reading – liberal or conservative – of *Desperate Housewives* is the more convincing is cheekily carried out in the Spring 2005 issue of *Ms.* magazine: Jennifer L. Pozner takes the position that the show perpetuates the right-wing agenda by 'reinforcing sexual, racial and class stereotypes' while Jessica Seigel argues that the show depicts empowered women by means of a 'winking subversion beneath [an] impossibly thin, nouveau-riche façade' (Pozner and Seigel 2005). Pozner's position is here relevant for its assertion that the reinforcement of stereotypes only feeds into the right-wing agenda:

It's no wonder right-wing culture warriors...love a show whose worldview harks back to a time when two-parent, middle-class families could comfortably thrive on single incomes, women's identities were primarily determined by the men they married and the children they raised, and husbands were not expected to trouble themselves with such pesky matters as child care and housework (ibid.).

The repercussions of a show speaking to 'right-wing culture warriors' will obviously affect *any* representation of homosexuality in *all* programmes that air on network television. On Wisteria Lane what can never be restored to order – meaning, what is too transgressive to fix or mould into the 'right' ideology – must eventually be relegated to the shadows, where the transgression is judged neither right nor wrong but merely (as the conservatives cross their fingers) forgotten about.

'I would love you even if you were a murderer'

Had *Desperate Housewives* been utterly irredeemable, filled with lascivious behaviour and 'sex, sex, sex' (quoted in Crawford 2004) without emphasising a return to family values, it seems fair to speculate that the show would never have seen the light of day on network, possibly appearing only on cable. And yet it is the *redeeming factor* of the transgressions, the fact that all is set to rights (at least, seemingly so), that allows *Desperate Housewives* to keep its prime-time slot. Far from being cancelled the show has an avid fan base, a large following that *Sex and the City*, because of its scheduling on cable, could only dream of. On public television, however, transgressions must always be contained and (heterosexual) order quickly restored. Homosexuality is an offence in this public realm, an irredeemable transgression that – in a prime-time slot – must either conform to the stereotypical view of what straight people think of gays (as in the ludicrously stereotypical depictions of gay life in NBC's *Will and Grace*) or else it must be repressed, re-establishing social Darwinian equilibrium.

On Wisteria Lane – whose set, incidentally, is the same as the 1950s comedy *Leave It To Beaver*, in which the Cleaver family embodied the best of American family and moral values – transgressions like adultery, suicide, statutory rape and prostitution abound, but homosexuality proves more textually problematic. During the first season queerness lurks in the shadows until the cataclysmic episode in which Andrew Van de Kamp 'comes out' to his parents, Bree and Rex (1: 18). But no sooner has he come out of the closet than he retracts, telling the Reverend Sikes (Dakin Matthews) that it has all been a big hoax to get out of boot camp (1: 19).

Andrew's uncertainty is in many ways symptomatic of a broader textual ambiguity towards homosexuality in *Desperate Housewives*. His outing is not followed with a sensitive and sympathetic exploration of the travails of a young gay man coming to terms with his sexuality, but instead is associated with criminality, violence, antisocial and sociopathic behaviour – and ultimately textual repression. While his father, Rex, is supportive – his sexual shenanigans with the local prostitute mean he is in no position to judge anyway – his mother's reaction is telling. Saying: 'I would love you even if you were a murderer' is meant to be reminiscent of what Cherry's own mother is reputed to have said to him when he came out (1: 18). But it also goes to the heart of the textual ambiguity surrounding queerness and how it is dealt with in the series.

The conflation of homosexuality with criminal behaviour is eerily reminiscent of the religious right's condemnation of homosexuality as a sin, as somehow a weakness in the individual character. Certainly, Andrew has been signposted from the start as a troubled teenager. He is known for smart-mouthing his mother and for his antisocial behaviour – for example, smoking marijuana in his bedroom and then storing the drug in his school locker (1: 9). Bree has more than once been called up to school to meet with the principal over her son's misdemeanours. But these misdeeds pale into insignificance when his most shocking transgression leads to manslaughter. Drunk while driving a new car given to him by his father to placate his parental guilt over the impending divorce, Andrew knocks down Juanita 'Mama' Solis in a late night hit and run (1: 7). Not only has he driven away without stopping but he shows absolutely no remorse. Bree, who comes up with the idea to cover his tracks, is concerned that his actions have aroused no emotions in her son (1: 8). 'Why do you care?' he says. 'Because I need to know that you're not a monster,' comes his mother's reply.

I feel bad that she got hurt. But I also feel bad that my car got dinged because somebody didn't have enough sense to look both ways before she crossed the street. And I also feel bad that now I'm gonna have to ride my bike to school... She's an old lady. Okay? She's lived her life. I have my whole life ahead of me, and now it might be screwed up! That's what you should be worried about!

Long before Andrew comes out to his parents (1: 18) he is positioned as trouble in the text, exhibiting sociopathic tendencies.

That the queer character is so 'against nature' as to be against society is reinforced elsewhere in the narrative. While Andrew goes without punishment two other gay characters are not so lucky. Suspicious of his wife's fidelity, Carlos Solis takes matters into his own hands when he goes after the cable guy (John Haymes Newton), whom he mistakenly believes to be having an affair with Gabrielle (1: 4). However, this could not be further from the truth, as not only is the cable guy not Gabrielle's lover but he is not even attracted to women. Queer is thus associated – and unconsciously punished – with (comedic) violence. For if the gay character is seen as a threat to the sociocultural norms of Wisteria Lane – and by extension to American moral values – then Carlos's behaviour is, while not necessarily exemplary, at least textually justifiable as a means of keeping queerness in check. Gay-bashing is played down on *Desperate Housewives* as about comic misunderstanding. Carlos's mistaken beating of two gay men, both of whom he misreads as straight, illustrates a textual ambivalence towards homosexuality. Because it is funny, we are not meant to take this textual retribution too seriously. While homosexuality is still there, Carlos's actions serve as a reminder that all will be set to rights – in this case through the recollection of just what kind of violent fate befalls queer folk on Wisteria Lane.

Textual recuperation of homosexuality also comes in the guise of Bree's attempts to 'cure' her son. In an illuminating *New York Times Magazine* article analysing the religious right's campaign against gay marriage, this idea of queerness and its 'cure' is seen in a broader context: 'Of course, this view of homosexuality – seeing it as a disorder to be cured – is not new. It was cutting edge thinking circa 1905' (Shorto 2005: 40). Bree, a Republican, member of the National Rifle Association (NRA) and a religious zealot, represents typical American right-wing attitudes towards homosexuality – that it can somehow be 'fixed' or cured – or at the very least suppressed. Inviting Reverend Sikes over for supper to counsel Andrew, Bree's actions illustrate a strand of ideological systems at work within contemporary America society (1: 19). In other words, religion and family values are *good* while homosexuality is *bad*; and their confrontation at the Van de Kamps' dinner table becomes one of 'good versus evil'. It is at this intervention that right-wing ideological values, a mixing of religion and state, are emphasised, as our attention is drawn to the image of Jesus and a portrait of the champion of the New Right, the late President Ronald Reagan. That the Reverend visually resembles, quite strikingly, Jerry Falwell is surely meant to drive the connection home.

Later Andrew meets with the Reverend after church and confesses that he is not gay after all. Telling him that he lied to his parents, Andrew says: 'Look, all I know is I wanted to get the hell out of that camp. So I lied to my parents and told them I was really worried that I was having feelings for other guys and they did exactly what I wanted them to' (1: 19). That Andrew might have lied about being gay could be narratively feasible if we choose not to recall Susan Mayer's discovery of him and Justin (Ryan Carnes) kissing in the Youngs' swimming pool (1: 15), if we forget Justin's remark to Gabrielle that he had a 'buddy', and if we also close our ears to Andrew's statement to Sikes: 'Look, I love vanilla ice cream, okay? But every now and then I'm probably gonna be in the mood for chocolate. Y'know what I'm saying?' (1: 19).

Immediately allaying the fear of homosexuality, Andrew's character becomes either bisexualised or just sexually confused, as so many 16-year-olds are. The transgression of homosexuality is therefore translated – via the use of 'vanilla' and 'chocolate' – into something more acceptable, be it bisexuality, or, what the religious right feel to be the same thing as bisexuality: normal teenage sexual confusion. Having followed the weight of the term 'murderer' from Bree's remark to sociocultural representations of homosexuality-as-pathology, it should come as no shock that Andrew – who may or may not be gay – intends to ruin his mother's life by saying: 'I'm gonna make her believe that God has delivered her this little miracle. Until one day, when she least expects it, I'm gonna do something so awful it is going to rock her world. I mean, it is really going to destroy her. When that day comes, trust me, I'll know paradise' (1: 19).

Andrew's case is where we are confronted with homosexuality in a pivotal plotline. But, just as quickly as it is introduced, it is covered over: it is veiled, concealed and erased from the scene entirely. For the rest of the first season, we see nothing more of Andrew – he is literally textually repressed. Instead, we are witness to another of Carlos's (unintentional) gay-bashings, as though his violence is the only way to restore heteronormative order on Wisteria Lane after homosexuality has had its turn in the spotlight. Justin is Carlos's second victim, the victim of male dominance and the assertion of power – by way of violence – to (re-)implement heterosexual order. While the first victim of Carlos's fist was an incidental character, it is Justin who seems to suffer for Andrew's queer confession. Andrew gets away, so to speak, but Justin (his 'buddy') is the victim of violence, of gay-bashing: Carlos's fist thus acts as a metaphor for the religious right's pounding out of homosexuality from *Desperate Housewives* and from America altogether.

Having left with a promise of vengeance against his mother, Andrew's reappearance in the second season is inevitable; we are even promised by Marc Cherry, in an interview with *USA Today*, that the 'narcissistic sociopath' Andrew will keep his word, and '[what] he'll do in the fall to get back at his mother is so unpleasant' (quoted in Lo 2005).

What now?

It is difficult, as this chapter has shown, to discuss the actual representation of homosexuality in a television programme that cannot commit itself to this issue: it is thrown into the shadows, veiled over, just as quickly as it was allowed its brief moment of visibility – in alignment with Sedgwick's remarks on Gothic transgression and the eventual restoration of order. Instead, the politically infested media, the current state of America's stress on family values and the indigestibility of homosexuality within a culture of increasing religious domination call for a reading of *Desperate*

Housewives as an ideology that stabilises and reasserts the 'right' way of things.

Recent attacks on gay marriage by fundamentalists are everyday news items despite the fact that they are likely not attacks on the allowance of same-class rights to homosexuals but attacks on homosexuality (versus American ideologies, versus religion) itself. Such Puritan attitudes are the basis for the aforementioned denunciation of *Desperate Housewives* by the American Family Association and yet, as we have seen, are paradoxically the attitudes reinforced in the show that supposedly appeals to right-wing viewers.

It will be interesting to see what the second season of *Desperate Housewives* will bring to the table. According to *The Swift Report*:

> In exchange for [Laura] Bush's high-profile visits to Wisteria Lane [in the upcoming season], producers are said to be exploring several new plotlines intended to appeal to conservative Christian viewers. One likely subplot: a religious conversion by Bree Van de Kamp's pharmacist lover, played by Roger Bart. In focus groups, conservative viewers gave low marks to the character played by Marcia Cross for engaging in an adulterous affair. But the traditionalist viewers warmed to Ms. Van de Kamp and her lover George in a subplot that has the pharmacist refusing to prescribe birth control pills to local ladies, citing religious reasons (D'Arby 2005).

The question of 'appeal' is of the utmost importance. Catering plots to a conservative Christian audience not only compromises a truly *public* media, forcing it to comply with right-wing ideologies, but it also precludes *any* further representation of homosexuality on Wisteria Lane. Should George refuse to fill birth control prescriptions as well will only validate many American family-geared companies (like Wal-Mart), which have already begun a similar campaign against women's reproductive rights. By incorporating new plotlines to appeal to the religious right, the inclusion (or continuation) of the homosexual subplot might be entirely out of the question. In fact, during the final editing of this chapter, the second season had already begun airing in the US. Andrew does, in fact, return. Just as he 'came out' at boot camp, Andrew finds himself back in the same camp again – this time for asserting the place (and law) of his father, Rex, which certainly carries with it severe Oedipal weight (2: 4).

Homosexuality was allowed to briefly appear – it had its day in the sun – but the veil has been thrown over it, and its reappearance in such a marked manner on Wisteria Lane is in question. Andrew's queerness is only presented in so far as it incites the anger of his mother (2: 11). If we are to understand that any liberal sympathy with Andrew's homosexuality is impossible, that it has now been turned into an alternative narrative – one in which his avowed maternal vengeance is a revenge *that is queerness itself* – we are called to witness the reassertion of heteronormative order over such deviant sexuality. In other words, there can be no sympathy for the queer – at least, not here. As quickly as he was allowed his place in the spotlight, the queer has just as quickly become a prop for the right-wing agenda inherent in the programme itself rather than a self-contained character, and with a narrative, of his own. The queer Andrew we saw 'come out' has now left the building or in this case, the sprawling suburban set that is Wisteria Lane, in favour of a caricature: a figure against whom the heterosexist narrative can revolve and continue to reassert its dominance as well as a figure that the religious right can more easily stomach.

9

Hunters, heroes and the hegemonically masculine fantasies of *Desperate Housewives*

Brian Singleton

The daytime spectacle for the wives of Wisteria Lane is constituted by samples of heroic masculinity that come to replace husbands and partners. These daytime arrivals are primary examples of male agency, with their often unclothed hard bodies, performing physical tasks and assuming the dominant role in sexual encounters. These men are offered for scopic delight, most as eye candy; they intercede in the drama of the lane from the periphery, entering the space of female desire, and they negotiate that space according to the housewives' needs. John Rowland, the gardener, and Mike Delfino, the plumber, are men of service who restore to perfection the domestic routine that husbands fail to, or are not there to, provide. These fixers are everything husbands are not: men of action, providers of resolution and instant satisfaction, and demanding of no more than a little short-term emotional investment. And what of the women who are attracted to them? Gabrielle Solis uses her man of action (John) as a distraction from a life of boredom, while Susan Mayer fails to commit because of her desired man's imperfections, dark secrets and uncontrollability (Mike). She wishes for a relationship but is only really comfortable with a lover. Both men are represented as models of phallic masculinity; they wear tight-fitting shirts (and often appear shirtless) to show off the spectacle of their sculpted bodies. They invariably carry the tools of their respective trades (hoes, rakes, wrenches, screwdrivers), further reinforcing their phallic hegemony by not simply existing for their bodies alone. These bodies perform tasks that add a three-dimensional agency to their image, and lend a degree of social practice to the fantasy that they embody. Their 'to-be-looked-at-ness' is fantasised as an ideal state of grace. With disappointing regularity, however, these men fall from that state of grace, only to rise up again to that state in a perpetual cycle of female desire interrupted by the fallibility of fantasy. The housewives of Wisteria Lane do not wish for masculinity to be negotiated by alternative forms of the hegemonic. Only the women are permitted to negotiate the masculine in a way that permits the spectacle to dissolve and disappoint. For it is only through the dissolution of the fantasy that the fantasy can be forever resurrected.

John, the Latino gardener with the looks and the body of a model, appears throughout the first season to embody the hegemonically masculine (Connell 2005). He is represented and used in the narrative literally as the 'stud', the iconic object of Gabrielle's desire. He is sexually attracted to Gabrielle (herself a former model and beauty icon) but the camera focuses on him, not her. For instance, John and Gabrielle meet accidentally while their affair is in suspension (1: 18). They are both jogging and listening to music, thus the whole scene is enacted in dumb show. Gabrielle is wearing a sweatshirt and pants while John is stripped to the waist to reveal his divinely sculpted body, which we have seen on many occasions before. The camera stays on Gabrielle's side of the street for the most part and focuses on John. There is nothing to see of Gabrielle's equally beautiful body as it is deliberately covered from the gaze. She puts a finger to her lips to prevent him from speaking and thus, silenced, he can only be looked at, admired and fantasised over. Throughout their relationship Gabrielle, through age and wealth, is perpetually in the ascendant. John may have the physical strength and apparent agency, but it is really he who is seduced; he is the dangling plaything of the older woman. And as the camera invites the viewers to linger over his body in this (and many other) shots, he represents an icon to be looked at and to provoke the agency of woman in the sex act. In fact, during the snatched moments of their affair in many episodes it is Gabrielle who pushes and pulls John into sexual compliance and not the other way round.

In the pilot (1: 1) John accidentally pricks his finger on a bush. Gabrielle's way of caring for him is to kiss his finger better maternally, and then kiss the rest of his body sexually. In the next episode (1: 2) she visits him in his apartment for the first time for a sexual encounter. She (and we) watch as he rips off his shirt in one spectacular move to reveal his perfect pectorals. But as she lies in the missionary position with John on top of her (a position that she has configured as her wish), she spots a photograph of John as a boy. This is a jarring reminder of the desire for John as an adult hero, and not someone who is technically under age. The spectacle of John's body connotes adult sexual prowess but the photo reminds Gabrielle and us of the falseness of the connotation. Together with the camera, Gabrielle constructs John for us as a spectacle of masculinity that is intrinsically phallic (Lehman 2001). John's is a hard body that never once suffers a blemish or a wound (apart from the aforementioned slight finger prick from a bush), and we learn from Gabrielle that sex with him is good as she engineers it in most episodes. Nevertheless, the phallic masculinity of John is not permitted hegemony. She controls the affair (its impetus, timing and location), he has no economic or social status (one pair of shoes and a credit card with a tiny limit), and his rare violent outbursts are benign. He kicks impotently at a pile of grass when he discovers Gabrielle is pregnant (1: 21), and later in the same episode is prevented from gaining entry to the Solis home to confront Carlos Solis by a dish of salsa in the face. This violence is 'expressive' rather than 'instrumental' (Hatty 2000), and always ineffectual. And so housewife Gabrielle creates for us an iconic male with all the physical attributes of the hegemonic 'true' male (Connell 2005) but with absolutely none of the agency.

The lack of agency attributed to John denies him the possibility of the heroic male in the same way that Carlos's electronic tagging device emasculates the possibility of the heroic within his dominant character. He works within possibly the most hegemonic of work situations, in acquisitions and mergers, with its predatory drives for takeover and annihilation all in pursuit of the acquisition of wealth and economic domination. His work is not defined in terms of location. The first and only possible location where 'work' might take place is in the home of his boss, Tanaka (1: 1). Carlos's trophy wife Gabrielle is reluctant to go because she fears his boss will try to grope her again. He responds by telling her she must let herself be groped by his boss. Despite his desire for children Carlos's masculinity is authoritarian in its complete espousal of patriarchy, to the point of treating his wife as a possession. He is also fiercely jealous of his wife's sexual attractiveness and fears his loss of control over her. Throughout the first six episodes he has his suspicions of Gabrielle's infidelity, but identifies wrongly a gay cable guy (John Haymes Newton) as the object of her desire (1: 4), and thus loses all his power and status as an alpha male. Some time later (1: 9) the police descend on his house and Carlos spends the remainder of the series either in jail or electronically tagged and confined to his home. Despite this image of the trapped male, he endeavours to assert control over his wife, but in so doing slides further away from his hegemonic status. He appears totally duplicitous by tampering with Gabrielle's birth control pills and later he resorts to physical violence to force her to sign a post-nuptial agreement (1: 18). Throughout the first season Carlos is captured on numerous occasions naked, getting into the bath or bed. He is a man who has continual sexual desires that need to be satisfied, and his constant naked body is a reminder of his sexualised character. But the image of Carlos is as pervasive for Gabrielle, too, and she uses this 'need' of his to assert her own power over him. Carlos can strip all he likes to satisfy his needs, but it is Gabrielle who tactically withholds or satisfies his needs as a way of negotiating her own agenda (of further acquisition of clothes, cars, necklaces, or even the gardener!). He may have made her pregnant, but in the wider ambit of their relationship he is completely emasculated.

Tom Scavo, too, is constantly being thwarted in the public sphere of work by Lynette and can only be a hero through 'play'. He offers his body as an archetypal heroic male in tiger-skin underwear, like Tarzan, the jungle animal-man (1: 21). We are first introduced to Tom as potent and fecund (1: 1). He has fathered four children, three boys and a young and notably silent girl. The boys are noisy and rough and drive Lynette demented. When he returns home after a business trip he instantly 'restores' the behaviour of the boys with a present of a football. Only the male with the male game can control the wayward younger males. He stands iconically in the doorway with the boys positioned all around him, as an über-father, a father who has fathered male children. He both physically and psychologically controls the male children and banishes them with a bribe to the outside world for 30 minutes. He does so not in order to give Lynette some respite from their boisterousness, but in order to satisfy his own sexual needs, and to reinforce his hegemonic fatherly status even further. He asserts his authority first over the children and then over Lynette by manoeuvring her into the bedroom ('I have to have you') and forcing her down on the bed. Lynette exists for him as someone who satisfies his needs, to the point of not wearing a condom and taking a risk of making her pregnant again. But this is his ultimate downfall, as the hegemonic male cannot conquer in this essentially female terrain and she socks him in the jaw. Similarly, dressed as Tarzan, he emasculates himself by asking Lynette to turn the lights off. His view of the hero is one that should not be objectified when we all know from films and television that the hero, first and foremost, provides an 'awesome spectacle of phallic masculinity' (Lehman 2001: 26) that feeds the fantasy of the beholder. The spectacle of the heroic male body is an essence in itself. It does not need to speak. It simply 'is', rendered speechless by the power of its corporeal presence (see Rutherford 1992). Sadly for Tom he does not realise this and wishes for the spectacle of his body to be invisible. This puts Lynette right off sex. The heroic male does not recognise the visual rules of being a hegemonic fantasy.

Similarly, the male voice is supplanted by the female and his discourse is imagined as hegemonic, also. For instance, Mary Alice Young's voiceover that tops and tails each episode, focuses on Susan's desire for a hero: 'We all honour heroes for different reasons; some for their bravery, some for their daring, and some for their goodness' (1: 17). The camera glides over Susan's watercolour illustrations of fictional heroes, and Mary Alice continues, 'But mostly we honour heroes because at one point or another we all dream of being rescued.' We then see Susan imagining various scenarios in which Mike Delfino might rescue her. In fact she is not being rescued in the literal sense from some danger, but she is being rescued from her own inability to make up with him. One scenario involves Mike with a gun and she hides behind her door, afraid of his phallic power. But in another she simply melts into his arms as he silences her prevarications with a forceful kiss. Her desire is for the silent male, the protector, and the hunter-gatherer of 'true' masculine hegemony. He embodies Roland Barthes's dictum to the fullest: 'I want to possess, fiercely, but I also know how to give actively' (1978: 126). He solves Susan's dilemma of the possible imminent forgiveness of his past transgressions with an active kiss. Her fantasy is that he knows what is good for her when she herself does not know. Being fiercely possessed, she imagines, is the cure for her equivocation.

When Mike is first spotted by the women of Wisteria Lane (and by Susan in particular in 1: 1), he is seen as a new male in what is set up to be very much a female space. The women control the lane by their act of community in response to Mary Alice's suicide. The new male, therefore, must be assimilated into the community of women and this is achieved through a mixture of fantasy and interrogation. Attempts by Susan subsequently involve her questioning of him in respect of relationships with other women. But not once do we hear of an extended family, and nor are the women interested. He is a rogue male caught between historic representations of other rogue males. He is the hard and tough 'cowboy' figure of the western genre, although our suspicions that he is not operating within the law are raised from the outset, simply because of his isolation. He exists primarily, in other words, in relation to the women of Wisteria Lane. Susan's love rival, divorcee Edie Britt, configures him also in hegemonic 'hard-body' terms (MacKinnon 2003). She washes her car wearing very little in response to Mike, shirtless, but it is Edie who is fore-grounded to remind us that the 'hard-body' is her fantasy, and hers alone (1: 4). To consolidate her fantasy she even sponges her own body, to make more of it visible, and to suggest that her inner uncontrollable passions also need cooling down. Mike's body never takes up the whole frame. Edie's presence stands in the way of Susan's desires but also bars the way for the homoeroticisation of Mike's body explicitly; her own wet body determines the fantasy. Mike is hers and hers alone. This is very much a heterosexual visual matrix of 'to-be-looked-at-ness' that disavows the gay male gaze, and reinforces the primacy of hegemonic masculinity in terms of compulsory heterosexuality (Connell 2005).

But it is no fantasy that Mike Delfino, for viewers as well, is the man-as-hunter (Whitehead 2002), the lone male who forsakes hearth and home for a heroic project. He even goes off on his project with his best friend, Bongo, the aggressive Alsatian, the hegemonic canine. That canine is aggressively protective of Mike to the point of scaring off predatory females such as Susan. Throughout the first six episodes Bongo can be heard barking out of shot. His presence permeates the lane and provides an index to the visually absent Mike. When we do see man and beast together they take up the whole frame. For instance, Mike has to square up physically to the active Bongo, and the frame is full of the spectacle of aggression (1: 3). Bongo quadruples the extent of Mike's masculinity as he is seen to be wrestling with and ultimately controlling animal passions. The fact that he can control them suggests that he might possess them himself. We do not know what Mike and Bongo's project is but we can imagine that it is a search for a woman. The woman, we also imagine, is the prize, either directly or indirectly. The hero's action will deliver the woman. But Mike's project is unclear for all and thus his 'cowboy' image does not last for long. He lurks in the shadows, operates mostly under cover of darkness, and quite often is captured at the edge of the frame. He thus becomes, again temporarily, a reflection of the male protagonist in classic film noir. He is caught between his loyalty to other males (to the father of his ex-girlfriend Deirdre Taylor [Joelie Jenkins], who turns out to be the woman-as-prize) and his attraction and attractiveness to alluring females (Susan and Edie). But, as the narrative of his quest becomes less murky and his own role within it is reinstated to that of hero (he is not a cop killer after all), Mike's body undergoes a very significant transformation from the 'hard-body' of fantasy to the wounded hero of actuality. Susan's attempts to turn the supposed bad man into good are constantly being thwarted by his continuing project of searching for the truth of Deirdre's disappearance. He continues unabated his 'hard-body' project. But that body image starts to break down halfway through the first season with a succession of mishaps that befall him. He is mistaken for a burglar, is shot in the abdomen and does not go to hospital but is tended to at home by a dodgy doctor (1: 14). The following evening he takes Susan out to dinner in a posh French restaurant, La Petite Fleur. The timing is auspicious as it is Valentine's Day. But the heroic male begins to bleed and he is rushed to hospital. Many images of the wounded hunter abound in Romantic painting and they invariably depict a shirtless man being tended by a doting woman. Here, however, Susan does not get that chance. Mike's actual wound is not shown as even in his hospital bed he is covered by a smock. Susan, in fact, is the one who reveals more flesh, in a party frock totally inappropriate for a hospital setting. When two male cops enter the room Susan is displaced and she can never play the carer to the wounded hero as the hero comes under suspicion. Later he is beaten up in an underground parking lot by a rogue cop who dropped the charges against him for Martha Huber's murder (1: 19). Later still he is spotted by Susan covered in bruises. How these wounds have come about create a disturbing dilemma for Susan, as her instinct in her fantasy is to tend those wounds.

These two scenes, however, form a device in the narrative of masculinity. In the first the phallic masculinity of Mike is overturned into 'its vulnerable, pitiable, and frequently comic collapse' (Lehman 2001: 26). But in the second it is also a deliberate masochising of the male body in that it is temporarily dephallicised 'in order to rephallicise it' (Robinson 2001: 141). This is a familiar trope of the western, in which injury plays an important role in the construction of masculinity. The male body, once injured, must then go through a period of convalescence and recovery. And, once recovered, the body is re-habilitated in order 'to establish the validity of masculine identity' (Hatty 2000: 168). This 'wound culture' (see Seltzer 1998) is a serious counterpoint to Susan being accident-prone. Her wounds are the result of her own innate klutziness. Mike's wounds are the result of external force meted out against him by others. Thus Mike, despite being wounded, emerges continually unscathed in the narrative of his own self-defined heroic project. In Susan's eyes, he is the hegemonic male rescuer from her singleton status only in her imagination (since she is not party to the details of his heroic project). Thus she has to learn from the omniscient wisdom of Mary Alice's voiceover that 'if the right hero doesn't come along, sometimes we have to rescue ourselves' (1: 17).

The wound culture extends beyond the self-rehabilitating heroic males to the subordinated masculinities, most notably those surrounding Bree Van de Kamp. If the heroic male body is configured as a 'low-maintenance proposition' (Hatty 2000: 121) that cannot take time out from the heroic project to take care of itself, then the bodies of the subordinated are extremely high-maintenance and do not recover quite so easily, if at all. Whereas Mike's wounds heal within the space of two episodes at most, these subordinated bodies spend inordinate amounts of time in hospital, in bed, on medication or on crutches.

Bree's husband Rex Van de Kamp has a body that is vulnerable by its very essence. He has an onion allergy that leads to his hospitalisation and near-death in the first episode. Throughout the first season what drives his particular narrative is his increasing medicalisation. He has a heart attack while being dominated by Maisy Gibbons (Sharon Lawrence) in an S/M sex game (1: 10), and finally there is his re-admittance to hospital in the final episode that leads to his death (1: 23). Metaphorically, Rex could also be said to embody a toxic masculinity (Robinson 2001) in which his emotional block with his wife has led to a somatic condition of the body. He has all the attributes of the hegemonically masculine given his social status as a doctor, his perfect wife, obligatory one child of each sex, and his membership of an expensive and elite country club. But his failure to control his children, let alone his own health (and this is doubly ironic given his own profession), undercuts his otherwise assured heroic status. He also fails to control his wife. Bree's choice of a love rival to make Rex jealous, the socially dysfunctional pharmacist George Williams, is an interesting one. If Rex is a subordinated male sexually if not socially, George is an even greater aberration within masculinity, being both socially and sexually subordinated. Bree's choice is just the ticket: she positions herself between the two rivals on a stroll through a gardening exhibition while the two men trade horticultural insults (1: 20). Further, Rex reminds George of his superior social standing that will always win out, reminding George of his position within the hierarchy of masculinities. The problem for Rex, though, is that the hege-monically masculine status that he clearly possesses does not extend to the bedroom, and this is where Bree's fantasy of the perfect masculinity breaks down. She does not want to handcuff and dominate him sexually. She wishes that role for herself. However, none of the men in her life (Rex the masochist, Andrew the gay son, and George the physically incompetent) can match up to the ideals of a masculinity she so desperately desires.

Throughout the first season masculinities are desired and dissected, probed and prodded into action, and emasculated more than once

(Tom, Carlos, Rex, George) by the women of Wisteria Lane. Men are categorised as having a compulsory heterosexuality. Andrew, Bree's gay son, has only one visible moment of his sexuality depicted by kissing Justin (Ryan Carnes) (1: 15), who first tried to 'cure' his homosexuality by blackmailing Gabrielle into providing him with his first heterosexual encounter. And he, along with a gay cable guy, offer a recurring joke by being comically mistaken for Gabrielle's secret lovers. But those masculinities so desired by Lynette, Bree and Gabrielle are impossible paradoxes. Their fantasies yearn for the authoritarian male, the hunter-hero, with a spectacularly phallic body, whose aberrant behaviour can be turned to good, and whose wounds of vulnerability can be tended in miraculously speedy acts of self-generation. But, when those masculinities appear in actuality, those hegemonic traits are reined in (Lynette and Tom), step over the boundary of hegemony and into total control (Gabrielle and Carlos), appear only as pale imitations of the fantasy (Bree and Rex), or continually elude the definition of the heroic by not operating within the law, or failing to solve the murder mystery (Susan and Mike). And at the end of the first season, as those hegemonic masculinities suffer catastrophic consequences of their partner's actions (Tom loses his job, Carlos goes to prison, Rex dies and Mike faces the gun of a child's rage), we are left with the women searching for new heroes (1: 23). One arrives in the form of a young African-American man, Matthew Applewhite. He is handsome and fit and immediately stimulates Edie Britt's fantasy. But his mother stands guard on her porch and keeps the new, seemingly available male, with the outward signs of the hegemonically masculine, guarded and protected from the machinations of those who might induce her son to fall from grace. And, with the men's hegemony successfully emasculated, the women of Wisteria Lane can seek further solace in sisterly solidarity.

Part 3:

GENRE, GENDER AND
CULTURAL MYTHS

I O

Disciplining the housewife in *Desperate Housewives*
and domestic reality television

Sharon Sharp

In an emblematic scene in ABC's prime-time breakout hit *Desperate Housewives*, Lynette Scavo, a stay-at-home mother who has been abusing her kids' ADD medication to keep up with the other Wisteria Lane mothers, has a physical and emotional breakdown and contemplates suicide to escape being trapped at home with her children (1: 8). Later, in a rare moment of sisterhood, Lynette's friends attempt to console her by relating their own moments of mommy trauma, and Lynette sobs: 'Why didn't you ever tell me? We should tell each other this stuff.' In an equally memorable moment about shame and secrets, Martha Stewart clone Bree Van de Kamp, who believes in the old-fashioned values of respect for God, the importance of family and love for country, removes freshly cleaned handcuffs, recently used to reluctantly dominate her husband in an S/M scenario, from the dishwasher (1: 14). These representations of the housewife are particularly notable in the way they offer a feminine perspective on the domestic sphere and the contradictions of lived female experience. But they are not limited to *Desperate Housewives*. A brief sampling of the housewife as represented in prime-time US television during the 2004 season marks the new fixation on the housewife, and domesticity in televisual discourse.[1] Domestic reality TV, a sub-genre of reality TV programming, has also trained its gaze on the housewife and home.[2] Lifetime Television's *How Clean is Your House?* humiliates housewives and others with the exposure of bad housekeeping such as cat faeces in the marital bed and mouldy food in the refrigerator. ABC's *Super*

Nanny and Fox's clone *Nanny 911* feature stern British nannies who give exhausted mothers and distant fathers strict parenting rules for raising their unruly children. Fox and ABC also have offered up their own versions of Britain's *Wife Swap*, which dramatise conflicted housewifery when two women from radically different social backgrounds swap households for two weeks. The housewife, relatively absent from prime-time programming since the departure of *Roseanne* in 1997, has returned with a vengeance.

Like *Desperate Housewives*, domestic reality television, in which traditional concepts of gender are dramatised and debated, invites viewers inside the domestic sphere, where they discover that house-wifery, motherhood and domesticity can be exhausting, empty and unfulfilling. Unlike the happy housewives idealised in sitcoms of the past, the housewives who are regularly swapped, scrutinised and shamed on domestic reality television are decidedly ambivalent, frustrated, overworked, neurotic and unhappy. The model of house-wifery put forward by domestic reality television is a contradictory one: the ambivalence of the domestic reality television housewife subverts the ideology that women should find domesticity and motherhood fulfilling, yet she is ridiculed for breaking the TV rule that women should never express dissatisfaction with motherhood and domesticity. Similarly, when the domestic reality television housewife exhibits an over-investment in domesticity *à la* Martha Stewart it is conceived of as a dysfunction that alienates her husband and children and she is punished with domestic discord.

This chapter explores how problems of housewifery and domesticity in *Desperate Housewives* resonate with the model of housewifery circulated in the current trend in domestic reality television. By examining the representation of housewifery in *Desperate Housewives*, as embodied in the characters Lynette and Bree, I focus on how these representations relate to cultural anxieties about the housewife and domesticity, and examine how they are indicative of the way the media currently construct the housewife. The key argument is that the cultural work being done in the televisual discourse of the housewife is both complex and contradictory. On the one hand, the emphasis on problems of the housewife in *Desperate Housewives*, like domestic reality television, seems to offer potential for feminist critique in their rebellion against what Susan Douglas and Meredith Michaels have described as the new 'momism' or 'the insistence that no woman is truly complete or fulfilled unless she has kids, that women remain the best primary caretakers of children, and that to be a remotely decent mother, a woman has to devote her entire physical, psychological, emotional being to her children 24/7' (2004: 4). On the other hand, *Desperate Housewives* and domestic reality television confirm dominant cultural beliefs about traditional gender roles as they ridicule housewives for their perfectionism and ambivalence about motherhood and domesticity.

The new television housewife

The idea for *Desperate Housewives* was born out of media coverage of a case of troubled domesticity that brought to the surface anxieties about social expectations of motherhood and housewifery. Show runner Marc Cherry's conceptualisation of the series originated in watching with his mother the news coverage of Andrea Yates, a mother convicted of systematically drowning each of her five children in the bathtub. As Cherry relates in his much-repeated origin story of the series, he turned to his mother and said:

> 'Can you imagine a woman being so desperate that she would hurt her own children?' And my mother took her cigarette out of her mouth and said, 'I've been there.' [...]Suddenly it occurred to me, 'Well gosh, if my mom had these moments, every woman has had a moment where she is close to losing it.' As I talked to her and found out these things, the genesis of this idea was born in that (Crook 2005:3).

The idea for *Desperate Housewives* thus begins with an ambivalent housewife and mother: a woman who had been discussed in the media (not always unsympathetically) in terms of her extreme deviation from normative conceptions of motherhood and housewifery but also in terms of how she exemplified the difficulties women face living up to the new momism.

Cherry's 'comic soap opera' exploits a limited range of anxieties about housewives and domesticity through its five upper-middle-class female protagonists who live on the suburban cul-de-sac Wisteria Lane, each with her own mommy trauma (none of which approach the trauma of Andrea Yates). Voiceover narrator Mary Alice Young's suicide, committed after performing her domestic routine and 'polishing her life until it gleamed with perfection', opens the pilot episode and introduces the five main characters. Susan Mayer, a divorced single mother who works from home as children's book illustrator and seems incapable of mothering her child; Bree Van de Kamp, who has a Martha Stewart complex and alienates her husband and children on her quest for perfection; Lynette Scavo, a former corporate powerhouse who is stay-at-home mom to four unruly children (even though she was clearly more successful than her husband in the corporate world); Gabrielle Solis, a nouveau riche Latina gold-digger trophy wife who has an affair with her teenage gardener and contemplates aborting her unborn child of uncertain paternity; and last but not least, real estate agent Edie Britt, the neighbourhood slut, without the attachment of husband, family or friends and whose self-esteem is derived from male sexual attention, rounds out the cast.

Despite the women's movement's efforts to liberate women from the exile of the domestic sphere, *Desperate Housewives*, like domestic reality television, returns women to the home. As in the domestic reality television series in which housewives are taught traditional concepts of gender, and in which wives and not husbands are swapped, *Desperate Housewives* puts forward the assumption that domesticity is a female-oriented sphere. The series showcases a decidedly ambivalent take on 'retreatism', which Diane Negra and Yvonne Tasker have identified as one of the most persistent themes of post-feminist representation: 'In the retreatist scenario, a well-educated white female professional displays her "empowerment" and caring nature by withdrawing from the workforce (and symbolically from the public sphere) to devote herself to husband and family' (2005: 108). While many post-feminist representations offer this choice as a form of empowerment and as the best option, *Desperate Housewives* obsesses over the anxiety of retreatism. As series creator and executive producer Marc Cherry describes the show:

I call it a post-post feminist take. The women's movement said, 'Let's get the gals out working'. Next the women realised you can't have it all. Most of the time you have to make a choice. What I'm doing is having women make the choice to live in the suburbs, but things aren't going well at all. The show is actually a love letter to all the women out there who have issues and are trying their best to be stay at home moms (Weinraub 2004: B7).

This 'love letter' to stay-at-home moms is most dramatically played out through the characters Lynette and Bree, who are, technically, the only stay-at-home mothers in the first season, as they do not participate in any work outside of the home. Lynette most clearly articulates the ambivalent housewife model advanced in domestic reality television. As if to emphasise her ambivalence a montage sequence featuring her washing dishes, feeding the baby and cleaning chocolate fingerprints off the window is accompanied by Mary Alice's voiceover, sarcastically informing us that her friend used to 'see herself as a career woman and a hugely successful one at that but she gave up her career to assume a new label – the incredibly satisfying one of full-time mother, but unfortunately this new label frequently falls short of what was advertised' (1: 4). Generally rumpled, exhausted and covered in baby spit, Lynette does not relish her role as housewife and mother and seems at times to hate her three unruly boys and young baby girl. Running into a former colleague, who tells her she would be running the firm by now if she had not left and asks Lynette how she likes domestic life, Lynette lies and tells her: 'It's the best job I've ever had,' (1: 1) expressing some of the contradictions of the ambivalent housewife: she is privileged enough to be able to retreat to home and family but once there finds it unfulfilling.

As domestic reality television's surveillance of the American home explores at length, the ambivalence of housewives almost always emanates from the wife's unequal shouldering of the domestic and childcare labour, and Lynette's ambivalence about being a stay-at-home mom has similar origins. Her husband, Tom Scavo, an advertising executive who spends much time away from home, is affably oblivious to Lynette's situation. Like the belligerent or distant patriarchs who make up most of domestic reality television's conflicts, Tom rarely helps with the childcare or domestic chores, and Lynette is often depicted pleading on the phone for him to come home, while her undisciplined children wreak havoc around her. In Lynette, *Desperate Housewives* comes closest to a feminist critique of patriarchy and the unequal division of labour. Without her husband's help, Lynette cannot keep up with the challenges of keeping house and keeping her unruly children under control, which leads her to abuse her children's Ritalin. When Lynette breaks down from her drug addiction (1: 8), she confesses to friends Bree and Susan that she feels humiliated and like a failure 'because the other moms make it look so easy'. Lynette's confession demonstrates an extreme ambivalence towards the role of motherhood, and satirises the ways women internalise the social pressures of choosing to be stay-at-home mothers and living up to unrealistic standards of domestic perfection. Indeed, this scene has become a common referent in the popular media – from *Oprah* to *USA Today* – that is used to introduce problems related to the mommy mystique. This cathartic moment of rewriting the housewife is remarkable because it speaks to women's lived experience in a way that has been verboten or demonised in popular media. This housewife, to some degree, rejects the contemporary ideology of femininity that insists women should feel maternal and should find motherhood fulfilling. However, this critique is constrained by the series' emphasis on competition between women and the internalisation of cultural values that insist women should be in charge of domesticity and find it fulfilling.

While Lynette makes it clear that part of the problem is that her husband does not share the burden of childcare, this is addressed not through reconfiguring the burden of parenting, but by 'scoring some high-grade nanny'. As in domestic reality television, which rarely suggests more equal parenting or state-supported childcare as a solution to the overburdened housewife's plight, Lynette and her husband decide to hire a young, white, attractive woman as a nanny (1: 9). *Desperate Housewives* presents a solution to the mommy mystique problem that is decidedly upper-class: as much as this series articulates the ambivalence of being a housewife and mother, it is a distinctly upper-middle-class ambivalence. It is important to note that it is precisely the women, who have the choice to retreat into the home or stay in the corporate world, through whom this discourse is mobilised and to some extent ridiculed. Narratively, this discourse that rebels against the ideology of femininity is recuperated in the text, as the network of friendship between the suburban housewives is used more to judge and shame each other rather than as a network of support for sharing and debating problems of domesticity and motherhood. Lynette is constantly judged by her neighbours: even her friend Susan, who, while watching Lynette unsuccessfully corral her children, gives her a look that narrator Mary Alice tells us says: 'You should learn to control your kids, after all, they're your responsibility' (1: 10).

If *Desperate Housewives* is careful to police the housewife's ambivalence, as demonstrated by Lynette, it also goes to great lengths to ridicule the housewife's over-investment in domesticity. Like domestic reality television's control-freak housewives whose fervour for domestic order alienates their families, Bree's impeccable domestic comportment is characterised as an obsessive-compulsive disorder that causes her children and husband to loathe her. Bree's teenage son, Andrew, accuses her of 'running for mayor of Stepford' and her husband Rex wants a divorce because he is tired of 'living in a detergent commercial' with his 'plastic suburban housewife' (1: 1). Like the exploration of the verboten ambivalence towards housewifery and motherhood that *Desperate Housewives* circulates in the representation of Lynette, Bree's characterisation at first glance reads as a critique of the images of domesticity and femininity that are measured by the quality of housekeeping and cooking. *Desperate Housewives* derides Bree's belief that spending three hours to cook osso bucco and basil purée for her family, zealously scrubbing toilets, and polishing the silver will lead to personal satisfaction and domestic bliss. And her retreat into the home and passion for domesticity demonstrate that home is not the site of love and fulfilment for many women but is, in fact, often based on repression of desires. In a session with her therapist Bree confesses that she would settle for a life of repression and denial with her philandering husband because it would allow her to continue to throw the dinner parties that she finds so 'elegant and civilised' (1: 14).

Much as Bree's investment in domesticity functions as a critique of social expectations about femininity and domesticity, it is also ridiculed as an investment in her upper-middle-class status. Her passion for domesticity is interwoven with her obsession with keeping up appearances and general upper-middle-class perfection. Rather than admit that her family has severe imperfections, Bree upholds a façade of perfection. When her son Andrew is involved in a hit-and-run accident, she arranges for his car to be stolen and uses chemical solvent to clean the blood from the pavement (1: 8). Rather than confide in her friends that she and Rex are in marital counselling, she tells them they are taking tennis lessons at the country club (1: 3). While *Desperate Housewives* ridicules the housewife's ambivalence by constructing Lynette as an abject, jealous woman, the series mocks the housewife's over-investment in domesticity by constructing Bree as a cold and deeply dysfunctional woman. Her obsession with domesticity is not based on genuine affection for her family but is a product of her dysfunction. When Rex, convalescing from a heart attack, observes that the tray with freshly laundered napkins, flowers from the garden and good china that Bree has prepared for him is proof of her affection, she coldly replies that he should not mistake her 'anal retentiveness for actual affection' (1: 13). Similarly, when Bree's argument with Rex causes him to suffer a second heart attack, she takes the time to neatly make the marital bed before driving him to the emergency room because she refuses to leave the house with an unmade bed (1: 22).

Like the Martha Stewart housewives in the domestic reality television series *Wife Swap* and *Trading Spouses* who are not welcomed home by their families upon their return from their swap, *Desperate Housewives* ridicules Bree's perfectionism as dysfunctional rather than validating her investment in domesticity and women's work at home in general. Further, even as *Desperate Housewives* ridicules the housewife's investment in domesticity, it also celebrates and glamorises it through the language of domestic lifestyle television in the show's *mise en scène*. However dysfunctional Bree may be, she enjoys a life of leisure filled with commodities; domestic labour, when performed, is depicted as an obsessive yet pleasant hobby.

The disciplining of the housewife as embodied in Lynette and Bree is most apparent with regard to their sexuality. While domestic reality television goes to considerable lengths to keep out of the bedroom (aside from reminding housewives that neither children nor cat faeces belong in the marital bed, and despite the sexual implications of titles such as *Wife Swap* and *Trading Spouses*), in *Desperate Housewives* the bedroom is where housewives are policed the most. Sex is another domestic duty that the housewives fail to perform without dysfunction and that provides little personal satisfaction. Lynette's ambivalence is manifest in her abject appearance: unlike the other housewives, who wear lingerie and miniskirts, Lynette is often wearing baggy soccer mom garb and smelling of baby vomit. Her attempts at seduction are played for laughs: she falls asleep in a sexy French maid costume while waiting for Tom, only to be discovered later by him and the business associate he has brought home for the night (1: 21). When Lynette does get sex from her husband, it is because he is aroused by a glimpse of their young nanny in the nude (1: 11).

Similarly, Bree's obsessive-compulsive disorder interferes with her sex life. In another failed seduction played for laughs, Bree's attempts to win back her husband's affection, by seducing him in La Perla lingerie and a fur coat, is thwarted by her inability to look away from a sloppy burrito perched on the night table and dripping onto the carpet while they are having sex (1: 6). Later, after discovering that Rex visits another suburban housewife for his S/M pleasures, Bree decides to keep her marriage together by dominating her husband, an activity that she finds unpleasurable, 'sick' and 'dirty' (1: 14). If domestic reality television tells us that domestic bliss is the woman's job, *Desperate Housewives* tells us that having a pleasing sex life is the woman's responsibility too, only it will probably not be pleasurable for her. Pleasure is hard to come by for the housewife: it is clear that housewives are punished for their ambivalence or over-investment in their roles as they are denied any pleasure in the domestic sphere.

While *Desperate Housewives* and domestic reality television that focuses on the housewife and home are certainly unique, they circulate similar cultural anxieties about the housewife. Surveying the American home, the new televisual discourse on the housewife tells us that the choice to retreat into the home has resulted in ambivalence and dysfunction. The image of the conflicted housewife and troubled domestic sphere appears at a time when ideas about housewifery and family are being questioned and even transformed. We can read the trend to fixate on the housewife as an effort to contain and normalise these changes through the rhetoric of shame and ridicule. Although domestic reality television and *Desperate Housewives* belong to different genres, they operate within the same logic: they represent women judging other women for not living up to traditional norms of femininity and domesticity, and often shame the women they feature. Rather than sounding a critique of the social pressures that demand perfection and place an unequal burden on women, the new televisual discourse on the housewife blames individual women for problems of domesticity and invites viewers to feel superior. While we laughed at the antics and physical comedy that ensued around the housewife of television's sitcom past, these new shows ask us to laugh at the housewife's predicament with a more malicious laughter.

Notes

1 Housewives have been on American television since its beginning. See Mary Beth Haralovich. 'Sitcoms and Suburbs: Positioning the 1950s Homemaker'. In *Private Screenings*. Eds. Lynn Spigel and Denise Mann. Minneapolis: University of Minnesota Press, 1992: 111–142; Patricia Mellencamp. 'Situation Comedy, Feminism, and Freud: Discourses of Gracie and Lucy'. In *Feminist Television Criticism*. Eds. Charlotte Brunsdon, Julie D'Acci and Lynn Spigel. Oxford: Oxford University Press, 1997: 60–73; Elspeth Probyn. 'New Traditionalism and Post-Feminism: TV Does the Home'. In ibid.: 126–137; Kathleen Rowe. *The Unruly Woman: Gender and the Genres of Laughter*. Austin: University of Texas Press, 1995; and Lynn Spigel. 'From Domestic Space to Outer Space: The 1960s Fantastic Family Sitcom'. In *Close Encounters*. Eds. Constance Penley, Elisabeth Lyon, Lynn Spigel and Janet Bergstrom. Minneapolis: University of Minnesota Press, 1991: 205–235.

2 For more on reality television, see James Friedman. Ed. *Reality Squared: Televisual Discourse on the Real*. New Brunswick, NJ: Rutgers University Press, 2002; Sujata Moorti and Karen Ross. 'Reality Television: Fairy Tale or Feminist Nightmare?' *Feminist Media Studies*. 4. 2. 2004: 203–231; and Susan Murray and Laurie Ouellette. Eds. *Reality TV: Remaking Television Culture*. New York: New York University Press, 2004.

II

Murder and mayhem on Wisteria Lane: A study of
genre and cultural context in *Desperate Housewives*

Judith Lancioni

The conjunction of the light-hearted and the serious in *Desperate Housewives* is evident in the phrases used to describe the series: 'dark and comedic' (Oldenburg 2004: E1); a 'frothy adult soap' combined with 'heightened drama' (Frutkin 2004); and 'mordant humour' (Poniewozik 2004: 20). Chief writer and executive producer Marc Cherry describes his creation as 'a dramatic soap opera that has more than a few laughs' (Jones 2004). Nicollete Sheridan, who plays Edie Britt, agrees, adding that 'it's touching and it's weird and it's funny and it's witty' (Carroll 2004). These descriptions are indicative of dramedy, which, as the name implies, fuses together two distinct genres: comedy and drama.

This generic fusion begins with the ingenious title sequence, which establishes the ideological context of the series and sets the tone for each episode. The title sequence was designed by yU+ co, with animated images drawn from famous works of art to show how women from Eve to the present have struggled under male domination ('yU+ co Opens ABC's *Desperate Housewives*' 2004). The sequence begins with Hans Memling's famous Renaissance painting of Adam and Eve after the fall. The two figures, clad in their fig leaves, stand under an apple tree. As Eve reaches up, a boulder-sized apple falls down and crushes Adam. Next comes a scene of an animated Egyptian hieroglyph – Nefertiti surrounded by children who pop up one at a time and disappear again as she gestures with her hands.

The next sequence provides an adaptation of Jan Van Eyck's wedding portrait of Giovanni di Arrigo Arnolfini and his wife. In the original portrait they are hand in hand (Jones 2000). In this updated version, he is eating a banana as she sweeps the floor in the background. He throws the peel on the floor and she – apparently pregnant, though not in the original (ibid.) – sweeps it up into a small pile of debris on the floor. She caresses her stomach and throws the broom into the air.

Giovanna is absorbed into an arched window that becomes the peaked roof of the building in an animation of Grant Woods's famous 'American Gothic'. The broom floats briefly through the painting, perhaps as a reminder that female independence is possible. A dour-looking man and woman stand side by side. He holds a pitchfork. The original painting occupies the screen for a beat. Then a broadly smiling, red-headed cartoon-type woman enters the frame and chucks the old man under the chin. Her bright red lipstick and sly wink contrast broadly with the rural couple's stolidity. Next the farm woman's head is tightly framed in what becomes a sardine can. The lid rolls up and she becomes the central illustration on the can's lid. Over her is the word 'canned' and under her is the logo 'aged sardines', a clever take on what can happen to ageing wives. The can is propelled onto a kitchen counter. A rosy-cheeked woman reminiscent of 1950s food advertisements enters the frame, her arms full of jars and cans. A Campbell's soup can falls out of the assortment, appearing between a cartoon couple reminiscent of Roy Lichtenstein's pop art. As the soup can drops out of the picture, the couple confront each other, their faces close. A tear cascades down the woman's cheek. Suddenly she pops the man with a right to the jaw, a purple burst indicating the power of the blow; this woman literally takes power into her own hands. This image is followed by that of a shaking apple tree; this time a snake is clearly visible in the branches. The smiling housewives appear under the tree as apples fall into their hands.

Lane Jensen, who produced the project, explains that each segment is designed to illustrate 'the gripes women have faced over the years from infidelity to a husband who can't pick up after himself' ('yU+ co Opens ABC's *Desperate Housewives*' 2004). The serio/comic construction of the sequence invites careful scrutiny: first, of the original artworks and the ideology they embody regarding the role of women; and, second, of their droll reinterpretation and the ideology implied. While the title sequence may just appear comical, the original artworks were serious and embodied an ideology in which men held the power. (It was Eve, after all, who, according to centuries of tradition, picked the forbidden apple, making her the first sinner and responsible for Adam's sin). In this modern reinterpretation, women have the power: Eve still picks the apple, but Adam gets crushed, suggesting that she will no longer accept the blame; Nefertiti's children seem to perfectly obey her commands; Giovanna throws away her broom (no more sweeping for her) and the cartoon woman tears up (traditionally passive response to being emotionally hurt by a man), then takes aggressive action to solve her heartache.

Clearly this is a post-feminist confection, since the women, all from different socio-political and historical contexts, are assertive and take charge. But in the final frame, as the female quartet from Wisteria Lane hold their apples, a snake hovers in the branches above their heads, suggesting in a comic way that vestiges of old myths remain. The credit sequence is comic, but the ideology it spoofs is not. It also suggests that this series, like its opening credits, will take a serio/comic look at various constructions of gender relationships and women's role in them.

The title sequence demonstrates how dramedy fosters the weaving together of comic and dramatic elements across storylines, thus creating a highly complex text – a complexity that lends itself to the articulation of ideological discourse. My purpose in this chapter is to explore the functioning of this blended genre in the first season of *Desperate House-wives* and to discuss the ideologies facilitated by it. My contention is that dramedy is especially effective in constructing a post-feminist text.

Dramedy

The term 'dramedy' first appeared in the 1980s and was applied to series like *Moonlighting*, *The Wonder Years* and *Hooperman*. Dramedies blend the comic and the serious in different ways; some separate comic and dramatic storylines, while others combine drama and comedy together.

Desperate Housewives does both. While the mystery surrounding Mary Alice Young's suicide and Martha Huber's murder, the dark relationship between Zach and Paul Young, and Mike Delfino's clandestine hunt for Deirdre's (played by Jolie Jenkins) killer are purely dramatic, Susan Mayer's competition with Edie for Mike's affection seems purely comedic. But comedy and drama interact within a single storyline as well. Lynette Scavo's struggle to control her children seems funny, but the maternal desperation and the drug addiction that result are not. Gabrielle Solis's adventures with her teenage lover are hilarious but potentially hurtful for everyone involved. Witness the scene in which Juanita 'Mama' Solis finally succeeds in catching Gabrielle in bed with John Rowland. The scene is funny because Gabrielle has escaped detection so many times before. But when 'Mama' Solis is run down by a drunken Andrew Van de Kamp the humour evaporates. As Cherry explains, 'We come at this show with an ironic twisted bent…' (Jones 2004). Those twists are the essence of dramedy.

As Cherry acknowledges, the series uses dramatic and comedic elements to reveal the tragedy beneath 'the antics these women face' (Lisotta 2004: 14). Bree Van de Kamp provides the best example of this serio/comic blend. Her obsessive/compulsive housekeeping, though comic, has a serious origin. She tells Zach that when her mother was killed by a car, she washed away the blood. It made her feel better (1: 5). So, while Bree's domestic achievements may be funny by virtue of their excessiveness, their effects are rooted in tragedy.

Sometimes the comedy/drama blend is brief but revelatory. In the pilot, for example, Martha Huber, licking red sauce off her finger, hears a noise, grabs the blender she borrowed from Mary Alice at least six months earlier, and, ever inquisitive, runs over to the Young's, presumed source of the noise. She looks through a window, sees Mary Alice lying in a pool of blood, and runs back to her home, swiftly ripping the label with Mary Alice's name off the blender. The scene is both dramatic and funny. By licking the blood-like substance off her finger (comedy), Martha symbolically links herself with Mary Alice's suicide, preparing viewers for the actual link revealed in a subsequent episode (drama), when in a twist of fate Paul uses the same blender to kill her. The blender, which was a source of humour in the pilot, becomes a tool for violence.

The discovery of Martha's corpse is also both dramatic and comic, funny and appalling (1: 12). Mary Alice remarks that since childhood Martha Huber has craved an exciting life – to be captured by pirates, or become a star, or marry a millionaire. But the only excitement in her life came when she died, the police officer kneeling over her grave promising that her face will be in newspapers across the state.

Often in dramedy, incongruity, idiosyncrasy, exaggeration and absurdity are used to foreground the polysemy of a particular scene, situation or character. Sometimes incongruity injects grizzly humour into the unnerving violence of Wisteria Lane, making it better (we can laugh) and worse (laughing seems inappropriate) at the same time.

Or incongruity may make us laugh and cringe, as when Felicia Tilman, Martha's sister, says to Paul: 'I hid the originals in a safe place. It seemed like a reasonable precaution seeing as you murdered Martha and all. Would you like a cookie?' (1: 21). Then there is Maisy Gibbons (Sharon Lawrence), stalwart PTA member who censors fairy tales while serving as the neighbourhood hooker on the side to earn extra cash.

Idiosyncrasy can be used to distance the audience, opening up narrative gaps that invite multiple and often conflicting interpretations (Nelson 2001: 45). 'Idiosyncratic' is certainly an apt term for Martha, who, out of spite and jealousy, drags a corpse from her own yard into Bree's so that her neighbour's oh-so-perfect lawn would be ruined. Mrs McCluskey (Kathryn Joosten), Lynette's elderly neighbour, repeatedly steals her own plant then accuses the Scavo boys.

Absurdity also plays a major role in the dramedy of *Desperate Housewives* – for example, the fact that John persists in calling Gabrielle 'Mrs Solis', even when he's proposing. Another example occurs in the pilot when he and Gabrielle have just made love. As Gabrielle lights up, John asks, 'Hey, can I have a drag?' She answers, 'Absolutely not. You're much too young to smoke.'

The eccentricities of these minor characters contribute to the carefully constructed mayhem of Wisteria Lane. In Martha's case, despite her seeming affability, her actions confirm her mean-spirited nature. Mrs McCluskey's idiosyncrasy is motivated by loneliness. Maisy is two-faced – bossy, huffy and politically correct at school and embarrassingly incorrect at home, although she seems to regard her own behaviour as defensible. Together, they raise questions about who these people really are, given the absurdity of their behaviour, and alert viewers to the multiple realities they will encounter at every house on Wisteria Lane.

The four major characters make even greater contributions to that mayhem. Gabrielle mows the lawn in an evening gown and high heels when her husband complains that John has neglected it (1: 1). To escape her mother-in-law's scrutiny she drops her at a casino, knowing that Juanita is a compulsive gambler (1: 6), and also has her arrested as a shoplifter (1: 5). Bree brings baked goods to Mary Alice's funeral then gives the grieving husband precise instructions about when to eat them, before asking him to return the baskets (1: 1). She is so distracted by the marriage counsellor's dangling button that she loses concentration (1: 3). She visits her husband's hotel room, hoping her sexy underwear will rekindle his interest, only to fixate on a sloppy burrito instead of him (1: 6). Susan's misadventures – breaking into Edie's house and accidentally setting it on fire (1: 1) or locking herself out of her house whilst naked (1: 3) – are legendary. Lynette is driven to desperate acts by her sons; abandoning them by the roadside when they fail to stop misbehaving in the back of the car (1: 2) and, in a dress and high heels, wading into the pool at Mary Alice's funeral, to retrieve them (1: 1).

While these scenes are hilarious, they are counterpointed by more serious interludes, drama and humour melding together like two sides of a coin. Funny as it may be, Lynette's being called to the principal's office because her twins have painted a classmate blue (1: 4) is one incident in many that will lead her to drug addiction and emotional breakdown (1: 8). Gabrielle's cat-and-mouse game with her mother-in-law leads to Juanita being run over (1: 7) and her fatal fall down the hospital stairs (1: 17). Nowhere is this counterpoint clearer than when Bree delays taking Rex to the hospital, following his heart attack, so she can make her bed (1: 22). She loves him, but cannot escape her own fastidiousness.

The editors of *Desperate Housewives* – Troy Takiki, Jonathan Posell and Andy Doerfer – point out that dramedy lends itself to the creation of a tapestry of moods. As Posell explains, a funny scene builds to a peak followed by a brief pause and then more serious material, or sometimes comedy can interrupt a serious storyline ('yU+ co Opens

ABC's *Desperate Housewives'* 2004). Dark alternates with light. For example, the scene in which Felicia finds out about her sister Martha's death is followed by a scene in which Susan rushes to Mike's house for a romantic rendezvous (1: 12).

Posell credits dramedy for the distinctiveness of *Desperate Housewives*. Combining two genres, he contends, facilitates 'multiple storylines, dramatic scenes, and comedic scenes that butt up against each other seamlessly' (ibid.). The characters, he adds, are likeable, even when they're bad. 'We love the fact that they can be evil and still get themselves into silly situations.' For example, the fact that George Williams is so conniving and malicious doubles the humour of his shooting himself in the foot, especially since his female companion (Bree) is an adept markswoman.

Feminism, post-feminism and dramedy: a tale of two ideologies

Thus far I have taken what Jason Mittel calls a 'textualist' approach to genre (2001: 5), using examples from *Desperate Housewives* to argue that this television series is a dramedy. However, Mittel contends that genre study should not be limited to the examination of a single text or even a group of texts. Genre study must instead analyse a text in relation to its cultural context, including the relevance of a genre to a particular community (12). Mittel stresses the importance of studying 'how genres operate as conceptual frameworks, situating media texts within larger contexts of understanding' (17).

Since *Desperate Housewives* centres on the lives of four suburban 'housewives', the appropriate cultural context would seem to be its portrayal of wives and mothers in the twenty-first century. In fact, Marc Cherry has described his series as 'a twenty-first century take on women at home', a 'postfeminist' tale about women's choices and their positive or negative results (Oldenberg 2004: E1).

The term 'post-feminism' came into vogue in the 1990s without any firm definition and so has been applied in contradictory ways (Negra 2004). It has been described as a 'cultural catchphrase' that refers to various theories about the relevance of first wave feminism (ibid.). Discussion abounds. Joanne Hollows (2000: 192), for example, disagrees with feminists like Susan Faludi (1992) and Susan Walters (1995), who seem to equate post-feminism with anti-feminism, agreeing instead with Charlotte Brunsdon's 1997 more positive assertion (101–102). As Hollows points out, these critics would disagree on the impact of a given text (192–193). For Faludi and Walters, films like *Pretty Woman* (1990), *Fried Green Tomatoes* (1991) and *Working Girl* (1988) and television shows like *Ally McBeal*, *Sex and the City*, *Moonlighting* (and presumably *Desperate Housewives*) represent a backlash against feminism (Hollows 2000: 193). Hollows, on the other hand, argues that these texts reflect 'many modes of femininity' and their relationship to feminism (ibid.).

Brunsdon and others agree that post-feminism repudiates feminism's rejection of traditional roles. While acknowledging the oppressiveness of patriarchy, post-feminists accept both the stay-at-home mom and the career woman paradigms, acknowledging that women can be traditional, radical, and even beautiful, at the same time (Press 1991: vxi). Thus 'meanings may reflect the influences of patriarchy and the influences of feminism' simultaneously. Post-feminism accepts these differences and explores 'feminism's contradictions' (Schriefer 'The Laughing Medusa').

I contend, that because dramedy integrates two genres that would normally be conceived as opposites, it is an effective vehicle for dramatising the 'negotiation of contradiction' characteristic of post-feminism (ibid.). In fact two popular dramedies, *Sex and the City* (Negra 2004) and *Ally McBeal* (Kim 2001), have been studied as post-feminist discourse, suggesting that this genre lends itself to the critique of multiple and often opposing ideologies.

None of the women in *Desperate Housewives* is overtly feminist; in fact, in some ways they are pre-feminist, showing no interest in issues of gender equality. However, the text constructs them in ways that address feminist issues with post-feminist concerns, including 'sexuality, subjectivity, and identity' (Kim 2001: 319).

Separately, each housewife seems to be living a pre-feminist paradigm. Bree fits the female stereotypes enshrined in the commercials and sitcoms of the 1950s, when mothers were domestic divas who never got mussed or muddled. Lynette is the stereotypical frazzled mother overwhelmed by her domestic duties. Susan, deserted by one man, is engaged in a desperate search for another. And Gabrielle is the beautiful, selfish conniver out to get everything she wants no matter what she has to do to get it. Together they comprise a panoply of stereotypes perpetuated by film and television and derided by feminists. Their difficulties can be traced to two sources: marriage and family. But rather than focusing on these social constructs, as a feminist text might, *Desperate Housewives* first concentrates on the individuals involved. 'Postfeminism is about individuals and their personal choices rather than career paths or job equity' (Cayse 2005).

Lynette embodies Susan Douglas and Meredith Michaels's claim that in many contemporary television texts (2004: 11–12) the working woman is pitted against the stay-at-home mom. But, in this text, both these lifestyles are at war in one person. Lynette illustrates the difficulties and the rewards of being a stay-at-home mom. Her desperation, Felicity Huffman suggests, 'comes from raising four kids under the age of six' while searching for her 'identity in motherhood' when all her experience has come from the boardroom (Carroll 2004).

Viewers learn in the pilot that Lynette was a highly successful businesswoman who chose to abandon the office in favour of domesticity. Now she is a mother, struggling and failing, or so she thinks, to control her kids. Two scenes, one dramatic and the other comedic, illustrate this. In the first, Lynette, hallucinating that Mary Alice is beckoning her to commit suicide, dumps her kids at Susan's before rushing off to reflect on what happened (1: 8). In the second, Lynette begs a reluctant Bree to babysit so that she can have drinks with her friends. 'Today I have a chance to join the human race for a few hours. They're actual adults waiting for me with margaritas. Look, I'm in a dress. I have make-up on' (1: 18). Given that Lynette spends most of her time in jeans or shorts and a shirt, her pleading is both funny and poignant. Does she regret her choice? Does she know who she is any more? Has she succumbed to cultural norms about what a woman and a mother should be?

She meets a former colleague and is visibly uncomfortable about her unkempt appearance and the boys' rowdiness (1: 1). Her reactions, though funny, raise serious questions about how fulfilled this former businesswoman is as a stay-at-home mom. Will Lynette, like Giovanna, abandon her broom and return to the boardroom, as the season one finale suggests? Clearly Lynette has not lost her business acumen. When Tom brings clients home to pitch a sales promotion, Lynette wows them by suggesting they advertise on dry-cleaning bags (1: 5). She steals his thunder and seems to enjoy it. Though Lynette tries to be the traditional wife and mother, this incident indicates her true milieu. Her character embodies one of 'feminism's contradictions' (Schriefer), an equally strong desire for fulfilment inside and outside the home.

Susan, too, illustrates these (ibid.). In some ways she seems to be imprisoned by patriarchy, especially in her desperate effort to find a man. She feels diminished by her husband's desertion and needs a man to help find fulfilment as a woman. Motherhood is not enough, but when Zach becomes obsessed with her daughter, Julie, Susan stops behaving like the older sister and slips back into the traditional role (1: 13). At about the same time, she accepts responsibility for her irresponsible mother, Sophie (Lesley Warren) (1: 18). But these choices coexist with her sexual assertiveness. She actively pursues Mike (rejecting the patriarchal paradigm, in which the male is the pursuer). She reconciles her own (feminist) needs with her 'duty' to care for her mother and daughter – but it is her choice. She is not a victim of a rigid patriarchal code, and, as the season progresses, she becomes much less klutzy, more sure of herself and her identity.

The meticulous Bree appears to capitulate to, rather than negotiate patriarchy. She takes great pride in her cooking, her cleaning, her gardening, her child-rearing. She is convinced that domestic perfection is the key to happiness, but Rex's divorce action and adultery, and her son Andrew's lack of remorse for his hit-and-run accident and disrespect for her, shatter her illusions. She fights back by first trying, unsuccessfully, to seduce Rex, then capitulating to his need for a dominatrix, before finally choosing a stereotypically female strategy: that of making Rex jealous by dating George Williams, the pharmacist. Unfortunately, this choice eventually leads to Rex's murder. It is interesting that, unlike Susan and Gabrielle, Bree seems to view sex as a strategy rather than a source of pleasure. After Rex dies she seems lost, her identity crumbling along with her pre-feminist ideology.

Gabrielle is a caricature of the beautiful, selfish woman who marries for money. She slept her way to a top-notch modelling career then went on from that into marriage with a wealthy businessman. He showers her with gifts, but in turn demands that she flatter and flirt with his business associates and ostentatiously model the opulent jewellery he gives her. Gabrielle feels used and abused, or so she tells her teenage gardener.

Unlike Susan and Lynette, Gabrielle is sure of who she is. She is not intimidated by cultural norms she doesn't agree with, and she revels in her sexuality. But, as the following three scenes demonstrate, there is another side to Gabrielle. In the first, after they have made love, Gabrielle tells John that Carlos has given her everything she ever wanted, but that she wanted the wrong things (1: 1). In the second, as she is admiring John's gift of a perfect rose, Carlos drives up in a brand new sports car with a red bow on it. 'Is it the best gift you've ever gotten?' he asks (1: 2). She answers with a wild embrace, but her gaze rests on the rose. Mary Alice remarks that few men can appreciate the worth of a perfect rose; but John did. The third scene involves an exchange with Father Crowley (Jeff Doucette), who knows about her affair with John. 'Don't you want to be a good person?' Crowley asks. 'What I want is to be happy,' she replies. 'That's the answer of a selfish child,' he says. 'I know,' whispers Gabrielle (1: 8).

What relationship does Gabrielle have to post-feminism? On one level, her character resurrects traditional prejudices against beautiful women – that they are selfish, vain, greedy, unmaternal – but these traits are conveyed largely through a humorous hyperbole that weakens their sting. On another, as Betty Mayhew suggests, media images of women exerting control over men and flouting 'social conventions, rules and boundaries' represent a challenge to patriarchy (The Media and Postmodernism). Surely Gabrielle fits this description. Furthermore, she challenges the patriarchal delusion that a woman who does not want children is unnatural and unfeminine. When Carlos intimates to the Van de Kamps that Gabrielle has changed her mind, she protests vociferously that she does not need a child to feel fulfilled. I am 'not negotiating my uterus,' she screams (1: 8). But she does. When Carlos successfully schemes to get her pregnant, she will not agree to have the child unless he, too, takes responsibility for its care. How this storyline will develop remains, at the time of writing, to be seen.

Despite her beauty, self-assurance and sexual freedom of expression, Gabrielle, like her friends, is not what she seems to be. Dramedy's melding of the comic and the dramatic facilitates what Robin Nelson describes as double-coding: the characters, their actions and their environments embody contradictory characteristics that produce a 'productive tension', evoking 'simultaneous affirmation and subversion' to critique competing ideologies (2001:45). Gabrielle's rejection, and then reluctant acceptance, of motherhood invites viewers not only to think about Gabrielle in a different way but to reassess the meaning of motherhood as well.

The other housewives contribute to this reassessment as well. Lynette loves her children, but is overwhelmed rather than fulfilled by the construct of motherhood she represents. Bree follows the traditional maternal ideal, but ends up rejected by her children, especially Andrew, whose rejection turns to hate. Susan starts out as her daughter's friend – or at times her daughter's daughter, since it is Julie who gives the advice and Susan who follows it. But, at a crucial moment, Susan ends the role reversal and reverts to a more traditional construct of mother as loving protector. Kim Akass lauds *Sex and the City*'s rejection of media stereotypes of motherhood and its portrayal of 'motherhood in all its ambivalence' (2004). I contend that *Desperate Housewives* provides a broader understanding of ambivalence. It goes beyond Miranda Hobbes's (played by Cynthia Nixon) ambivalence about the desire to be a mother and her rejection of the romantic illusions perpetuated by a patriarchal society (which corresponds to Gabrielle's experience) to encompass other stages of motherhood: Lynette's struggle with pre-schoolers and a frequently absent husband; Bree's experience with teenagers and what seemed like the perfect nuclear family; Susan's struggles as the single mother with a teenage daughter and an irresponsible mother. Each woman is ambivalent about her own experience of motherhood (and occasionally of others'; Bree and Lynette do not always agree about motherhood). Each is double-coded, permitting a critique of alternatives within her own experience, and the women together provide a broader critique of what motherhood has and might mean. Pre-feminist and feminist practice are critiqued from a post-feminist perspective.

The same can be said about marriage. Each housewife represents a slightly different paradigm of marriage. Both Lynette and Bree have nuclear families, though at different stages of development. Susan is a single mother. Gabrielle is childless and wants to stay that way. Not surprisingly, as the following examples demonstrate, Bree has a romantic vision of marriage and the fulfilment it should bring. The serious scenes suggest that Bree is disillusioned about those ideals, even as she tries to conform to them. Rex had once asked her what had happened to the carefree, wind-blown girl he had married (1: 1), but when that girl reappears, Rex does not recognise her. Bree tells her would-be suitor George about the wonderful times she and Rex had on a romantic trip to Italy, but when she reminds Rex of the trip, he only remembers disasters (1: 20). Bree's eyes fill with tears. Later she asks her husband, 'Honey, do your hands still tremble when they touch me?' Rex replies, 'No. But come on, we've been married eighteen years.' Bree's plaintive reply is: 'Yes, we have. And you still don't know when I need you to lie.'

Susan had a difficult divorce, but still believes she needs a man to be happy – though whether she needs marriage is open to question. Lynette has a healthy sex life with Tom, and what seems to be a happy marriage (despite her difficulties with the kids). She calls on Tom occasionally when she cannot cope anymore, and he does help. But she has difficulty sorting out their roles, especially as her self-image deteriorates, and she starts interfering in his professional life until, in desperation and anger, he resigns; a move which forecasts a role reversal in the second season. Gabrielle would seem to operate under a pragmatic paradigm: marriage is for fun and profit. When the fun stops, she makes adjustments. Despite the wide range of models presented, each woman is negotiating a place for herself within marriage. Yet none of the models are condemned outright because double-coding enables viewers to see all sides of each situation. Thus viewers are given the opportunity to critique both the institution and the different instantiations of it.

Diane Negra praises *Sex and the City*'s 'ambiguity and ambivalence about those dilemmas that are most likely to be oversimplified, caricatured and romanticized within a proclaimed "postfeminist" popular culture…' (2004). I believe that *Desperate Housewives* achieves these goals as well, using dramedy to construct a post-feminist critique of marriage, motherhood and friendship. (The housewives are always there for each other, but not in a sentimental or idealised way. Even when they go to console Lynette after her breakdown, the interchange grows naturally out of the friendship that has been portrayed through poker games and through the dependability they offer each other).

While some feminist critics label *Ally McBeal* feminist and others anti-feminist, Hollows considers the show a 'product of a historical context that was partly formed by feminism' (2000: 198); an argument that could be similarly applied to *Desperate Housewives*. The series mirrors 'the influences of patriarchy and the influences of feminism at the same time' (ibid.). Marc Cherry begins with male fantasies and uses humour to crack the stereotypes, and drama to show what lies beneath. The housewives (the name itself is patriarchal) begin as patriarchal fantasies, but they do not stay that way. Bree's embodiment of the patriarchal ideals of the housewife bring her to the verge of feminism when her realisation that they have brought her nothing but unhappiness make her attempt to renounce them. Lynette embodies post-feminist awareness that choosing between a domestic career and a position outside the home is problematic. Susan, like Bree, has been jolted out of the stereotype of the happy home and is trying to refashion her life as a woman and a mother. Gabrielle may seem enmeshed in the patriarchal archetype, but she, too, is aware of her wrong choices and is trying to reinvent herself.

Charlotte Brunsdon asserts that post-feminism can provide a 'changed context of debate on feminist issues', and thus have a positive influence on popular culture's construction of femininity and female roles (1997: 101–102). The series certainly has engendered debate, much of it on the imaginativeness of the concept, the cleverness of the writing, and the complexity – and quirkiness – of the characters; in other words, the most visible aspects of dramedy. There has been less commentary on the ideological critique that dramedy promotes. James Poniewozik comments that *Desperate Housewives* foregrounds 'what our unrealistic ideals of domesticity do to women' (2004: 20) then labels the series 'smug' because its writers imply that, if stay-at-home moms realised how meaningless their lives were, they too would commit suicide. Germaine Greer insists that *Desperate Housewives* holds no interest for feminists, asserting that the female characters must have been concocted by misogynists (Adamson 2005: 9). Rondi Adamson of the *Christian Science Monitor*, challenging Greer's view, points out that feminism is supposed to be about choice, whereby a woman can still be a feminist and stay at home with her kids (2005: 9).

This commentary, and I hope there will soon be more, confirms that popular culture provides a venue 'where meanings are contested' (Gammon and Marshment 1988: 1) and contradictions are tolerated as an inevitable by-product of a culture in transition (4). Culture, in this case, must include post-feminism and its construction on Wisteria Lane. Hopefully, the success of *Desperate Housewives* will encourage increased analysis of post-feminism and dramedy, a blended genre that has not yet received the critical attention it deserves.

12

White picket fences, domestic containment and female
subjectivity: The quest for romantic love

Sherryl Wilson

The official *Desperate Housewives* website describes the drama thus:
'A primetime soap with a truly contemporary take on "happily ever
after," this new hour-long drama takes a darkly comedic look at
suburbia, where the secret lives of housewives aren't always what they
seem' (abc.go.com/primetime/desperate). The use of the phrase
'happily ever after' denotes the fairy-tale ending, which then promises
to be subverted through the 'darkly comedic look'. As viewers of the
programme will know, the main setting for the drama, Wisteria Lane,
does have a fairy-tale quality about it: the houses are perfect, the
lawns immaculate, the sun always shines, its inhabitants lead privileged
lifestyles and are beautiful (well, the younger ones are; older women
are stereotypically battleaxe-like).[1] These markers of success add up
to an articulation of the American dream in which individuals have
the right to life, liberty and the pursuit of happiness.[2] However, the
claim that the programme offers a 'contemporary take' on women's
lives is rather more problematic. The show does reveal some of the
'desperation' of women's lives once caught within the traditional
domestic sphere, but when we explore the narrative arc that shapes
our understanding of two key characters, Gabrielle Solis and Susan
Mayer, contradictions emerge. Each woman is driven by a desire for
the attainment of romantic love despite the fact that both have
experienced it as a failure in the past. Both women continue to buy
into ideas of romantic love – the romance, the courtship, the
wedding, the happy-ever-after – locking themselves into a loop

that diminishes their capacity to move beyond the patriarchal ideal of the domestic.

In addition to being bound by the quest for romantic love, the overarching detective/crime narrative further contains the individual stories played out in Wisteria Lane. However, these narratives of containment are mitigated by the deployment of playful irony and aesthetic pleasures; the lush visuals – the clothes, the bodies – and a satisfying ironic knowingness speak to contemporary tastes. As such, *Desperate Housewives* uses comedy and postmodern nostalgia to *close down* possibilities of transgression rather than open up new female subjectivities. So, although the show reveals the flaws in the patriarchal ideal of marriage, the possibilities for representing a feminist argument are foreclosed by the female protagonists themselves. This chapter explores the notion that the space that is Wisteria Lane and the quest for romantic love re-articulates traditional middle-class femininities and sensibilities.

Romantic love is a form of attachment that is distinguishable from a solely sexual attraction or lust; it is indicative of a love that is both emotional and sexual. Romantic love has been historically emphasised in Western societies, having become a recognised passion in the Middle Ages and identified by insurmountable barriers of morality or convention that separated the lovers. The tension produced through physical attraction and the impossibility of intimacy gives rise to an 'excessive regard of the beloved'. Properties of romantic love purported by Western culture include: the element of surprise; lack of control; sex is not predicated as a solely physical act; it forms the basis for a lifelong commitment; it is the highest form of self-fulfilment (Wikipedia.org). This definition of romantic love serves well to provide an analysis of the ways in which Gabrielle and Susan negotiate their respective romantic relationships within the domestic confines of Wisteria Lane.

While the ideal of romantic love pre-dates the mid-twentieth century, it became a part of the processes of post-war domestication and the development of American suburbia. Estella Tincknell (2005) discusses the rise of the companionate marriage in 1950s America, when the concept became increasingly tied to meanings attached to the family structure with its emphasis on a partnership based on mutual commitment. Accordingly, for 'women especially, the idea of romance as a cultural entitlement became part of the more general expectations produced around marriage' (14). For Gabrielle and Susan the quest for romantic love is made manifest in different ways: the former locks herself into a gilded cage expressing her yearnings through an extra-marital affair, while the latter is contained within an adolescent notion of romance that refuses to accommodate the less than perfect actuality of her love object. In their respective ways, both women reinvest in the expectation that marital relationships will be prefaced and sustained by physical and emotional attraction.

Enclosures, containment and the domestic ideal

Raymond Williams's 1974 concept of the room as a televisual space that both structures and infuses with meaning is a useful formulation through which to consider *Desperate Housewives'* narrative of contain-ment. Emerging from theatrical conventions, he suggests,

> The room is there, not as one scenic convention among all possible others, but because it is an *actively shaping environment* – the particular structure in which we live…the solid form, the conventional declaration, of how we are living and what we value. This room…[is] a set that defines us and can trap us: the alienated object that now represents us in the world (1989: 12;) (emphasis added).

Williams is identifying a continuity between the naturalist dramatists' creation of 'enclosed rooms on enclosed stages' (6) and us watching television in our rooms at home. As such, the room is infused with meaning, a structure that is 'declamatory and active' (Wheatley 2005: 146). So, and as Helen Wheatley points out, Williams's argument marks 'the room…[as] television's definitive space' (ibid.). This focus on the room as a determining structure is an interesting notion that enables an exploration of the female subjectivity articulated though *Desperate Housewives*. The 'room' most dominant in the programme is not an internal area such as kitchen or living room, but that which is created through the lines of picket fences as they criss-cross Wisteria Lane, marking out each character's private, domestic space encapsulating the women's individual dramas. The fences erect a room, or series of rooms, which construct both Susan and Gabrielle in ways that more closely adhere to the 1950s perception of ideal womanhood – albeit with some elements of 'desperation' to unsettle the picture – than is more commonly the case with contemporary TV dramas such as HBO's *Sex and the City*, and *Six Feet Under*. For example, the 'queer postfeminism' identified by Jane Gerhard (2005) in relation to *Sex and the City*, which, she argues, works to problematise and destabilise gender identities and relations, is a complexity that is absent in *Desperate Housewives*.

As argued earlier, Wisteria Lane and the characterisation of its female inhabitants invoke nostalgia for an earlier time while the theme of romantic love simplifies the complex realities of domestic relationships. This recuperation of the past has been identified by Fredric Jameson (1991) as a defining characteristic of the postmodern sensibility. Discussing the medium of film he argues that the 'past' is appropriated 'through stylistic connotation, conveying "pastness" by the glossy qualities of the image, and "1930s-ness" or "1950s-ness" by the attributes of fashion...' (18). While the *style* of *Desperate Housewives* – the clothes, the houses, the bodies – are contemporary, pastness is evoked through what Raymond Williams calls the 'structure of feeling', which defines and determines subjectivities and identities limiting and exerting pressure on ways of being.[3] Here, the structure of feeling is produced through the 'rooms', the picket fences, creating a declaration about the ways we are living now and what we value. What is evoked are traditional notions of the domestic that are premised on the desirability of romantic love. Gabrielle's and Susan's quests define them as characters, trapping them (and, by extension, us as we watch) within a value system that evokes sensibilities of the past.

The quest for romance: Gabrielle

I want to now look more closely at Gabrielle. For the purposes of my argument here, it is noteworthy that this character has sought to escape the confines of deprivation through the construction of the feminine ideal, which, as a model, she both embodies and perpetuates.

However, her achievement on these terms is only partial: she has sought completion through her marriage to über-macho Carlos Solis, who, while able to provide abundantly materially, is also drawn as a stereotypical Latino: emotionally inarticulate, hot-headed and prone to violent outbursts. Gabrielle's subsequent disappointment with Carlos lies in her failure to achieve the highest form of self-fulfilment attained through romantic love. This is made evident by her affair with John Rowland, her teenage gardener, revealing a yearning for a romantic attachment that transcends that offered by material comfort. Although constructed to conform to the 1950s ideal, Gabrielle does buck this through her refusal of the nurturing role prescribed for her: she does not have children, nor does she want them. More, her lively, sexual relationship with John calls up references to D.H. Lawrence's 1928 novel *Lady Chatterley's Lover,* which, on publication, provoked scandalised responses to its narrative of adultery across the barriers erected by social class. John, in an old-fashioned mode of deference, always calls Gabrielle 'Mrs Solis', signalling the barriers that threaten to separate the lovers. This barrier is what often produces the tension between them and, as the series continues, reveals the degree to which Gabrielle relies on their relationship for the attainment of romantic love denied in her marriage.

The episode entitled 'Ah, But Underneath' (1: 2) is particularly interesting due to the leitmotif of loneliness that runs throughout, and gives a narrative shape to the observations offered by the recently deceased Mary Alice Young in the form of the voiceover. The notion that romantic love within marriage is often a chimera is indicated by Mary Alice when she says 'Loneliness was a thing my friends understood only too well.' As we cut to the various nocturnal activities of the women who live in Wisteria Lane, Gabrielle is seen wallowing in the sensuous luxury of a deep, hot bath that stands in the middle of her huge and beautiful bathroom. The *mise en scène* positions her as a woman without wants and is reinforced by the aesthetics of the soft focus and the warm, rich colour palette. The shock of surprise comes when Mary Alice's voiceover overlays this scene and cuts across this reading as, in a soft voice, she describes Gabrielle as 'a drowning woman desperately in search of a life-raft'. So now we know: the loneliness of her marriage to Carlos provides the impulse behind her relationship with John. The motif of water invocated in the verb 'drowning' is underpinned and repeated through the numerous scenes in which she shares her huge bath with John, her life-raft. Later that same night we see Gabrielle in bed when Carlos arrives home, very late, after having attended to a work commitment. She tells her husband: 'You know, Carlos, I didn't marry you so I could have dinner by myself six times a week.' The poignancy of this observation stands in contrast to the lavish lifestyle of leisure that Gabrielle inhabits, and articulates the emotional realism identified by Ien Ang (1985). Even though we may not identify with the luxury of Gabrielle's home and clothes, we are able to connect through the palpable sense of sadness in this statement. More than this, it reveals to us that, although Gabrielle did not marry Carlos for material wealth alone, hers seems not to be a companionate marriage based on the romantic ideal. However, the turn to playfulness disrupts the moment. Her next statement repositions Gabrielle as spoilt and work-shy: 'You know how bored I got today? I came this close [fingers held up, millimetres apart] to cleaning the house!' Thus the potential for emotional realism becomes emptied out of any of the meaning articulated though her declaration of loneliness. While we are left with a deeper understanding of Gabrielle's isolation, she is equally positioned as the architect of that isolation.

Of course, in order for this characterisation to be maintained Carlos needs to be drawn as an unreconstructed male who measures his masculinity by his ability to provide material goods and through the acquisition of a trophy wife. Arguably, the lack of sensitivity and emotional intelligence speaks to the stereotype of Latino machismo that makes for good comedy but is similarly restrictive in terms of character development. The conversation continues once Gabrielle has established that she is not in the mood for sex.

Gabrielle: But we could stay up and talk.

Carlos: [laughing] What is the matter?

Gabrielle: It's not exciting any more.

Carlos: What do you want?

Gabrielle: Like it used to be. Surprise me, take my breath away.

Carlos: OK, OK [moves away from Gabrielle].

Rather than initiating a conversation about her loneliness and emptiness, Gabrielle returns to the default position of wanting breathtaking romance – characterised by surprise and excitement – to be provided by her man. And surprise her he does, by buying a very expensive sports car all tied up with ribbons. But not before John has surprised and moved Gabrielle by presenting her with a painstakingly selected perfect red rose, which he tells her is 'just like you'. Carlos would not understand why the car was not the 'best gift' Gabrielle had ever had because, as Mary Alice tells us, 'it's a rare man who understands the value of a single, perfect rose.' The obvious symbolism of the rose reflects the romantic ideal, in which surprise is provided while that also articulating the barrier separates John from Gabrielle. In her recognition of the meaning provided by the rose Gabrielle is awakened to her desire for emotional intimacy absent in her marriage to Carlos. The tension between what is desired and what is possible provides much of the narrative movement in Gabrielle's personal drama as she vacillates between ending/maintaining her relationship with John and through her ambivalence towards Carlos. As such, Gabrielle's narrative is contained within this movement and by the overarching mystery that accompanies Mary Alice's suicide.

Carlos's repeated beatings of the wrong men in light of his suspicions that his wife is having an affair provide a series of comic representations of the masculine, Neanderthal responses to a troubled marriage; this provides a viewing pleasure but one that precludes any serious comment on contemporary gender relations. Meanwhile, Gabrielle's character is somewhat recuperated at the end of season one when, unexpectedly pregnant, she decides to keep the baby while her yearnings, defined by the rose, remain at the level of fairy-tale romantic love. However, it should be said that she is bound to surprise us in the future.

The quest for romantic love: Susan

Arguably, Susan offers us a more contemporary look at the 'desperation' of women's lives. As a divorced single mother she represents a figure common in the contemporary cultural landscape. She works at home as a children's illustrator, and although we do not know what stories she illustrates it is possible that they are those that perpetuate the fairy-tale of romance and the happy-ever-after. Although her ex-husband, Karl Mayer, does not pay child maintenance the real stresses and tensions of juggling a work life with single parenthood are eclipsed in favour of Susan's central narrative function, which hinges on her developing relationship with Mike Delfino, the very desirable, apparently widowed plumber who has moved into the neighbourhood. What is interesting about Susan is that, despite her life experiences, she remains bound by her investment in the adolescent ideal of romantic love. While Gabrielle's quest is given physical form in her relationship with John, Susan's dream of romance constructs barriers that enforce a separation between herself and her object of desire. This is established in the pilot episode, when Susan's daughter, Julie Mayer, watches her mother watching Mike. While the *mise en scène* constructs Mike as the object of Susan's gaze, her regard for masculine chivalry that is the corollary to romantic love closes down possibilities that she may transgress normative codes of conduct. Despite Julie's encouragement that Susan should ask Mike out on a date she (Susan) replies that she would prefer Mike to do the asking. So she, like Gabrielle, wants to be taken by surprise, or at least wooed in a traditional manner.

In 'Ah, But Underneath', during Gabrielle and Carlos's own nocturnal drama, Susan is unable to sleep and gets up for a drink of water. She is seen standing at her sink in the kitchen looking through the window. Described as 'parched' by Mary Alice in her voiceover, Susan sees 'the tall drink of water she needs to quench her thirst'. This 'tall drink of water' is Mike. Walking his dog along the street, the man is surrounded by white fences that stretch both horizontally and vertically across the screen. The *mise en scène* is fascinating. Although it reinforces Mike as the object of Susan's gaze, it also positions him as one whose physical attractions are enhanced by his homeliness; walking his dog in his own neighbourhood suggests not just a care of and for domestic pets but also signals his connection with Wisteria Lane. Of course, as the series progresses, this connection develops an increasingly sinister tone as elements of Mike's past are revealed to unsettle the picture and to spoil Susan's romantic hopes. While Mike is contained within the matrix of picket fences, Susan remains contained within her ideal of romance, which refuses to be dislodged despite urges to do so from her date advice-giving daughter; the window that she gazes through symbolises her separation from the thing that she desires. Mary Alice's choice of metaphors, of Gabrielle drowning and Susan's thirst is interesting because each invoke the life-giving or -taking property of too little or too much water. What this connotes is that the life's force for each woman is the promise of the life-giving self-fulfilment attained through romantic attachment, the pursuit of which defines their characters and contains their individual stories.

Susan's narrative is more complicated than that of Gabrielle because her pursuit (and eventual gain) of Mike's romantic sensibilities is enmeshed with the murder/detective mystery that serves as the central fulcrum for key inhabitants of Wisteria Lane. Mike's implication in the crime mystery comes to re-present the barrier that defines romantic love, an obstacle that, for Gabrielle, is constructed by her emotionally inarticulate husband and her illicit desire for John.

A key moment occurs in 'Pretty Little Picture' (1: 3), revealing the degree to which Susan is defined and contained by her quest for romance. The moment follows the disastrous dinner party hosted by Bree Van de Kamp, which, in turn, is preceded by the slapstick scene in which a naked Susan, locked out of her house, has fallen into the bushes. This happens just when Mike appears to accept the invitation to accompany Susan to the dinner party; however, embarrassment becomes good fortune when he turns saviour and gets her into her home. Walking home after the dinner party Susan explains that her ex-husband Karl treated her 'so badly at the end, I haven't been able to get over it'. Mike replies: 'Maybe he did you a big favour ... Just look at it as a starter marriage, you know, boot camp preparing you for something better next time.'

Suggestions of a future premised on matrimony rather than, say, the joys of single life or of an enriched relationship with Julie return us to the notion of companionate marriage premised on romantic love. An emboldened Susan thanks Mike 'for being such a perfect gentleman' when he saw her naked in the bushes. Mike: 'Oh, I wasn't a, perfect, gentleman. I went and snuck a peek. And, uh, for what it's worth, wow!' So, not only is Mike (more or less) a gentleman, he believes in the possibility of happy marriage *and* desires Susan sexually! The dreamy smile lingering on Susan's face as she re-enters her house signals her delight. But it also reminds us that not only is she imprisoned by disappointment in her erstwhile marriage, escape from this prison is premised on *rescue* through the acquisition of romantic love. Although Susan does behave in an autonomous fashion, she does so in her quest for Mike – the love-o-war between Susan and Edie Britt for Mike's attention, the accidental setting fire to Edie's house, the attempts to befriend Mike's dog, and so on.

Gabrielle and Susan each point to the romantic, pre-feminist sensibilities that characterise the housewives who inhabit Wisteria Lane, a space that presents us with a kind of dream image in which the pleasure is located in the detail – of the perfectly appointed houses, the clothes, the bodies. Identifying pleasure in detail as feminine, John Caughie argues:

> The important point is that pleasure in detail is a pleasure in profusion, and, for analysis, this pleasure has to be thought differently than a pleasure governed by the Law of the Father and driven by desire or lack. It is, if you like, a small pleasure, a pleasure ... in the ornamental and the everyday which the history of aesthetics has assigned to the feminine, a pleasure which the academy, and academic film and television theory, has not regarded as manly, noble, or dignified (2000: 215).

The small, pleasurable, feminine details offered through *Desperate Housewives* are contained within the white picket fences that mark the boundaries of each domestic dwelling and the individual dramas that take place within them. The structure of feeling produced by these 'rooms' returns us to a world containing us – as well as the characters – within the 1950s American suburban ideal typified by the feminine desire for romantic love. The comedy is similarly contained within this structure of feeling. Rather than offering transgressive possibilities in which alternative views of female subjectivity are offered, disrupting and/or challenging women's traditional position, the humour in the programme reinforces the domestic containment symbolised by the fences and by the fantasies of romantic love that produce a haze blinding the women to wider realities.

The omnipresence of the deceased Mary Alice evoked through her voiceovers does not call up the magical realism evident in, for example, *Six Feet Under*, where the dead frequently reappear to reveal complex and hidden aspects of key characters. Rather, Mary Alice's presence contains the activities in Wisteria Lane by presenting a continual reminder of the crime/detective story that frames the series, while Gabrielle and Susan's quests for romantic love serve as distractions from worrying about conflicts and contradictions that beset women in the twenty-first century. The impulse behind producing these strategies of containment and the reasons for the popularity of the show can only be speculative. But I would posit that, in addition to the pleasurable detail and the comic situations, *Desperate Housewives* offers a retreat from the unease and instability of women's *real* lives in contemporary culture, recuperating the dream of domestic, wedded bliss premised on the promise of romantic love to produce the 'happily ever after'.

Notes

1 Space prevents a fuller discussion of the ways in which older women are represented in *Desperate Housewives*, but it is noteworthy that the more-than-slightly-demonic Martha Huber and her sister occupy the position of 'old hag' or 'crone'. Whether or not these women can be seen to embody Mikhail Bakhtin's positive formulation of the grotesque body would require further analysis.

2 The term 'American dream' is a loose and rather lazy phrase when used to describe aspects of American culture. However, for the purposes of clarity I should state that I am referring to the sensibilities enshrined in the Declaration of Independence, written in 1776, which proclaims that 'all Men are created equal, that they are endowed by their Creator with certain unalienable Rights, that among these are Life, Liberty, and the Pursuit of Happiness'. In 1787 the same men congregated to write the Constitution, the preamble to which states: 'We the People of the United States, in order to form a more perfect union, establish justice, ensure

domestic tranquillity...and secure the blessings of liberty to ourselves and our posterity, do ordain and establish this Constitution for the United States of America' (emphasis added).

3 Williams describes a structure of feeling 'as firm and definite as "structure" suggests, yet it operates in the most delicate and least tangible parts of our activity. In one sense, this structure of feeling is the culture of a period: it is the particular living result of all the elements in the general organization' (cited in Caughie 2000: 4).

13

Desperation and domesticity: Reconfiguring the 'happy housewife' in *Desperate Housewives*

Anna Marie Bautista

It is no longer possible to ignore that voice, to dismiss the desperation of so many American women.

Betty Friedan 1963: 26

This is the thing you need to know about Bree. She doesn't like to talk about her feelings. To be honest, it's hard to know if she has any. Does she feel anger, rage, ecstasy? Who knows? She's always...pleasant. And I can't tell you how annoying that is. Whatever she feels is so far below the surface that...that no one can see...she uses all those domestic things.

Rex Van de Kamp on Bree Van de Kamp (1: 2)

The plight of the desperate housewife was critically explored in 1963 by Betty Friedan in *The Feminine Mystique* – the 'desperation' that she claimed had afflicted 'so many American women' (1963: 26) has recently been given a significant amount of media attention, most notably in the representations of the title characters in the ABC television series *Desperate Housewives*. In addition, the popular media has been saturated with images of the housewife, most of them 'desperate' in some way or another; these include the housewives being compared and contrasted on the reality show *Wife Swap* as well as the trials of domesticity encountered by the hapless Jessica Simpson on *Newlyweds*. This focus on the figure of the housewife and the domestic experience is particularly noteworthy following popular culture's previous inclinations to reflect the experiences of the single woman (*Sex and the City*, *Ally McBeal*, *Bridget Jones's Diary*) who is rarely, if ever, defined by her proximity to the domestic space. In contrast, the figure of the housewife has commonly been associated with the space of the home, and the desperation that has come to signify domesticity has arguably become an integral component of her construction.

This desperation did not define previous constructions of the housewife – the most iconic of these was arguably the figure of the 'happy housewife' that was popularised in the 1950s. This 'happy housewife' was perhaps most aptly personified by *Leave It To Beaver*'s June Cleaver (Barbara Billingsley) – 'a patient mother, loving wife, and cheerful consumer, dispensing love and cookies to husband and madcap sons alike' (Walters 1992: 74). Images of the nuclear family in 1950s America are often associated with the always smiling and cheerful figure of the housewife/mother who is completely satisfied with her role of happy homemaker – an image of domestic bliss that is distinctly absent from the representations of domesticity on *Desperate Housewives*.

This chapter will focus on how *Desperate Housewives* deviates from such notions of domestic bliss as exemplified by the 'happy housewife' and how the show comments on the various myths concerning women and domesticity, many of which are arguably based upon nostalgic images of the 'ideal' housewife and mother portrayed on 1950s television. Interestingly, in her *Ms.* magazine article 'Housewife Wars', Catherine Orenstein describes the women in *Desperate Housewives* as '21st-century women, with 21st-century wardrobes and attitudes, but they're dropped into 1950s suburbia…' (2005). The housewives on Wisteria Lane encounter a range of issues, such as marital infidelity, single parenthood, the dichotomy between working and stay-at-home motherhood, sexuality and familial dysfunction – none of which were ever likely to have been confronted by June Cleaver and her 1950s television counterparts. In this respect, the analysis will focus on the character of Bree Van de Kamp, as she is clearly a parody of the perfect 1950s sitcom mother – the perpetual 'pleasantness' that her husband Rex describes is a direct throwback to the constantly cheerful demeanours of June Cleaver, Margaret Anderson (Jane Wyatt) in

Father Knows Best and Harriet Nelson (Harriet Hilliard) in *The Adventures of Ozzie and Harriet,* among others. However, Bree incorporates contemporary discourses concerning domesticity and motherhood into her characterisation of the 'perfect' housewife; some of these evolving discourses will be discussed and I will illustrate how they influence the often subversive and 'desperate' traits that complicate Bree's embodiment of the 'happy housewife'.

The figure of the 1950s housewife has largely been defined by her 'contain[ment] within the domestic space of the home' (Haralovich 2003: 72). This space of the home has long been the subject of feminist analysis concerning woman's place and domesticity. As Linda McDowell and Joanne Sharp state in their summary of the dichotomy between the public and private spheres that have traditionally defined male and female spaces:

> The social construction of the home as a place of familial pleasures, a place of leisure and rest – for men a sylvan and tranquil respite from the rigours of the city or the workplace and for women a supposedly safe haven – has a long history in the west. The dualism of home/workplace, the public sphere and the private arena, is mapped onto and constructs a gendered difference between male and female that has taken a particular spatial form in western nations since the industrial revolution (1997: 263).

Desperate Housewives would seem to both reiterate and dismantle this idea of the home being a safe haven for women in its representation of the domestic environment, recalling Cara Mertes's suggestion that the home 'is alternatively a site of disenfranchisement, abuse and fulfilment' (1992: 58). The contradictions between these aspects of 'disenfranchisement, abuse and fulfilment' engendered by the home have had a significant impact on perceptions of the housewife.

This ideology of separate spheres for men and women was crucial to the institutionalisation of motherhood, and resulted in the construction of the housewife/mother being closely related to 'woman's proper place' within the domestic space. These ideas have generally persisted, despite the redefinition of women's roles that took place largely as a result of the feminist movement in the 1960s and 1970s. This movement was greatly influenced by the publication of Friedan's 1963 book, when she brought 'the problem that has no name' to public attention and several women attempted to address the question 'Is that all there is?' as they struggled to reconcile the ideology of domestic bliss with the reality of their situations. This ideology had been strongly pushed immediately after the Second World War, in response to the increase in married women's employment that had been necessary during the wartime period. However, as Marilyn Yalom notes, this 'transformation was intended to be temporary. Everyone understood that as soon as the war was over, she would return to her primary occupation as wife, mother and homemaker' (2001: 322).

Upon the end of the war it became necessary to ensure that things reverted to 'normal', and the ideology of the 'perfect' housewife and mother was vehemently endorsed in order to do so. The 'happy housewife' figure was thus constructed as women were encouraged to return to full-time homemaking, and this renewed focus on domesticity was aided by a booming economy, which promised to revolutionise housework as domestic appliances became more easily accessible. The fixed gender roles established in the Victorian period were summarily reinforced in order to counter female employment opportunities that had been introduced during the war and continued to be available to women outside the home. Annagret Ogden observes:

> The renewed focus on domesticity and homemaking led naturally to the evolution of a role that complemented and completed that of Mrs. America. The wife of the 1950s saw herself – and was encouraged to do so by the media and the pressure of society – as supermother, pure and simple (1986: 174).

The media's promotion of this 'supermother' notably included television's popular representations of the ideal suburban nuclear family and the contented housewife/mother within it.

Such notions of the supermother are no longer as prevalent and the genial image of the happy housewife has long since been challenged and critiqued. However, domesticity has seemingly enjoyed a revival of sorts within popular culture, though its presentation varies from its earlier idealisation in the post-war era. The cultural visibility of the housewife has increased as a consequence of the success of *Desperate Housewives* as well as the aforementioned reality shows *Wife Swap* and *Newlyweds*, which also portray the various tribulations experienced by women within the domestic space. The prominence of Martha Stewart's domestic empire has also elevated domesticity to a form of expertise, augmenting the status of the private sphere of the home within culture. However, this renewed focus on domesticity is notably different from the 1950s 'cult of motherhood' (Dow 1996: 90), in that women are not generally presented as being naturally disposed to the domestic sphere, challenging the assumptions within the separate spheres ideology. Domesticity and motherhood are now largely depicted in terms of skills and abilities to be acquired and cultivated; thus, while domesticity and motherhood might still be idealised in many ways, the efforts required to achieve these ideals are also exposed.

Current discourses about motherhood and domesticity are typically associated with notions of ambivalence, anxiety, confusion, guilt and of generally being overwhelmed, which all exemplify the desperation that has come to be aligned with the domestic arena. Writers such as Judith Warner (*Perfect Madness: Motherhood in the Age of Anxiety*) and Susan Douglas and Meredith Michaels (*The Mommy Myth: The Idealization of Motherhood and How It Has Undermined Women*) have recently described the numerous difficulties that women experience in reconciling the myths of 'perfect' and 'natural' motherhood and domesticity with the legacy of feminism. As Abby Arnold delineates in her article 'The Rhetoric of Motherhood':

> Myths of motherhood still permeate our culture and are the lens through which we frame and discuss mothering. The lens may not be as outwardly restrictive as it was in the past and include the language of choice, but it is still centered around the unachievable myth of the perfect, all-available Mother (2003: 1).

Arnold and others would suggest that, in spite of the 'language of choice' offered to women as a consequence of the feminist movement, motherhood and the traditional domestic role are still being idealised and revered.

This continued mythologising and idealising of the maternal and domestic role have seemingly extended to the portrayal of the women on *Desperate Housewives*. Indeed, each of the four main characters has her own respective struggles with the unachievable myth of domesticity and motherhood. The trials of domestic life have previously been depicted on prime-time television, albeit within the generic structures of situation comedy: earlier television housewives, most notably Lucy Ricardo (Lucille Ball) on *I Love Lucy* and Samantha Stevens (Elizabeth Montgomery) on *Bewitched*, have rebelled against their prescribed domestic roles, their efforts usually thwarted and contained by their husbands by the end of each episode. More recently, the grittier aspects of motherhood and domesticity were sardonically projected onto the character of Roseanne Connor (Roseanne Barr) on *Roseanne*. These and other 'desperate' predecessors hinted at the desperation within domesticity, but *Desperate Housewives* is arguably the first to dramatically explore the complexities and contradictions behind the constructions of woman's place in the home, particularly as they relate to women in the post-feminist era. The show has summarily been dismissed by certain critics as a soap opera, variously described as 'stylized camp', 'kitsch', and Germaine Greer has gone on to proclaim that it has no relationship whatsoever with feminism (2005). The representations are indeed clichéd and stereotyped to a certain extent, particularly with respect to Bree.

The (desperately) happy housewife

At the outset, Bree would appear to be the most superficial and caricatured of the *Desperate Housewives*, but I will argue that she is the most complex and possibly the most desperate. The character evidently recalls the perfect 1950s sitcom mother. Indeed, the pilot (1: 1) introduces Bree as Wisteria Lane's 'perfect wife and mother' (to everyone except her family), who was 'known for her cooking... making her own clothes... doing her own gardening... reupholstering her own furniture...'. She takes pride in her domesticity as if it were an art form, her meticulousness offset by her immaculate appearance and mechanically upbeat demeanour. As her husband Rex complains during a marriage counselling session, it is virtually impossible to determine 'if she has any [feelings]', so mired is she in maintaining pleasant appearances and honing her domestic abilities (1: 2). However, unlike the experience of the happy housewife of previous eras, her constant striving for domestic perfection ultimately has disastrous effects on her relationships with her husband and children. Later in the pilot, Rex asks for a divorce, likening their marriage to a 'detergent commercial' and lamenting the 'cold perfect thing' she had seemingly become. True to form, Bree responds by retreating to shed a few private tears and then re-emerging with her smile and emotions seemingly intact.

Although she might initially appear to be little more than a caricatured stereotype, various dimensions gradually become apparent within the character, including the desperation shared by the other housewives. The positioning of the idealised figure of the perfect housewife in the current era would inevitably be complicated by contemporary discourses of domesticity and motherhood. Bree's apparent embracing of the domestic role echoes Cynthia Fuchs Epstein's argument in *Deceptive Distinctions: Sex, Gender and the Social Order* (1988) concerning women's willingness to subscribe to the 'separate spheres' ideology.

> Women participate in the conspiracy; they protect men and help maintain the myths...Women who 'prop up' men...also protect their own sphere (the home) from male control by arguing that they have special competence for their domain as men do for theirs – asserting that women manage the home better and are more suited to it. Women prevent men from becoming competent in the home, holding that men's personality traits are not suitable for women's roles and that men's biological makeup impedes their acquisition of the required attributes such as nurturance or home management (Tucker September 2005).

In an era that commonly questions preconceived ideals concerning women's association with domesticity and the private sphere, Bree is strangely anomalous in her apparent insistence on asserting this 'special competence' for the (domestic) 'domain' and on perfecting the 'required attributes' of 'nurturance [and] home management'.

However, in her protection of her own sphere Bree arguably brings a rather monstrous and subversive element to earlier incarnations of the perfect housewife. Her competence within the domestic domain is somewhat demonised in her presentation as a 'control freak'. This competence enables her to wield a considerable amount of power within the domestic realm, which her husband is seemingly unable to challenge – her 'mistaken' inclusion of the onions that Rex is dangerously allergic to when fixing his salad immediately after his request for the divorce ('I can't believe you tried to kill me…') is a strong testament to this (1: 1). While June Cleaver and Margaret Anderson may have seemed eerily plastic at most with their fixed smiles and exaggeratedly cheerful dispositions, Bree's updated version encapsulates a threatening aspect that is absent from her 1950s counterparts, suggesting that too much control and competence within the domestic arena might not be so desirable for women after all. The final episode of the first season ends with Rex mistakenly believing that Bree has killed him by purposely administering the wrong medication (1: 23), accentuating the darker and more sinister aspects within current discourses of domesticity not commonly alluded to in popular representations of the housewife.

Such darker elements within domesticity recall the trope of 'momism' coined by Philip Wylie in his 1941 book *Generation of Vipers*, which accused American women of being 'overbearing, domineering mothers who turned their sons and husbands into weak-kneed fools' (quoted in Spigel 2001: 51). This would seem to be an apt description of Bree and her tendency to dominate Rex and their children, Andrew and Danielle. While June Cleaver and Margaret Anderson happily deferred to their husbands on practically all domestic and familial matters, it is clear that Bree is the decision maker in the Van de Kamp household. In spite of the disintegration of their marriage throughout the first season, Bree stoically insists on maintaining a harmonious front, and Rex helplessly complies. Even when his involvement with the neighbourhood prostitute Maisy Gibbons (Sharon Lawrence) becomes open knowledge on Wisteria Lane, Bree refuses to crack, as illustrated by the incident at the restaurant in which she threateningly forbids Rex to acknowledge the stares and whispers of the other diners (1: 16). Bree complicates the perfection and apparent contentment embodied by former happy housewife icons with a coldness and determination that obscures her pride and expertise in her domestic role. Her mechanical response to Rex's heart attack (making the bed) as her daughter Danielle looks on in stunned bewilderment starkly attests to this (1: 22).

Initially, the complexities that Bree adds to the perfect housewife figure are largely limited to such aspects of control and extreme fastidiousness. However, as the series progresses, the character is gradually developed, and the domesticity that Bree personifies becomes truly desperate as it emerges that the appearance of perfection she so adamantly maintains is a façade for the sadness and desperation within her. In describing Bree, the posthumous narrator Mary Alice Young recollects 'the easy confidence of her smile … the gentle elegance of her hands … the refined warmth of her voice' but remembers most 'the look of fear in her eyes.' (1: 1) This fear belies the power she holds within the domestic space of the household: as Mary Alice continues in the narration, Bree's domestic 'world is unravelling' as her marriage and her relationships with her children disintegrate. The revelations that Rex has been having an extramarital affair and that her son Andrew has homosexual tendencies shatter her perceptions of domestic harmony and satisfaction, and make it increasingly difficult to maintain the appearances that are so important to her. During one of her sessions with marriage counsellor Dr Albert Goldfine (Sam Lloyd), Bree refers to psychoanalytic theory and Freud's disdain for his mother to comment on the thankless domestic tasks that are often taken for granted.

> His mother had to do everything by hand, just back-breaking work from sunup to sundown. Not to mention the countless other sacrifices she probably had to make to take care of her family. And what does he do? He grows up and becomes famous, peddling a theory that the problems of most adults can be traced back to something awful their mother has done … She must have felt so betrayed. He saw how hard she worked; he saw what she did for him. Did he even ever think to say thank you? I doubt it (1: 2).

She is specifically referring to the actual work, the drudgery and effort required behind the image of the perfect housewife rarely acknowledged in the earlier popular incarnations. Later in the series, the expression of her grief and disappointment over the failure of her marriage also reveal a softer facet to the implacable veneer that she typically projects. Indeed, although she does not explicitly defer to Rex in the same way that June defers to Ward Cleaver (Hugh Beaumont), she is curiously accepting of Rex's infidelity and even submits to his sexual fetishes, in spite of her deep disdain and reservations (1: 13). Also, her relationships with her children are strained at best, particularly with her rebellious son Andrew (who does not hesitate to demonstrate his contempt for his mother at any opportunity), illustrating that the control she wields within the household is not so pervasive after all. This is most aptly illustrated during her breakdown upon learning of Rex's death, where all traces of her steely control have been completely stripped away (1: 23). Perhaps more so than any of the other housewives, Bree's desperation reflects the myriad complications and contradictions that define current perceptions of women in relation to the domestic realm.

In spite of the subversive elements that Bree invokes in her contemporary incarnation of the happy housewife, the agency and fulfilment she fails to achieve in her family relationships suggest that her construction is not really so different from the earlier models that she parodies. Although the show's narrative explores and interrogates the desperation within her domestic prowess and obsession, its simultaneous devaluation and reclamation of domesticity ensure that she is merely another desperate housewife at heart. Thus, although the show complicates the iconic image of the happy housewife, ultimately it offers no solutions to the desperation that informs current inter-pretations of the domestic role.

Part 4:

NARRATIVE, CONFESSION
AND INTIMACY

14

Dying to tell you something: Posthumous narration and female omniscience in *Desperate Housewives*

Deborah Jermyn

An odd thing happens when we die. Our senses vanish. Taste, touch, smell and sound become a distant memory. But our sight? Ah, our sight expands. And we can suddenly see the world we left behind so clearly.

Mary Alice Young (1: 2)

It is curious that Mary Alice Young, the posthumous narrator of *Desperate Housewives*, should situate sight as the pre-eminent sense with which she experiences and understands the world. In time-honoured tradition, vision, when precisely honed, is privileged as the sense that most reliably and cogently brings with it insight and knowledge. It seems that, for Mary Alice, a picture, when perceptively examined, really might endeavour to 'speak a thousand words'.

The relationship she poses between herself and sight is curious, first, since her voiceover situates her as a kind of omnipresence who evidently both sees and *hears* all. Second, it seems strangely at odds with the audience's comprehension of her, since this relationship is so predominantly marked by our aural knowledge of her, by an over-whelmingly auditory familiarity, by *voice*. It is her voice, in conjunction with image, which provides and *enhances* irony, humour, pleasure, insight and suspense throughout *Desperate Housewives*. Through the conceit of a dead woman narrator, writer Marc Cherry has constructed a strikingly inventive characterisation, which is quite without parallel in the history of television, for the manner in (and degree to) which it privileges female subjectivity, knowledge and ownership of the text, even despite emanating from a male writer. Clearly, in one respect the fact of her physical absence from the world of the story could be said to constrain and delimit the tangible extent of her power and influence within the text. Nevertheless, through Mary Alice, *Desperate Housewives* undermines the constraints of woman's more ubiquitous function across audio-visual culture broadly as an object of vision, by situating her instead as omniscient observer, auditor and narrator. In doing so, the programme critically engages with the long history of women's complex and conflictual relationship with language in patriarchal culture, a culture where women's voices have so often been marginalised, discredited or silenced within mainstream representation.

This chapter examines the uses and affects of the female voiceover in *Desperate Housewives*, and the manner in which it creates a knowing and critical female subjectivity in the text. Moving on from the body of critical work that has long recognised the problematic and complex relationship women hold to language and speaking, and the cultural privilege generally afforded to 'male' discourses (see for example Coates 1998), I argue that *Desperate Housewives* undermines and plays with many of these notions and traditions. The gendered stereotype of women as gossips and 'storytellers' is an established convention in Western patriarchy. As Fern Johnson and Elizabeth Aries put it:

> Folk wisdom has long denigrated women's talk as 'idle chatter', 'yackedy yack', 'hen cackling', 'gabbing' and 'gossip'. Such folk wisdom pejoratively places women in the position of having nothing better to do with their time than talk and of having nothing important to talk about (1998: 216).

In *Desperate Housewives'* narration, the negative connotations of such cultural associations are inverted, and the sense of 'having nothing better to do' and 'having nothing important to talk about' becomes the very substance, the essential pleasure, of the voiceover. Rather than denigrate it, the text foregrounds and celebrates women's oral culture, in large part through the voiceover.

The sounds of generic hybridity

Desperate Housewives is a text rich in intertextuality, making a wealth of allusions to texts drawn from both film and TV history. These range from the suburban dystopia of *The Stepford Wives* (1975); to the narrative conventions of soap (such as multiple storylines, domestic milieux, cliffhangers); to the festering dysfunction of David Lynch's small-town America (both *Twin Peaks* and *Blue Velvet* [1986]); and to the female camaraderie of *Sex and the City*. Of course, *Sex and the City* is also where one finds one of television's prime instances of female voiceover narration prior to *Desperate Housewives*, a key feature of this very recent and landmark series, which *Desperate Housewives* appears to have quite consciously capitalised on in an effort to similarly capture female viewers.

Generally, though, the voiceover is a narrative device primarily associated with cinema rather than television fiction, perhaps most notably and consistently utilised by classical Hollywood's film noir movement and, to a lesser extent, by a relatively small body of films within the 'women's picture' in the 1940s. In the latter category, far more unusually for classical Hollywood, women protagonists were given the voiceover, in films such as *Rebecca* (1940), *The Snake Pit* (1948) and *A Letter to Three Wives* (1949). With its narrative preoccupations surrounding murder, suspense and convoluted plotting on the one hand, and its domestic settings, female protagonists and (an often Gothic-style) romance on the other, *Desperate Housewives* clearly owes a narrative debt to both film noir and the woman's film. Hence the body of work on these cinematic oeuvres offers some useful starting points from which one might start to conceptualise the role and place of Mary Alice's voice in *Desperate Housewives*, particularly given the dearth of critical work on the voiceover in TV drama.

The evocation and reworking of film noir's male investigative voiceover, so emblematic of the movement, is one of the crucial features of *Desperate Housewives*' reflexive play with multiple generic precursors and genre hybridity. While Mary Alice's voice, like the male protagonists of such films as *Double Indemnity* (1944) and *Out of the Past* (1947), 'creates a mood of *temps perdu*: an irretrievable past', crucially it abandons the accompanying sense of 'all-enveloping hopelessness' embedded in noir (Schrader 1996: 58). This is replaced instead with quirky humour and bemused meditation, which repeatedly point to the inherent ridiculousness and pettiness of suburban life. At a superficial level, the male voiceover of film noir serves to anchor the male protagonist as the proprietor of the text, placing his subjectivity at the core of the narrative. But, in fact, the male voice of film noir frequently works to cast doubt on his own mastery of events, carrying connotations of obsession and powerlessness. When Joe Gillis (William Holden), longing to escape his sordid lifestyle in *Sunset Boulevard* (1950), observes 'Maybe I could get away with it, get away from Norma, maybe I could wipe the whole nasty mess out of my life...' we never doubt he is doomed to fail. In contrast to the noir style of narration, where knowledge is often restricted or overtly subjective, Mary Alice claims omniscience ('To understand Maisy Gibbons, you first need to know how she spent her afternoons...,' she tells us, before confiding the routines of Maisy's [played by Sharon Lawrence] family life and the clientele who visit her home to pay for sex [1: 10]). Where in film noir there is confusion and discord, Mary Alice speaks with calm authority and wisdom ('Competition, it means different things to different people... the trick is knowing which battles to fight,' she informs us following a series of major rows on Wisteria Lane [1: 7]). Where in film noir the male voice carries an oppressive sense of doom and loss, in *Desperate Housewives* lies wry humour (when Edie Britt notes at the fashion show rehearsal that Martha Huber 'wouldn't be seen dead in black', Mary Alice observes: 'Sadly for Mrs Huber, this was no longer the case,' as we cut to the image of her corpse wrapped in a bin liner [1: 9]).

Looking more closely at these filmic precedents, what seems most remarkable about Mary Alice's voiceover when comparing it to its cinematic forerunners is the lack of disjuncture between her voice and the image. Critical work on both the woman's film and film noir has pointed to how the narrators' voices frequently operate in a kind of tension with 'real' events or with what we see. For example, Sarah Kozloff notes that film noir often uses voiceover to 'stress the narrative's subjective source' and observes, 'Their stories, which have to do with crime and adultery, are almost always confessional and often these confessions revolve around problems of seeing and perceiving – they have been too trusting or too suspicious – they have misjudged themselves and the lay of the land' (1988: 63). In regard to the woman's film, Mary Ann Doane has argued that the female voiceover is 'not infrequently subjected to a loss of unity, coherence and consistency. Quite often…it is completely separated from any notion of the authority of the female protagonist and, in fact, turned against her', often being subverted by a male character who completes or reinterprets the narration (1988: 151). Karen Hollinger argues that such tensions in the woman's film challenge any easy interpolation of the spectator into a patriarchal subject position by enabling, 'a distancing awareness that makes a less ideologically complicit reading of the texts possible' (1992: 36). But she nevertheless agrees that the female voiceover is recurrently bound up in 'narrative battles for control of the story between various competing elements in the text, a dichotomy between word and image' (35).

Out-of-body experiences – the disembodied woman's voice in Desperate Housewives

There is no such conflict evident around Mary Alice's voice in *Desperate Housewives*, which exudes calm authority and composed wisdom throughout. Partly this is a result of the quality of Brenda Strong's vocal delivery, which exudes an ironic kind of 'all-American' enthusiasm in artificial fashion. But, beyond this, it emanates from the particular peculiarities of the voiceover and Mary Alice's place within the text, which are structured in an unusual and highly distinctive manner. At a pragmatic level, she frequently helps ease the seguing between scenes. More interestingly, each week her voice also frames the story, providing the opening prologue – often a pithy tale about the misplaced values of suburbia – and the epilogue – often extracting some sage lesson based on what we've seen or tantalisingly pointing to the next twist in the tale. She approximates what Kozloff calls a 'frame narrator' in that she begins her narration with the first images of the text and her actual act of narrating is not visualised; nor can it be, since she is dead at the start of the story – and herein lies the unusual nature of Mary Alice's place/presence in the text. Robert Stam et al. observe that Kozloff's category of frame narration 'in Genette's system would probably be labelled heterodiegetic' (1992: 100), i.e. a character-narrator who does not appear in the story he or she recounts. But, of course, Mary Alice *does* appear in the story – in flashback, in photos and home movie footage, on audiotape, in dreams – though the time of the unfolding plot is time 'outside' of her. While it is concerned with the events of the past, the time of *Desperate Housewives* is set in the present, a present that Mary Alice's suicide precludes her from being physically present in.

Yet she still has knowledge, awareness, insight into this time. As well as having a heightened sensitivity to her friends' emotional states ('Susan suddenly had an awful feeling in the pit of her stomach…,' she tells us as she watches Susan Mayer watching Edie Britt ingratiate herself with Mike Delfino [1: 2]), she appears to be actually present at events; when Gabrielle Solis observes 'Guess we found the skeleton in her closet' on discovering the size 8 label on Mary Alice's old clothes, Mary Alice interrupts, 'Not quite, Gabrielle, not quite,' as if actually there interacting with her friends (1: 1). She can cue flashbacks, such as scenes of a dinner party at the Van de Kamps' prior to her death (1: 3). Mary Alice can even anticipate developments and exchanges; in the aftermath of a break-in on Wisteria Lane she observes, 'Gabrielle was about to experience a home invasion of her own,' just as Juanita 'Mama' Solis pulls up in a cab (1: 5). She thus enjoys a superior position of knowledge in relation to the text, above that of both other characters and the audience.

Furthermore, I want to argue that residues of Mary Alice's curious and oddly empowered present-absence go further, making her a significant structuring presence in the programme despite her death. Mary Alice *is* embodied in the text, albeit in an abstract sense, not merely through her voiceover but through her association with particular and recurrent forms of distinctive camera movement and visual aesthetics. Firstly, the edit at the end of each week's 'Previously on…' montage, which leads into her opening prologue, is recurrently made through a fade to *white*, whereas the dominant televisual convention is to fade to black. This white screen carries with it connotations of the celestial, suggesting the movement towards a bright light that survivors of near-death and out-of-body experiences often describe, making Mary Alice's 'presence' oddly visible. Indeed, she is seen by us bathed in this white light on more than one occasion; for example, when she appears to an exhausted Lynette in a vision at her broken window, where, floating in the celestial ether, she hands her a gun (1: 8).

Secondly, *Desperate Housewives* features an unusually fluid camera for a TV production. It recurrently draws on an elaborate dolly to move from high-angled shots above Wisteria Lane down to individual houses, or pans and tracks across the street. Following the credits the programme often opens (and, indeed, later ends) with a shot above the houses and trees before travelling down to street level, as if Mary Alice, in communion with the camera, were moving down from the heavens to accompany us into the scene. For example, in the second episode of season one this association between the camera/Mary Alice/heavenly omniscience is particularly notable at the end of the episode, when she berates the way people 'so rarely stop to take a look' at the world. As if enacting her words, the camera moves from an exterior shot of Wisteria Lane, accompanied by a refrain of angelic choir music, swooping up to the skies and gazing at the stars, before crossing an expanse of space to sweep down to the river, where the chest containing her deadly secret bobs to the surface. The panning/tracking shots often frame the scene or look at the houses from behind a white picket fence, as if Mary Alice were still there, discreetly watching the homes and residents of Wisteria Lane from among them.

Finally, the camera also turns up in unexpected or hidden places in *Desperate Housewives*, secreted in the cupboards at Mike's house or the Mayers', waiting in the mailbox for Susan or Mary Alice to collect their post, lurking behind fences or outside windows and creeping inside through them. While serving to enhance the general air of mystery and secrecy in the programme, in these small moments the camera also mirrors Mary Alice's apparently limitless bounds. In all these aesthetic motifs, her disembodied freedom can be felt at a physical level. Thus, even while dead, she inhabits the text fully, enjoying a conspicuously high degree of knowledge of, access to and movement in and around its constituent parts.

In this sense, Mary Alice *shares* characteristics with the hetero-diegetic voiceover narrator, who is 'given a kind of free-floating, bodiless status, "a voice from on-high"' (Stam et al. 1992: 100), and who enjoys a heightened degree of 'authentication authority' (99). The disembodied voiceover is unusual in classical cinema, but particularly so in terms of women's voices; Kaja Silverman is able to trace just one example, that of Addie in *A Letter to Three Wives* (1988: 48–49).

Desperate Housewives' privileging of female/feminine subjectivity in its willingness to give Mary Alice such a role is especially striking for this reason. This 'subjectivity' exists, though, not in terms of an overtly subjective account of events and characters, since we never have object cause to doubt her reliability despite the notable silence she generally maintains in regard to her husband and son. Even the revelation about her deadly secret in the series finale does not discredit the truth of the observations on suburban life she has shared with us for the previous 22 episodes. Rather, this female/feminine subjectivity exists in terms of what is deemed to be 'worth' talking about. The details and observations we might expect a male narrator to be concerned with, bound up in the masculine, classical drive towards resolution, are often peripheral to Mary Alice.

It's good to talk – reclaiming gossip on Wisteria Lane

Indeed, from the very start she holds all the answers to the mystery – the motive for her own suicide, the fate of baby Dana, the reasons for Paul Young's secrecy – but she never seems hugely interested in divulging this information or deliberating over these events with us. In a 'male', noir-style investigative drama such as *Double Indemnity*, narrated by the hapless Walter Neff (Fred MacMurray), the acquisition of these truths and 'facts' from the past, alongside the 'solving' of the woman, would take pre-eminence. In contrast, Mary Alice is more concerned with her neighbours' lives, their rows, their gossip and affairs of the heart. 'Suburbia is a battleground, an arena for all forms of domestic combat,' she tells us (1: 6), and herein lies the territory she is primarily concerned with. She revels in this tangential terrain, telling us all about the petty-mindedness of Martha Huber sabotaging Bree Van de Kamp's lawn through jealousy (1: 7), the crotchety complaints of Mrs McCluskey (Kathryn Joosten) against Lynette Scavo's family (1: 14), as well as the 'deliciously sordid' scandal of Maisy Gibbons' arrest (1: 16).

This is not to say in any sense that women's talk precludes engagement with the concerns of 'serious' or 'high' culture. Rather, in its attention to the quotidian conflicts and routines of women's lives,

Desperate Housewives takes time to reflect on some of the everyday negotiations and experiences lived out by these women (albeit women of a largely privileged milieu). All these narrative diversions, however seemingly banal or removed from both 'serious' culture and the quest to resolve Wisteria Lane's mystery, are nonetheless about the politics of women's lives. Johnson and Aries argue that 'talk is the substance of women's friendship', and it is precisely the kinds of everyday subjects and gossip dear to *Desperate Housewives* that constitute much of this talk. Their research into women-only conversation found, 'In adulthood, close female friends converse more frequently than close male friends about personal and family problems, intimate relationships, doubts and fears, daily activities and hobbies and shared activities' (1998: 216–217). Crucially, the pleasures of *Desperate Housewives* lie as much in these detours as they do in our edging ever closer to the 'solving' of Mary Alice's suicide, to the extent that the 'diversions' become equally the subject of the narrative. In this way, just as much as in the exchanges between the group of women friends (and 'enemies') at the text's centre, Mary Alice's gossipy, meandering voiceover fosters and relishes women's talk and a female/feminine subjectivity.

Speak up dear – the housewife talks back

Of course, despite everything I have argued here, *Desperate Housewives'* use of a female narrator does not lend itself entirely unproblematically to the possibility of a feminist reading of the text. It would be remiss not to acknowledge that the effort to mark this text as 'owned' by women through its address is part of a larger commercial strategy, rather than an avowedly feminist project. Furthermore, one might also critique the fact that, paradoxically, in order to give Mary Alice a voice, the text simultaneously has to 'silence' her. She has to die in order to speak. Her subsequent 'empowerment' comes in a peculiarly ineffectual form, then, in that she is able only to make commentary on the unravelling narrative rather than instigate *change* within it or function as a narrative actant in any tangible sense. One might also ask where the season finale's revelation that Mary Alice was, in fact, a murderer leaves the audience *vis-à-vis* their relationship with her. This revelation comes largely from 'within' the denouement of the plot itself, others' investigation and Paul's confession, rather than her own willing admission. Like Mildred Pierce, is her story 'revealed as duplicitous' (Cook 1998: 73), has she 'failed' in some sense to keep faith with her listeners?

Or perhaps, rather more radically, might one of the more provocative and potentially subversive aspects of the text be precisely that it has led its audience to trust, empathise and collude with a murderous woman? In this way, the text leaves the audience to ponder how many other apparently ordinary housewives encountered in our daily lives might similarly share Mary Alice's hidden capacity for rage and violence. Here we might again bring a comparison to bear between *Desperate Housewives* and film noir, and specifically its archetypal destructive woman, the femme fatale. Clearly, the difference between these women is that the femme fatale murders to escape the constraints of the family, while Mary Alice murders to remain within them. Nevertheless, they are closer to one another than they might initially appear. Feminist readings of the femme fatale have embraced her 'excess' for the manner in which it brings the stifling ennui of culturally sanctioned femininity into stark relief, a conflict typically embodied in film noir by a dichotomy which contrasts the femme fatale with the figure of a 'good' girlfriend/wife/daughter (see Place 1998). In a similar vein to this earlier feminist work, Mary Alice's destructive impulses might likewise be said to enable a reading that conceptualises the text as undermining patriarchal order, rather than revering it.

Like the femme fatale, her behaviour destabilises and discloses the rocky foundations on which the institution of the family is built within patriarchal culture, while exposing the peculiarly damaging and acute pressures it places on women. As in film noir – where the women who constitute the positive inverses of the femmes fatales are pallid substitutes for the vitality and sensuality of their iconic sisters – by the time we reach *Desperate Housewives'* end the 'good woman' is also far from being an aspirational figure. Though dominant culture continues to endorse marriage and motherhood as worthy and desirable choices for women, the allure of this lifestyle is left somewhat tarnished by *Desperate Housewives*. Indeed, perhaps even more radically than in film noir, in *Desperate Housewives* it is precisely the 'good woman', Mary Alice, who is unveiled as having been the murderous impostor, the very nemesis of suburban equanimity, all along. Mary Alice had appeared, even to her closest friends, to live a life of comfortable, conventional, middle-class contentment; by the series' end, this life is revealed to have been built on repression, anxiety and the destructive drive to fulfil a superficially beguiling but ultimately untenable vision of domestic bliss. That contemporary TV is willing and able to make some headway towards reflecting on female identity and experience in such a fashion speaks of the impact of post-feminism on popular culture – and a moment in television that is to be embraced for the rich and intriguing material it offers feminist criticism.

Acknowledgements: Thanks to Caroline Bainbridge, Su Holmes and the editors of this collection for their thoughtful feedback during the writing of this chapter.

15

Desperation loves company: Female friendship and the façade of female intimacy in *Desperate Housewives*

Sherianne Shuler, M. Chad McBride and Erika L. Kirby

> Behind a façade of female intimacy lies a terrain travelled in secret, marked with anguish, and nourished by silence.
>
> Rachel Simmons 2002: 3

'Hey, did you watch that new show *Desperate Housewives* last night?' Chad asked. 'Loved it!' exclaimed Erika, while Sheri listened in horror, saying: 'You've got to be kidding me. That show is so offensive!' 'Did you watch it?' asked Erika, rolling her eyes at Chad. 'Well, no, because I object to the premise. It's anti-feminist,' Sheri insisted. 'I think you need to watch – it surprisingly has really interesting, ironic messages about gender,' urged Chad, 'and we need to write about it.' 'You two *American Idol* fans want ME to listen to YOUR television watching suggestions?' Sheri exclaimed. 'Granted, we're a little more pedestrian than you in our pop culture tastes, but Chad's right that if you actually watched you might have a different view,' Erika replied; 'this is an article begging to be written.' At this point we were mostly 'work friends', with Erika officially assigned as mentor to Chad and Sheri. Chad and Erika had worked together for one year, and Sheri was a brand new faculty member. It did not take long for us to develop deep affection and involvements outside work. In addition to the social aspects of our friendship, we began travelling together to conferences and collaborating on research projects. Chad finally persuaded Sheri to watch the first several episodes of *Desperate Housewives*. Despite her initial misgivings, she was hooked, and we eagerly awaited each episode and our discussions of them at work.

Bonnie Dow (1996) argued almost 10-years ago that television representations of female characters in community were rare. Then in 1998 *Sex and the City* emerged as a hit show where 'the value of female friendships and the role of these friendships in helping each of the women characters to understand herself and her life' was central, and many episodes '[suggested] that platonic female friendships are more important than sexual and romantic love' (Henry 2004: 67–68). Fast-forward six years to the debut of *Desperate Housewives*, a show touted as *Sex and the City* for suburban, married women. If true, it makes sense that female friendship and community would be a centrepiece of the show. As fans of the characters and the friendships on *Sex and the City*, we celebrated this possibility. We bristled at knee-jerk reactions (like Sheri's) that seemed to miss the series' irony about suburban life. We rejoiced in the focus on women's lives and relationships, especially women who (albeit attractive) were not young singles. There were other potentially transformative messages too, like exposing the difficulty of motherhood, the darker side of the 'American dream', and of moving up and into the suburbs. Yet for us, as both fans and feminist communication scholars interested in gender and relationships, the nagging question has become are the women of Wisteria Lane really 'friends' in an authentic sense? The longer we watched, the more we began to trade our 'rabid fans' hats for our 'communication scholars' ones, and our doubts about their friendships strengthened. As we compared literature and our experiences to the portrayals of female friendship on *Desperate Housewives*, we found that the women of Wisteria Lane fell short. While there certainly are moments of genuine, positive, adult female friendship, what we see more often is a façade. We argue that the women of *Desperate Housewives* are more aptly compared to adolescent *Mean Girls* (2004) than adult *Sex and the City* women. In making our case, we first examine the friendship characteristic that matches the literature (and thereby promotes the façade of female intimacy): the quantity of talk.

Female friendship: closeness through talk

Perhaps one reason the friendships portrayed on *Desperate Housewives* are compelling is the housewives' constant conversation, which squares with the research on female friendships. 'Talk is at the very heart of women's friendships, the core of the way women connect. It's the given, absolute assumption of friendship' (Goodman and O'Brien 2000: 34–35). Thus, 'talk is the substance of a women's friendship' (Johnson and Aries 1983: 354), and, in terms of the centrality of talk, relationships among the main characters on Wisteria Lane are typical of the constant connection we expect from female friends. This important aspect of friendship matches ours: when we are not talking face to face at work, we are constantly in contact via email and cell-phone. The women of *Desperate Housewives* talk about their own and neighbours' lives over coffee, in their driveways and at dinner parties; they chat on the phone when passing along juicy gossip or during their weekly poker game; they also converse in response to crises in each other's lives.

In addition to the quantity of talk, close friendship is often defined by its quality. The constant talk on Wisteria Lane not only provides support for everyday venting about problems with kids and/or other relationships, but also provides emotional support in crisis situations, such as when Susan Mayer comforts Gabrielle Solis after her husband Carlos's arrest (1: 9) or when all three arrive at the hospital in the middle of the night to support Bree Van de Kamp after husband Rex has had his heart attack (1: 23). As Mary Alice Young narrates, 'They came with their uncombed hair and their unmade faces. They came because after all these years... they were no longer just neighbours.' As the women huddle around Bree in the waiting room, they seem the picture-perfect image of close women friends offering this kind of emotional support. However, the scene turns this idea on its head when Bree tells her friends to stop their comforting behaviours because she might 'lose it'. Her response is unfortunate, given that women tend to listen non-critically and offer support (Brehm 2001; Johnson and Aries 1983). However, in rejecting this cornerstone of female friendships, Bree shows she would rather 'be strong' than be emotionally open and lean on her friends.

In addition to the emotional support offered by the housewives, instrumental support, or materially helping one another, is commonplace. They bring food to Mary Alice's wake and help by going through her things for donation (1: 1), they watch Lynette Scavo's kids (1: 8; 1: 18) and Bree lets Gabrielle store furniture in her garage to avoid it being repossessed following the investigation into Carlos's business dealings (1: 10).[1] While the housewives offer and accept emotional and instrumental support, they do, however, seem to have difficulty in asking for help. This difficulty seems to be tied to their reluctance to self-disclose, as receiving social support requires being vulnerable by sharing needs. Research suggests that women's talk is more self-disclosive than men's, so their friendships therefore are also characterised as more intimate (Brehm 2001). This does not seem to be the case in *Desperate Housewives*, as while there are scenes where the women do provide support, it is important to note that more often than not they keep their most dire problems to themselves.[2] In the pilot, Gabrielle tells her teenage gardener John Rowland that their affair keeps her from '[waking] up one morning with a sudden urge to blow [her] brains out' due to her disillusionment with how her life as a married woman living in the suburbs has turned out. Even though her unhappiness is serious enough for potential suicidal urges, she keeps this from her close friends. When Rex visits the local prostitute to satisfy his S/M fetish, Bree does not discuss his sexual proclivities or their marital problems with her friends. In fact, she specifically asks Rex to maintain the façade of tennis lessons to hide their marital counselling while hosting a dinner party for their friends (1: 3).

When the women of *Desperate Housewives* do self-disclose it is only when they feel compelled to do so by a public humiliation or a crisis point. Lynette cracks only after becoming addicted to her kids' ADD medication and desperately attempts to get help – by leaving her kids with Susan and taking off (1: 8). This situation ends in the sort of self-disclosure we would expect from female friends, but it is significant that Lynette's first instinct is to remove herself from her friends and be alone. When Bree and Susan eventually find her, she tells them: 'Other moms don't need help – other moms make it look so easy. All I do is complain.' Choosing this moment to tell the truth behind their experiences of motherhood has both Susan and Bree disclosing their own moments of despair. Susan confesses that 'when Julie was a baby, I was out of my mind almost every day'; and Bree adds, 'I used to get so upset when Andrew and Danielle were little. I used their nap times to cry.' Lynette sobs. She asks why nobody ever told her this, to which Bree responds: 'Nobody likes to admit they can't handle the pressure.' One of our favourite scenes, this is a poignant example of what women's friendships can be – women being honest, self-disclosing and offering support without judgment. While scenes like this appear occasionally, they are few and far between. And even this scene is based on the premise that the women usually do not self-disclose about their inability to cope with their children. We recognise that showing weakness is difficult, perhaps particularly hard when combined with the pressure to be the perfect mother (Wolf 2001). We also acknowledge there are plenty of real women who bottle up things inside and do not reap the benefits of support from friends. What we do find troubling, though, is that these women are touted as the *Sex and the City* girls all grown up, as if the *Desperate Housewives* friendships are of the same character and quality as the intimate comradeship forming the centrepiece of *Sex and the City* – or even as our friendship of barely one year. What looks on the surface like intimacy and close friendship, indeed what is called 'best' and 'good friendship' by *Desperate Housewives* characters, seems to us a pale imitation.

'Mean Girls' and the façade of female intimacy

Despite glimpses of genuine female friendships, *Desperate Housewives* is no *Sex and the City*. We should note that the comparison to *Mean Girls* was not in our original plan for this chapter. But, when Sheri exclaimed 'I'm beginning to hate these bitches!' after what seemed like the umpteenth viewing of an episode, Chad and Erika reluctantly agreed. We set out to praise the focus on female friendship. But, when we looked more closely, we were disappointed with what we saw through the lens of our friendship. As we repeatedly watched episodes, cracks in the intimacy façade became more and more apparent. Gabrielle may assure Bree that 'good friends support each other after they've been humiliated. Great friends pretend nothing happened in the first place' (1: 16). Lynette may try to explain to Edie Britt how friends should act – 'They call, they're sympathetic, they ask about the pain the other person is going through, and then they listen' – but Edie still has a problem with this definition, and wonders how to be a friend 'if you want to be supportive, but you just can't stand listening to people bitch'. Lynette's answer – that 'it's good to know how to bluff' – serves as the representative anecdote (Burke 1989) of how female friendship is most often depicted on *Desperate Housewives*: as a façade.

Fern Johnson (1996) characterises knowledge about female friendship prior to the late 1970s as folk wisdom 'about women's jealousies of one another; their "yackety-yak" with each other; and their idling away of time' (80). What we find on *Desperate Housewives* seems closer to this stereotype of yesteryear than the reality of women's friendship experiences. Overall, while the women of Wisteria Lane display some of the characteristics of authentic female friendships, we more often see them masking the real truth of their lives in creating a façade of intimacy. And, despite scholars' strides since the 1970s to recognise the depth and closeness of women's friendships, the house-wives seem to more closely emulate an older and less flattering stereotype of cattiness, competition, gossip and shallowness. This superficiality may be best illustrated by Gabrielle's reaction to finding out the secret of Mary Alice's closet when the ladies are helping to pack up their dead friend's clothes: 'Size 8, ha! She always told me she was a size 6. I guess we found the skeleton in her closet.' (1: 1) While this portrayal is disheartening to us as feminist scholars, we must acknowledge that many women do talk about other people. Leora Tanenbaum (2000) asserts that girls endlessly gossip about each other by fifth and sixth grades, culminating in the ultimate way to put other girls in their place: calling them sluts, for example. Gossip abounds on Wisteria Lane, often focusing on Edie, who is referred to as a slut from the start. The opening montage exposes the various men Edie has bedded, and even her 'best friend' Martha Huber comments that 'Edie may be trash, but she's still a human being' (1: 2). Tanenbaum (2000) argues that threatening females are often labelled sluts to discredit them – even if they are not more sexually active than other women. Despite committing adultery and statutory rape, Gabrielle is not seen as a slut, while Edie, a single woman and a threat to the other women, is.

As has been noted, the housewives try to keep many things about their lives private. If their neighbours are supposedly their best friends, what are they afraid of? An answer may be found in the way the women are often portrayed in immature, adolescent roles. Gabrielle is spoilt and wants to be kept by her husband. Even her priest, Father Crowley (Jeff Doucette), calls her 'a selfish child' (1: 8). Bree goes on a date with George Williams, who makes small talk with her husband in the living room as if Rex were her father (1: 11). A recurring example is the way Julie Mayer is portrayed more as Susan's mother than her teenage daughter. The women of *Desperate Housewives* seem to be no more than teenagers with families and large houses, and a comparison can be drawn between their friendships, the relationships among adolescent girls and the darker side of female friendships – gossiping, competing, teasing and forming cliques in what is known in the literature as 'female aggression' or 'girl bullying' (see Pipher 1994; Simmons 2002; Wiseman 2003). Tanenbaum explains that 'tension between covert competition and the social pressure to be nice to other women ... pushes the competitive spirit into the surreptitious realm of gossip and backstabbing and undermining' (2000: 193), so that girls 'are not innocent bystanders in some grand, patriarchal battle for their souls [but] are complicit in bringing each other down' (200).

The potential for aggression among teenage girls was recently highlighted in the 2004 hit *Mean Girls*, and in the spate of guidebooks published to help girls survive (see Dellasega and Nixon 2003; Shearin Karres 2004; Wiseman 2003). This competitive sabotage and underlying potential for manipulation in female relationships seems to be learned early in life (Simmons 2002), and traces of these painful adolescent memories are highlighted in Edie and Susan's animosity towards each other. Edie tells Susan: 'Girls like you were always cheerleaders. Clear skin. Honor roll. Popular. In high school, I was the girl that hung out with the freaks at the loading dock. And smoked. Everyone hated us.' (1: 12) Despite Susan's reassurances that at least they have left high school behind, Edie replies: 'See, I don't think we do ... I'm still the outsider that doesn't get invited to the cool parties, and you're still the perky cheerleader who thinks that she can pull the wool over everyone's eyes ... we're still in high school. The old rules apply. The cool kids only want to talk to the freaks when they need something.' This pattern of comparing social status is typical in a patriarchal society, when women often measure themselves in relation to other women, and competitive sabotage can occur over men, power, networks and social opportunity (Ivy and Backlund 2004).

The concept of competitive sabotage and 'intimate enemies' – those you keep close for manipulative reasons (Simmons 2002) – is clearly illustrated by Susan and Edie's competition over Mike Delfino (and later Susan's ex-husband Karl Mayer). It begins when Susan fakes concern for Edie, as she stands outside her neighbour's burning house, which she has accidentally set fire to after breaking in to find out if Edie was sleeping with Mike (1: 1). It continues when Susan accompanies Edie to scatter Martha's ashes under the guise of being a caring friend, but really it is because she feels guilty and wants to confess to burning down Edie's house (1: 12); and Edie returns the favour later when she 'innocently' expresses concern over Mike moving in with Susan (1: 22). Organising an intervention, Edie enlists the others to talk Susan through her decision. Of course it backfires on her when Susan convinces the others that she is in love with Mike: 'This is the worst intervention I have ever been to' concludes Edie. And, as if to prove the point, when Lynette asks Edie for advice about how to deal with the reappearance of her husband Tom's ex-girlfriend, Annabel Foster (Melinda McGraw), with whom he is now working, Edie recommends that she 'pull her in' and 'make her [your] best friend' in order to 'keep your friends close and your enemies closer' (1: 20).

Another aspect of 'intimate enemies' is also demonstrated by Edie's attempt to join the women's poker games. The literature on girl bullying asserts that girls squelch their own self-interests to 'get in good' with the popular clique (Simmons 2002). The four women friends of *Desperate Housewives* definitely seem a clique; at a book club meeting, Bree 'couldn't wait to get rid of' those other than her close friends (1: 7), and even other neighbours are outsiders. Their status is clearly demonstrated after Susan admits to Edie that she burned down her house (1: 12). In return for not going to the police, Edie wants only a simple (and sad) favour: to be invited to the clique's poker game, from which she has been excluded. But it is never made clear if she is making an effort to 'get in good' with the popular clique or whether she is taking her own advice and keeping her own friends close and enemies even closer.

Will they ever grow up?

While one hopes that the *Mean Girls* behaviour is something left in the high school locker room or the sorority house, television programmes are often guilty of playing up these negative character-isations of female friendship. Much of the controversy surrounding the *Sex and the City* women focused on their flaunting of appropriate female sexual behaviours. But perhaps the show's more revolutionary message is the elevation of female friendship. As Astrid Henry notes, 'While the programme shows women arguing over difference[s] of opinion, the way they handle their relationships, and their individual life choices, it never shows them fighting over a man or being competitive with each other, as is routine in most depictions of female friendship on TV' (2004: 69). Against the backdrop of outlandish murder mystery plot twists and the campy satire of suburbia, women's friendships look rather different in *Desperate Housewives*. The housewives regularly refer to one another as close friends, and yet it is only Mary Alice who really knows them (and then only posthumously). Perhaps most disturbing is that the show uses the trappings of intimacy, and then offers a bait and switch – namely, scenes that non-verbally indicate sharing and concern, complete with mugs of coffee at the kitchen table, are often filled with exclusion, secrets and mixed motives. The programme fails to demonstrate the sort of true community that many women experience in their female friendships. Further, it promotes stereotypes of women's camaraderie by portraying (even promoting) the darker side of some adolescent relationships as typical behaviour for adult women. Thus the comparison between *Sex and the City* and *Desperate Housewives* proves faulty.

Perhaps the intention of the show was never to portray ideal female friendships but, rather, a farcical account of them. Even if this is true, the danger lies in the way the show has been framed and received. Popular press articles abound with women claiming that Wisteria Lane is just like their neighbourhood, or that *Desperate Housewives* represents the *Sex and the City* women when they grow up, marry and move to the suburbs. The ABC website even sells T-shirts that say 'I'm a Bree', or 'I'm a Gabrielle'. As fans, we acknowledge the show is compelling, but we perceive a danger in reading it as anything but a façade of women's real relationships. So, as we mourn *Sex and the City* and continue to get to know the *Desperate Housewives*, let us hope the *Sex and the City* women do not really grow up to be manipulative, lonely, adolescent women. While true female friendship can challenge gendered structures (Johnson 1996), the interaction between the desperate housewives in the first season largely perpetuates them. We have hope, however, that in future seasons the women will come together to challenge the societal structures that too often separate and promote competition between them, that the show's small glimmers of true friendship will shine more brightly, and that the *Mean Girls* will outgrow their ways.

Notes

1 Likewise, we buy lunch when someone is short, Chad has minded and chauffeured Erika's kids, and Sheri serves as the voice of the 'tooth fairy' for Erika's daughter, who refused to keep believing unless she could call her. Erika and Chad even spent an afternoon rearranging Sheri's office furniture as a surprise during her recovery from foot surgery. Good friends do these sorts of things for one another (Roberto and Scott 1986).

2 In trying to understand the strong urge for self-protection among friends, we turned to our own friendship for comparisons and are somewhat puzzled. We have shared deeply personal information with one another – from Sheri and her husband's frustrating attempts to conceive, to Chad's ongoing familial issues, to a serious misunderstanding between Erika and her husband. Like friends who meet in the neighbourhood as a result of geographical proximity, we were thrown together in a common workplace and yet emerged as 'good friends' (as the characters refer to one another). Unlike the women of *Desperate Housewives*, who have supposedly been neighbours for years, we are relatively new friends. And also unlike them, we are not all female, which research suggests should make intimacy more difficult to establish. Nevertheless, despite these facts, we seek out one another for comfort and instrumental support and, regardless of who initiates it, our emotional and instrumental needs are met by one another with kindness and generosity. This is not what we automatically expect of colleagues, or of neighbours, but it is what we expect of good friends.

16

'Mother, home and heaven': Nostalgia, confession and
motherhood in *Desperate Housewives*

Stacy Gillis and Melanie Waters

The tropes of female friendship and maternal tension have long been
staples of female fictions, from the eighteenth-century Gothic novel
to contemporary chick lit, from Mary Wollstonecraft's 1798 novel
Maria (1994) to HBO's *Sex and the City*. Premiering in the autumn
of 2004, it quickly emerged that *Desperate Housewives* was concerned
with these same tropes. The show is predicated upon the act of
confession, a key strategy of female fictions. As a staple of the
(post-)feminist text, confessions reveal the tensions that swirl around
the figures of contemporary femininity, keeping women's 'desires and
motivations the focus of the story' (Mabry 2005: 195). Indeed, as
Shari Benstock points out, these contemporary accounts should be
located within the long history of debates about women's identities,
private space and domesticity: 'Chick lit's use of the diary form,
journals, letters, and e-mail links it to the epistolary tradition and to
the novel that emerged out of private modes of writing commonly
associated with women' (2005: 254). Televisual chick lit, *Desperate
Housewives* maps contemporary accounts of domesticity and motherhood, demonstrating how life in the American suburbs can be one rife
with angst, suspicion and deception. Through the confessional voiceover
of Mary Alice Young, secrets are revealed, although rarely to the female
inhabitants of Wisteria Lane. Peter Brooks argues, 'Confession evidently
comes easily in our culture – so easily that it may provoke scepticism
about its truth values' (2000: 74). While *Desperate Housewives* does
engage with this vexed issue of confessional 'truth', the residents of

Wisteria Lane are primarily interested in confession as a commodity, and customarily calculate the worth of confessional information in accordance with its suburban exchange value.

Confession in the show functions primarily as a way in which to explore female friendship and maternal tension. The friendships of the five women who make up the focus of attention in the first season appear, at first glance, to have much in common with their obvious urban counterparts, the women of *Sex and the City*. Over time, however, *Desperate Housewives* reveals itself to be much more reactionary than its televisual forerunner. The soap's testimonial format, which draws on a long and gendered history of fictionalised confessions, contributes to a nostalgic evocation of the white, middle-class American suburbia of the 1950s. Yet, while the thinly veiled hysterics and lush green lawns of Wisteria Lane are initially suggestive of a postmodern, ironic treatment of the suburban terrain found in the 1950s melodramas of Douglas Sirk and shows such as *Father Knows Best*, the soap all too often replicates the politics of this former era. Moreover, *Desperate Housewives* speaks to concerns about surveillance, privacy and the suburban environment that typically informed cultural representations of American domestic life during the decades following the Second World War. Given this referentiality, the politics of the show should be considered alongside the convergent Cold War ideologies of containment and conformity, and, more specifically, in relation to social anxieties about the threats posed by the insidious 'enemy within' that have resurfaced in the American cultural imagination in the wake of 9/11. This chapter discusses how nostalgia and confession are used to construct gender in *Desperate Housewives*, providing a reading of how motherhood is positioned as a causative factor in various forms of sacrifice, economic prostitution and psychological instability.

Domesticity and the politics of confession

In *Troubling Confessions*, Peter Brooks discusses contemporary American culture's reliance on 'confessional discourse and multifarious therapeutic practice' and refers to the 'high value [that] has come to be placed on speaking confessionally' (2000: 140). Citing the popularity of the talk show, Brooks comments upon the number of people who use the tropes and strategies of confession to talk about themselves in ways that would be incomprehensible to earlier generations. The 'talking cure', he argues, 'has evolved into a generalized belief in the catharsis of confession, of the value of telling all, in public' (140). The currency of confession in contemporary culture cannot be disengaged from its long association with feminist practice and, more specifically, its implication in the (re-)mobilisation of the US women's movement in the early 1960s. Confession, after all, was central to the operations of consciousness-raising groups in the 1960s and 1970s, in which private female experience formed the impetus for political awareness and, ultimately, action. As Sheila Rowbotham, Lynne Segal and Hilary Wainwright have noted, it was women talking to other women across the private/public divide that initially marked out the political terrain of second wave feminism:

> Much oppression takes place 'in private', in areas of life considered 'personal'. The causes of that oppression are social and economic, but these causes could only be revealed and confronted when women challenged the assumptions of their personal life, of who does the housework, of the way children are brought up, the quality of our friendships, even the way we make love, with whom. These were not normally the subject of politics. Yet these are the problems of everyday life, the problems about which women talk most to other women (1979: 13).

The boundaries and politics of personal experience were thus negotiated within this context of collective consciousness-raising, which allowed for the creation of non-hierarchical and supportive environments in which women could recount their 'private' experiences.

With its roots in confessional discursive practice, second wave feminism worked to transform the social organisation and capital economy of the United States. The movement was not, however, about excavating female psychology for elusive and intangible 'inner truths', but about identifying the political operations that were at work in the private lives of women. Johanna Brenner has accredited this particular phase of the women's movement with 'substantially dismantling the legal and normative edifice which had mandated women's subservience in marriage, denied us rights in our bodies and reproductive capacity, and legitimized our economic marginalization' (1996: 20). In nostalgically echoing a pre-1960s (and, thus, pre-second wave feminism) account of suburbia, gender politics and motherhood, *Desperate Housewives* is not required to reflect the legal, economic and biological enfranchisement that followed on from second wave feminism. This ready dismissal of the politics and praxis of second wave feminism is a common element of (post-)feminism and its willingness to valorise 'traditional' models of femininity, whether ironically or otherwise (Gillis and Munford, *passim*). The dominant women of Wisteria Lane – Gabrielle Solis, Lynette Scavo, Bree Van de Kamp and Susan Mayer – are persistently represented in terms of their economic, social, physical and/or psychological dependence upon men. In this respect, the series fails to account for transformations in the sexual division of labour that have taken place in the United States since the 1960s.

More significantly, perhaps, the eponymous housewives also eschew the confessional speech acts that Brooks identifies with Western culture in the late twentieth and early twenty-first centuries, and which Brenner associates with community and catharsis. Given its location in the suburban heartland of contemporary America, the show is tellingly contingent upon a radical occlusion of community: that is, the confessional acts, which are traditionally ascribed to femininity, are resisted and transgressed by the female characters. For Michel Foucault, confession is

> a ritual that unfolds within a power relationship, for one does not confess without the presence (or virtual presence) of a partner who is not simply the interlocutor but the authority who requires the confession, prescribes and appreciates it, and intervenes in order to judge, punish, forgive, console, and reconcile (1979: 62).

In this seminal account of confession, it is configured as an act of reciprocation: information is given in exchange for an absolution or similar negotiation of this information. The economic exchange that constitutes the confession is, however, problematised by the category of gender. If, as Irene Gammel has argued, confession has traditionally been regarded as a feminised act – an account that draws upon a 'history of confessional readings [which] has created the perception of women obsessively confessing their secrets, reinforcing stereotypes of the female psyche as fragmented and, what is perhaps even worse, as "needy'" (1999: 4) – then how, we should ask, are (gendered) economies of power reinforced or subverted within the confessional exchange?

The restrictive models of feminine identity that mark the protagonists of *Desperate Housewives* are established in the first episode, in which Susan, Lynette, Bree and Gabrielle are introduced through their actions during Mary Alice's wake. Susan is characterised by her culinary incompetence, and is tacitly, but repeatedly, infantilised through her teenage daughter's manifestly sophisticated understanding of adult social and emotional relationships. In the case of Lynette, who, at her husband's instigation, has sacrificed corporate success for motherhood, domesticated social status is shown to be precariously contingent upon the good behaviour of her children as she is forced to bribe her young sons in order to ensure that she is 'not humiliated in front of the entire neighbourhood'. Bree makes no direct references to the social tensions that underwrite suburban existence, but they are writ large upon the downcast faces of her husband and two children, who trail awkwardly in her rigidly composed wake. Proficient in the classically feminine arts of cooking, sewing, homemaking and gardening, Bree is, as Mary Alice states in her voiceover, believed by everyone to be 'the perfect wife and mother. Everyone, that is, except her own family'. The relationship between Gabrielle, an ex-model, and her husband Carlos is structured around a strictly economic exchange. In their first dialogue of the season, Carlos requests that she mention the price of her necklace to an acquaintance. Gabrielle responds with a comment that has resonance beyond the value of her jewellery, asking: 'Why don't I just pin the receipt to my chest?' As Carlos asks her to keep her voice down, she sarcastically retorts that she 'wouldn't want people to think we aren't happy'. This foregrounding of the necessity of appearance strikes at the heart of *Desperate Housewives*, speaking to the emotional subterfuges that the women on the street practise among themselves: the desire for personal privacy is presented as both a broad suburban phenomenon and a defining feature of the most intimate relationships. This not only functions to illuminate the importance that is ascribed to social ritual and conformity in the suburban world of Wisteria Lane, but also, through the narration of the deceased Mary Alice, exposes the dichotomy between surface appearances and emotional realities that the inhabitants of this neighbourhood contrive to conceal.

The dissymmetry of outward appearances and concealed truths that is established in this formative sequence is crucial to the plot trajectories of the first season. In the opening episode, a flashback to a scene before Mary Alice's death has the five women sharing a coffee and providing emotional support as Susan discusses her husband's infidelity. Recalling this support, she is annoyed that Mary Alice could not share her problems with her friends: 'I'm just so angry. If Mary Alice was having problems, she should have come to us. She should have let us help her.' What Susan refuses to recognise, however, is that a resistance to public confession is hard-wired into the female inhabitants of Fairview. When the women find the anonymous letter that spurred Mary Alice's suicide they are both horrified and tantalised by its reference to secrets and confessions: 'I know what you did. It makes me sick. I'm going to tell.' It is Susan who, in asking the question – 'Oh, Mary Alice, what did you do?' – speaks to the way in which secrecy, and the *absence* of confession, governs the dynamics of suburban relationships. While the friendship between the principal female characters is, superficially, organised along the lines of confessional problem solving, their friendship lacks the intimacy and therapeutic exchange that has often distinguished televisual representations of female friendship.

The women of Wisteria Lane host weekly poker games in each other's homes, generating the potential promise of intimate female disclosure. The poker sessions do, however, foreground the importance of confession as a strategic exchange of information: exploiting the 'privacy' of the games, the women use the sessions to gossip about their neighbours and to indulge in speculation about Mary Alice's suicide. This weekly 'confessional', upon which female friendships in Wisteria Lane are based, is, in fact, characterised by deceptions and silences. As a matter of course, the participants withhold information about themselves while circulating information about anyone who is not present in the room. Based on the exchange of personal information about other people, suburban female friendship emerges as a strictly *anti*-confessional phenomenon, from which the discussion of any authentically subjective experience – of anything that might jeopardise existing domestic arrangements – is necessarily precluded. The art of silence, of withholding personal information, is thus represented as essential to the maintenance of suburban life. Accordingly, then, authentic confessional statements – those 'true' secrets, such as what Mary Alice did – are repeatedly equated with social and personal disempowerment.

When characters do engage in confessional exchange, it is always marked by the parameters of gender. Masculine confession in Wisteria Lane, for example, is always punished. Rex Van de Kamp's confessions to his wife always result in horrific situations. Confessing that he wants a divorce, he nearly dies when Bree adds onion to his salad – a vegetable to which he is highly allergic. Likewise, at a dinner party hosted by the couple, Rex, ignoring his wife's desire for secrecy, confesses to the fact that they are seeing a marriage counsellor. Having thoroughly misunderstood how confession works within the friendships of Wisteria Lane, Rex is forced to endure a very public punishment when Bree makes her own confession – 'correctly' using the information contained within the confession as a means to an end, she reveals to the dinner party that 'Rex cries after he ejaculates.' (1: 3) Other men in the show regularly misconstrue the purpose of confession: Andrew Van de Kamp horrifies his mother by confessing that he does not care about running over Juanita 'Mama' Solis; Zach Young confesses to killing a sister he never had; Tom Scavo confesses to his father that he has a secret he can never share with Lynette; John Rowland repeatedly attempts to confess to Carlos that he is having an affair with his wife. Indeed, masculine confessional practice is shown to be effective only within institutionalised spaces. Andrew uses his confessional exchange with a priest to disclose the fact that his newfound piety is an elaborate ruse. Similarly, it is to a priest that Gabrielle confesses her unwanted pregnancy. Bound by the rules of the institutionalised confessional, however, the priest is unable to reveal the details of these disclosures to those who might be affected by them – namely Bree and Carlos. When confession occurs in these traditional contexts, then, there is nowhere for the information to circulate; in other words, it does not have the audience it needs. These exchanges reveal the ineffectitude of institutionalised confession within the secretive and 'private' environment of suburbia while also, once more, articulating the way in which masculinity is somehow incompatible with the confessional practices of *Desperate Housewives*.

The gendered economy of confession, as it circulates between the female characters, differs substantially. When Gabrielle encounters financial difficulties as a result of her husband's federal indictment, she does not tell her friends. Similarly, Bree attempts to keep her husband's involvement with a local prostitute a secret from the entire community. In an interesting exchange between the two women, in which it emerges that each knows – but has not previously spoken about – the other's 'secret', Gabrielle articulates the code of suburban relationships: 'Good friends support each other after they've been humiliated. Great friends pretend nothing happened in the first place.' (1: 16) Again, the female–female confession is designated as an economic exchange, in which the revelation or concealment of information is, above all, a useful bargaining tool. Consequently, these women rarely confess on behalf of themselves, but instead confess on behalf of other people. It is perhaps Bree and Edie Britt who understand the uses of this confessional strategy most clearly. Bree's theft of Mary Alice's therapy tape – in which the latter 'confesses' her real identity – demonstrates clearly that it is the *exchange* of information that is crucial in the act of (female) confession. That is, unlike the priest, who is bound by the rules of institutionalised (masculine) confession, Bree has few scruples about stealing the tape from the therapist's office – another traditionally sacrosanct institution of the confession – and playing it to her group of friends. Likewise, having blackmailed Susan into letting her join the weekly poker game, Edie openly uses the confessional exchange of information to gain knowledge about others. For all the text's adherence to the confessional narrative, it is counter-confessional in its reliance upon secrecy and privacy. In this way, the confessional praxis and (post-)feminist politics of *Desperate Housewives* are curiously intertwined, and gesture meaningfully towards the conformity culture of the 1950s, a culture that pre-dates both second wave feminism and the testimonial age to which it gave rise.

Nostalgia and the politics of motherhood

In Arthur Marwick's formulation, social life in the formative years of the Cold War was, for the middle classes at least, defined by 'rigid social hierarchy, subordination of women to men and children to parents, repressed outlooks on sex, … respect for the flag, government, and law, formal language and etiquette' (1998: 3). Trading on the classic 1950s theme of suburbanisation, *Desperate Housewives* enacts a problematic return to a retrogressive and outmoded system of values that is redolent of the post-war social life that Marwick describes. The integrity of this value system is entirely contingent upon a binarisation of public and private space, which would guarantee that what takes place behind closed doors – which, in the context of *Desperate Housewives*, includes Rex's sadomasochism, Gabrielle's infidelity, and the murders of Zach's biological mother (Deirdre Taylor, played by Jolie Jenkins) and Martha Huber – is prevented from rupturing the respectable surface of civic life. As *Desperate Housewives* persistently demonstrates, however, suburbia is an environment in which the distinction between public and private is eminently collapsible, and confessional discourse is positioned as dangerous precisely because of its capacity to initiate this collapse. Even the earliest accounts of suburbanisation remark upon the association of suburban architecture with a dream of privacy that is inconsistent with the 'profound *deprivation* of privacy' that structures social interactions within the suburban environment (Nelson 2002: 84–85; emphasis in original). This paradox is embroidered into the fabric of suburban life, and is evidenced in the types of anxieties that came to characterise the decade of the 1950s, during which the suburban explosion took place. Just as communism represented a threat to the American ideal of liberty, it also imperilled the privacy that was widely perceived to be indissoluble from this liberty. In this context, the preservation of capitalist liberties became increasingly synonymous with the successful fortification of the private realm. Paradoxically, however, as communism was widely interpreted as an insidious, internal danger, the Cold War generated a social climate in which surveillance – the violation of personal privacy – was increasingly admissible. Codified in the concept of privacy, civil liberties were at once preserved and infringed in the name of domestic security.

In *Desperate Housewives* the precariousness of domestic security is translated into spatial terms, as the architectural borders of the home – which formalise the boundary between public and private – are persistently violated. During the course of the first season, Susan secretly enters the properties of both Edie and Paul Young: overhearing the former in the throes of that most private of exchanges – sexual intercourse – Susan 'accidentally' burns her house down. Julie Mayer raids Martha's home for the measuring jug that proves her mother's involvement in the fire at Edie's while Mike Delfino gains illegal access to a number of local properties in the course of his secret 'investigation'. Similarly, Zach trespasses upon the Van de Kamp and Mayer properties before breaking into Mike's house in the season finale (1: 23). In this way, the threats that are mounted against the security of Wisteria Lane are located primarily within the circumscribed geography of that same suburban street. This situation is clearly redolent of the climate of anxiety that pervaded America in the early years of the Cold War, in which 'millions of Americans [were persuaded] to interpret their world in terms of insidious enemies at home and abroad who threatened them with nuclear and other forms of annihilation' (Whitfield 1991: 118). If the retroactive dimensions of *Desperate Housewives* allude to this historical moment, they also work to imitate the socio-political dynamics of a post-9/11 United States, in which the threat of international terrorism has been constructed, in the most explicit terms, as a threat from within. In the American ideology of the 1950s, the home was regarded as central to issues of national security, and was situated as the 'best bulwark against the dangers of the cold war', and the site at which the 'potentially dangerous social forces of the new age might be tamed' (May 1988: xviii; xxv). This model of domesticity has been notably re-emergent in this post-9/11 era, in which the Bush administration has repeatedly remarked on the importance of home and family in the fight against radical ideologies.

Central to the domestic politics of *Desperate Housewives* is the figure of the mother. Given that Marc Cherry's inspiration for the series emerged from a conversation with his mother in which she expressed sympathy for Andrea Yates, a Texas woman who murdered her five children because she was, in her own words, a 'bad mother', it is perhaps no surprise that ambivalence is the governing principle in the show's depictions of maternity, and in the attitude it assumes towards the 'good' mother/'bad' mother binary (Goodman 2004). In order to examine the construction of motherhood in *Desperate Housewives*, it will first be necessary to explicate the terms of this binary by providing a brief account of how the divergent notions of 'good' and 'bad' mothering have grown up within American culture. Reflecting on the early capitalist period in the United States, Nancy Chodorow, in *The Reproduction of Mothering*, usefully identifies the ideological inception of the 'moral mother'; the bourgeois female who is required to act 'both as [the] nurturant moral [model]' to her children and as nurturant supporter and moral guide to her husband on 'his return from the immoral, competitive world of work' (1978: 5). Historically, then, the 'good' mother has been constructed within American culture as the figure upon whom the stability of the family, the community and society (in the broadest sense) is radically contingent. Writing in the late 1970s, Chodorow argues that the ideology of the 'moral mother' remained embedded in the structures of the American family, extending its influence 'throughout society', and providing the standard by which an increasingly diverse population of women were to measure domestic competence (1978: 5).

While this strategic installation of the 'moral mother' as the guarantor of domestic well-being seems, superficially at least, to elevate the social currency of motherhood, it simultaneously elicits another, concomitant circumstance: if the mother is to be exalted for the favourable effects of her domestic influence, then it follows that she must also be held to account for any negative outcomes that might be ascribed to her mothering praxis. For Betty Friedan in *The Feminine Mystique* (1963), the acknowledgement of the importance of maternal agency is awkwardly coalescent with the post-war absorption of Freudian thought – with its well-established centralisation of the mother figure – into popular cultural forms. This convergence, Friedan suggests, gave way to a situation in the 1950s (and beyond) in which 'the mother could be blamed for almost everything. In every case history of troubled child [and] otherwise disturbed American could be found a mother' (1992: 165). Taking our cue from Friedan and Chodorow, we would suggest that the intense cultural focalisation of the maternal function, and the distinction between 'good' and 'bad' standards of mothering to which this rationale gives rise, remains problematically operational in *Desperate Housewives*. Although it is too simplistic to suggest that *Desperate Housewives* turns on the vexed binary of the good/bad mother, there is clearly a sense in which each of the women in the show are tacitly indicted for their various maternal shortcomings.

In *Homeward Bound* (1988), Elaine Tyler May examines the extent to which Cold War political ideologies – particularly those of containment and conformity – intersect with the sentiments that fuelled the domestic-familial revival of the 1950s. In this post-war context, motherhood was idealised as the 'ultimate fulfilment of female sexuality and the primary source of a woman's identity' (1988: 25). Motherhood, through its potential to contain the destabilising forces of unregulated female sexuality, is similarly codified within *Desperate Housewives* as an integral component of respectable suburban femininity. Of the women who feature prominently in the series, only the narcissistic and adulterous Gabrielle is (initially) childless, but she must battle furiously (and futilely) with her husband to remain so. Even Edie, the neighbourhood 'bad girl', has a son, though her sexual empowerment casts her as a 'bad', neglectful mother – a foil to the legions of dedicated maternal figures that populate the Fairview landscape. In the case of the 'perfect' mother, Bree, her meticulous fulfilment of the maternal function is equated with a domestic automatism that alienates her from the emotional lives of her teenage children. Her son questions her investment in the domestic life of the family, commenting that she acts as though she is 'running for mayor of Stepford' (1: 1). When the Van de Kamps embark upon divorce proceedings and their children display a reluctance to live with their mother, her maternal role is placed in direct peril. Falling victim to her blackmail – employed to ensure that she retains custody of the children – her son confesses to a priest that he will one day wreak a horrible revenge upon his mother and 'do something so awful [it] is really going to destroy her' (1: 19). Bree's conformity to a socially constructed standard of maternal perfection is not only shown to be irreconcilable with private familial harmony, but is also represented as directly endangering the (re)production of standard codes of morality.

Despite the trials that motherhood poses to the women of Wisteria Lane, the urge to confess to the frustrations and ambivalences that attend the daily business of mothering is rarely indulged. As Simone de Beauvoir comments in 1949 in *The Second Sex*, secrecy is written into the maternal contract. This secrecy is motivated by the mother's 'delight in surrounding with mystery an experience that belongs exclusively to [her]' and a darker impulse to conceal the 'inner contradictions and conflicts' that might vex the status of the 'good' mother (1997: 510). In accordance with de Beauvoir's observation, the female protagonists of *Desperate Housewives* rarely allude to the precariousness of their maternality, and especially avoid confessing to their (potential) maternal shortcomings. Indeed, the only maternal confessional exchange of the first season is prompted by Lynette's dramatic desertion of her children. Addicted to her children's Attention Deficit Disorder (ADD) medication, Lynette has a suicidal hallucination while standing at the kitchen sink (1: 8). Looking out of the privacy of the kitchen where the 'therapeutic' poker parties often take place, an angelic, light-haloed Mary Alice moves across her lawn and hands Lynette the gun with which she committed suicide. Raising the gun to her own head, Lynette experiences a fleeting identification with Mary Alice, whose suicide she clearly (mis)reads as an act of domestic isolation. Lynette is so traumatised that she leaves her children with Susan and runs off. When Susan and Bree finally locate her, it is her despair at her (lack of) child-rearing instincts that precipitates a discussion about motherhood and its cult of secrecy. Lynette confesses her perceived maternal failure and, for once, this confession is met by similar confessions. Susan divulges that when her daughter was a baby she was 'out of [her] mind almost every day', and Bree comments that she used her children's nap times to cry. Yet this frank acknowledgement of the difficulties of motherhood is a brief, unrepresentative moment in the trajectory of the first season, and the women are quickly returned to the privacy and secrecy of their homes and respective mothering praxes.

The figure of the ruthless, overprotective mother casts a dark shadow over the inhabitants of Wisteria Lane, and suburban motherhood is constructed as an underhand, and often brutal, enterprise that poses a distinct threat to the norms and values that it outwardly upholds. In this way, motherhood, as it is represented in *Desperate Housewives*, is strongly echoic of Philip Wylie's cult of 'momism', which is pitched by May as 'the result of frustrated women who smothered their children with overprotection and overaffection' (1988: 64). The viewing audience is exposed directly and indirectly to various exemplars of this 'momistic' existence. The detective hired by Paul Young makes pointed reference to a 'PTA mom [who] was hell-bent on landing her daughter a spot on the parade float [and] fed antifreeze to half the homecoming committee' (1: 7). It is Mama Solis and Bree, however, who provide the most chilling illustrations of this overzealous mode of child-rearing. Mama Solis, attempting to solicit evidence of her daughter-in-law's suspected infidelity, warns her of the lengths to which a mother will go to ensure the happiness of her offspring: 'All mothers know they have to protect their children, but some of us take our job more seriously than others.' This, coupled with the enigmatic confession that she, by some vague but nefarious means, made sure her abusive husband 'never hurt my son or me again', evokes a network of injurious praxis that is not only veiled, but also mitigated and absolved by the protective function of motherhood (1: 5). Within the feminised context of the suburban environment, motherhood is thus poised as the major source of women's agency within the domestic-familial matrix, and manifests itself in everything from Susan's surreptitious surveillance of her daughter's telephone conversations with Zach, to Bree's instrumental role in sabotaging her son's chances of a college swimming scholarship as a means of punishing him for his persistent displays of arrogance and insensitivity.

In this way, motherhood is placed in the register of endangerment: a condition in which the mother is always, simultaneously, threatening and under threat. While Mama Solis is run over – an incident that leads indirectly to her death – following her successful attempt to procure proof of her daughter-in-law's adultery, Bree's outward status as the perfect mother earns her nothing but contempt within the ranks of her own family (1: 1; 1: 7). Ultimately, however, these extreme manifestations of motherly emotion must remain clandestine. It is, of course, Mary Alice's unchecked maternal instinct, and her husband's attempts to conceal its most violent expression, which organise the revelatory story arc of the first season. In the first instance, it is Mary

Alice's intense desire for a baby that prompts her to 'buy' Dana, the child of Deirdre, the drug-addicted girlfriend of a young Mike Delfino, who is known to Mary Alice from her work as a nurse at a Utah hospital. Relocating from Utah to Fairview, and forging new identities for herself, her husband and her recently acquired infant, Mary Alice operates in a conventional, and demonstrably protective, maternal mode. Within the potentially distorting frame of her husband's flashback, Mary Alice is shown cooking dinner for her family and asking Paul to erect a fence in the backyard to prevent Zach from falling into the pool (1: 23). It is only when a rehabilitated Deirdre traverses the borders of the Young home, demanding the return of her biological child, that we witness Mary Alice's second and catastrophic display of motherly fervour. As Deirdre attacks Paul with a poker, thus foiling his attempt to prevent her gaining access to her child, Mary Alice grabs a knife and coolly stabs her maternal competitor to death. Paul's astonished exclamation of 'Oh, Mary Alice. What did you do?' replicates Susan's innocent questioning of Mary Alice's suicidal motive in the opening episode (1: 1; 1: 23). While Susan's question expresses regret that Mary Alice felt unable to disclose the reasons for her suicide to her friends, Paul's repetition of the question (re)asserts the ultimate inexplicability of maternal emotion, which is finally established as something dangerous and irrational that must remain concealed.

Gendered economies

Given the ways in which confession is central to both the friendships and the social fabric of Wisteria Lane, it is not surprising that the series is held together by the confessional voiceover of Mary Alice. Willing to kill to keep her child and her dream of domestic bliss – although not willing to let this truth emerge for the scrutiny of her suburban neighbours – she acts both as an über-confessor and confessant. Able to hear the secrets of her former neighbours and to weave them into the narrative that is *Desperate Housewives*, Mary Alice also reveals tantalising fragments of her own secret crime as the season progresses. Indeed, in a text in which bad things happen when men confess, nothing happens when women try *not* to confess. Although the confession of the clue to the season-long mystery – what did Mary Alice do? – is diegetically provided by a man, it is presented as the long-withheld statement of Mary Alice. This withholding of a confession within a text that is marked by its confessional framework is evidence of the way in which the (feminine) confessional paradigm facilitates evasion. Although a text that is ostensibly predicated upon female friendship, the reliability, truthfulness or usability of feminine confession in *Desperate Housewives* is rejected. The season ends with the dismissal of any authority that had been ascribed to the female confessional narrative, and the maternal is again silenced through the aggressive assertion of masculinity. The answer to Susan's question – 'Mary Alice, what did you do?' – is revealed by Mary Alice's husband, Paul, to Mike, in a space other than Wisteria Lane, and one which is strongly evocative of the masculinised world of the hard-boiled detective thriller. The women of Wisteria Lane are not, however, privy to the answer, as Paul's version of events becomes 'the' truth about Mary Alice and her motherhood. The season ends with the only male confession that does not result in punishment, as Mike's dazed realisation that he may be the father of Zach means that he does not kill Paul as he intended. In this way, paternality replaces maternality, and masculinity is ultimately valorised as the site of authority in *Desperate Housewives*.

17

Desperately debating housewives

Jennifer L. Pozner and Jessica Seigel

Dear Jessica,

Say it ain't so! I hear you love *Desperate Housewives*, ABC's hit series that cynically reinforces sexual, racial and class stereotypes. If that's true, you're in some questionable company.

On the episode of CNN's *Crossfire* during which he mocked 'grouchy feminists with moustaches', Tucker Carlson praised *Housewives* as 'good entertainment'. *Washington Times* columnist Suzanne Fields described it as 'sophisticated, edgy television for the era of the values voters who kept George W. on Pennsylvania Avenue' (2004).

It's no wonder right-wing culture warriors such as Carlson and Fields love a show whose world-view harks back to a time when two-parent, middle-class families could comfortably thrive on single incomes, women's identities were primarily determined by the men they married and the children they raised, and husbands were not expected to trouble themselves with such pesky matters as childcare and housework.

Housewives' Wisteria Lane is even set on the same Hollywood back lot where *Leave It To Beaver* was filmed.

Hyped as a cunning parody, *Housewives* is light on actual satire and heavy on the sorts of cultural clichés that play well at red state country clubs. Of the four main characters, three are white, all are wealthy and only one has a job – divorced mom Susan Mayer, supposedly a children's book illustrator. The only non-white wife,

Gabrielle Solis, plays into every tired cliché about oversexed, 'spicy' Latina gold-diggers.

On Wisteria Lane, female friendships are shallow and only superficially supportive, and the rare woman who doesn't conform to an ultra-thin, waxed ideal of beauty gets strangled in her kitchen (literally, as happened to a plump, nosy neighbour).

Jessica, when you find yourself enjoying a show that the *Chicago Tribune* encouraged readers to watch by saying, 'Women viewers may find it offensive to wives, mothers, suburbanites and feminists alike. Definitely stay tuned', it may be time to re-evaluate your analysis. Is there something I'm missing?

Desperately Hating Housewives,
Jenn

* * * *

Dear Desperately Hating,

Yup, you're missing plenty, Jenn, like the delicious Sunday evenings I spend coffee-klatching with my best friend over this madcap send-up of the *Leave It To Beaver* American dream. This show doesn't 'hark back' to the past – it skewers the myth of motherhood and suburban bliss with *Feminine Mystique*-inspired irony so sly that conservatives are as divided as liberals over whether to love it or hate it.

Its stealth feminism has not been lost on the 'values' crowd, including Rev. Donald Wildmon's American Family Association (AFA), which predictably denounced the show as immoral. Not surprisingly, Wildmon's group condemned its adulterous antics but not the murderous ones, singling out Gabrielle's affair with a hunky teenage gardener. Disgusting, isn't it? Adult women finally get to ogle hottie jailbait without feeling like Mrs Robinson – a visual *droit du seigneur* long enjoyed by men.

Yeah, adultery is bad. I'm against it. But *girl talk*? The AFA condemns that, too, as spokesman Randy Sharp told the *Chicago Tribune*: 'Our objection to *Desperate Housewives* is that ... discussion of intimate details between individuals is open for "girl talk," for lack of a better phrase.'

Real ladies, we know, shut up and suffer in silence. Girl talk, in fact – formalised as consciousness-raising groups – helped fuel the women's movement. The personal was political, then and now. *Desperate Housewives* dramatises the 'Second Shift' realities of an America in which even full-time working women do most of the housework and only 5 per cent of men take primary responsibility for childcare. Girl talk is subversive, and it's the emotional heart of *Housewives*, as our four heroines lean on each other to navigate troubled marriages, divorce, children and romance.

Male characters are peripheral on the show, which has resurrected the careers of three fine actresses over age forty – a rarity on sweet-young-thing-obsessed prime-time television.

I think you confuse the starring quartet's long-time, sometimes ambivalent friendships – as in real life – with their spicy conflicts with secondary characters such as the neighbourhood biddy (true, the only fatty). Still, when men fight we call it politics; when women fight it's derided as backbiting or catfighting – words that denigrate females jockeying for position and power.

This show exposes a *Diary of a Mad Housewife* reality and the power of sisterhood. For example, when former corporate honcho Lynette Scavo's four unruly children make her suicidal, she confesses to her buddies that motherhood is driving her crazy. 'Why don't they tell us this stuff?' she whines. 'Why don't we talk about this?'

So they talk. When we finally get a prime-time hit about women's domestic struggles – previously relegated to sappy daytime soaps – why is it a lightning rod for everything wrong with TV and America, including racism, classism and lookism?

Jenn, come on, join our coffee klatch – but no talking except during commercials. Can't you see the winking subversion beneath the impossibly thin, nouveau-riche façade? Or are you lining up with family-values conservatives on this one, like some feminists did in the 1980s anti-pornography movement?

Desperately Loving Housewives,
Jess

* * * *

Hey Jess,

If you want 'family-values conservatives', don't look to me – look to *Desperate Housewives*' creator Marc Cherry, a gay Republican who believes the real problem facing today's post-feminist women is too much freedom.

As he told the *Contra Costa Times*, 'We've reached the point where we realize that no, you really can't have it all … Long ago, it used to be easier: Society laid down the rules for you. Now, there are a lot of choices, but sometimes choices can lead to chaos.'

Where, exactly, does the 'skewering' come in? Certainly not from the show's majority-male writers, or from its creator, who says *Housewives* is darkly comic but not satirical.

'Satire sounds like you're making fun of something. And the truth is, I'm not making fun of the suburbs.' Cherry told The Associated Press, adding to *Entertainment Weekly*, 'I love the values the suburbs represent. Family, community, God.'

But since 'stuff happens', the 'fun' comes from watching women 'making bad choices' and suffering the repercussions. That's not 'stealth feminism', it's just vindictive. Nor is it new – the right loves punishing female sinners. Sadly, you're buying into regressive stereotyping gussied up as female empowerment.

It's fabulous that it illuminates the frustrations accompanying stay-at-home motherhood. But while writer Ellen Goodman points to Lynette as a 'signpost of a slowly changing society' and the *Pittsburgh Post-Gazette* branded her a 'Generation's Truthsayer', they (and you) are ignoring the show's fundamental premise that childcare is solely women's responsibility. Doesn't it bother you that Lynette is the very model of silent suffering?

In a key flashback, she nods in queasy acquiescence when her husband tells her to quit her career to stay at home with her babies. And no matter how low she sinks under the pressure of raising four kids – popping their ADD pills, self-medicating with red wine – she never asks her husband to share the burden.

As the former hostess of weekly *Xena, Warrior Princess* and *Buffy, the Vampire Slayer* parties, I'd happily join a coffee klatch centred around subversive, kitschy girl power. Friendships between intelligent, fleshed-out female characters were powerful enough to save the world on those shows; in contrast, the *Housewives* keep secrets from – rather than lean on – each other.

Look, I appreciate a good comedy as much as the next gal, but this show is more dangerous than a simple guilty pleasure – it's backlash humour hawking conservative ideology. For example, biological determinism explains a PTA mom's back-stabbing behaviour:

'It hasn't really changed since Girl Scouts. Girls smile at you to your face, but then behind your back they make fun of you,' Susan complains.

'That never would have happened in Boy Scouts,' answers Lynette. 'A guy takes his opponent on face to face, and once he's won, he's top dog. It's primitive but fair.'

'Isn't it sexist of us to generalize like this?' Gabrielle asks.

'It's science, Gabrielle' says Lynette. 'Sociologists have documented this stuff.'

'Well, who am I to argue with sociologists,' Gabrielle shrugs.

This is what passes for 'girl talk' on Wisteria Lane – too bad it sounds so much like the Best of Dr Laura.

Desperately Missing Roseanne,
Jenn

* * * *

Dear Jenn,

At least we agree that *Desperate Housewives* is 'darkly comic'. Webster's says comedy is 'the representation of human error and weakness as provocative of amusement'. That means screw-ups and bad choices – which you seem to see as 'vindictive' to women. Does that mean Jerry Lewis, the Marx Brothers and Three Stooges are 'vindictive' to men? But I won't suggest you 'lighten up', because 'Can't you take a joke?' is often used to undermine legitimate social critique.

Instead, I will deconstruct the joke. On *Desperate*, we're in the land of camp, that often gay, exaggerated aesthetic the late Susan Sontag so brilliantly pegged in her 1964 essay 'Notes on Camp'. *Housewives* is a textbook case, beginning with the 'double sense in which some things can be taken' – a 'private zany experience' for insiders.

Sontag's characteristics of camp also include exaggerated sex roles, shallow characters, overweening passion, heightened glamour, even pleasure in the 'psychopathology of affluence'. That's exactly life on Wisteria Lane: murder, suicide, paedophilia, adultery, prostitution and drug abuse, all on one fabulously landscaped suburban street.

Desperate creator Marc Cherry – who began his career writing for another woman-centred camp classic, *The Golden Girls* – claims to be a gay Republican (what could be campier?) while creating a show that's cul-de-sac Sodom.

You 'got' the tongue-in-cheek aesthetic of *Xena* and *Buffy* because you liked the subject of superheroes fighting evil. I loved them too. But you're so offended by stay-at-home moms that *Housewives'* camp style doesn't register. Yet it's crucial. The show is not making policy recommendations about childcare any more than it is recommending fornication and a multitude of sins yet to come (stay tuned!).

But enough critical theory – let's get to the burrito sex scene, my favourite. To win back her husband, domestic diva Bree arrives at his hotel room wearing only red lingerie under an overcoat. At that very moment, however, he is chowing down on a giant burrito. The husband takes the bait, but, no surprise, the burrito topples from the table and distracts her. His wife's concern with a teetering bean wrap symbolises how she makes him feel stifled.

The camera steps in as feminist, zooming in on the cheesy mess about to hit the floor. Who could think of sex at a time like that? Not us. As Infuriated Husband escorts her out, Bree quips: 'Obviously you've never had to clean a cheese stain off a carpet.'

'You bet, honey,' I tell the TV. I've also urged Lynette to go back to work part-time, even while I identify with her pleasure in feminine arts I love, like sewing. These are women's concerns in a fortysomething woman's world, so rarely seen on prime-time television. That's my 'zany private' experience as a feminist who believes women are good enough to be bad.

Still Loving Housewives,
Jessica

* * * *

Hey Jessica,

What's with your accusation that I'm 'offended by stay-at-home moms', rather than by a show which treats them so shabbily? I'm surprised you'd dust off the tired, misguided media chestnut, painting feminists as anti-mother. I never implied that mothers shouldn't stay home if they want to (and if they can – that choice is a luxury in today's economy).

Jess, I don't need you to deconstruct the joke for me – I just don't buy it. When Roseanne Barr wrestled Meryl Streep in the film *She Devil*, that was camp. But when a bunch of conservative guys create a show in which every female character is portrayed as self-indulgent and incompetent, that's just good old-fashioned Hollywood crap.

Can you really be so elitist as to think that burrito stains and arts and crafts are the 'woman's world' concerns that most deserve celluloid attention? As for Lynette's 'pleasure' in sewing school-play costumes, please – that 'feminine art' drove her to drugs!

The Golden Girls played by their own rules, letting no societal code (and no man) dictate their behaviour. Twenty years later, Lynette lives her husband's choices, Gabrielle trades sex for jewellery, 'good girl' Susan is pitted against the 'town slut', and Bree would rather keep a cheap motel's carpet clean than have an orgasm.

Yet that's why corporate media finds Wisteria's women so appealing. Remember when *Time* cited neurotic, micro-miniskirted Ally McBeal as the poster girl for the supposed death of feminism in 1998? Seven years later, it's the same old story: reviewers from *The Washington Post* to *The Jerusalem Post* insist *Housewives* represents 'reality' in a 'typical' American neighbourhood, and proves feminism has 'failed' or been 'killed'.

By the time Oprah Winfrey and Dr Phil paraded around 'Real-Life Desperate Housewives', I was ready to throw up. This show and its 1950s politics are being used against us; don't confuse that with feminism.

At least Buffy's *on DVD,*
Jenn

* * * *

Dear Jenn –

You have tried to indict *Desperate Housewives* and its fans with charges of male oppression and elitism. I beg to differ.

Hardly a male cabal, the *Desperate* writing staff is one-third female – slightly exceeding the percentage of women in the Writer's Guild of America, and much higher than that of, say, the popular sitcom *Everybody Loves Raymond* (only one of ten writers is a woman this season).

As to elitism, in today's economy, stay-at-home parenting is no 'luxury', as you claim, but a savings for many families, considering childcare costs, income taxes and commuting expenses. So much for *Housewives = haute bourgeoisie*.

You also imply that sewing is elitist. Careerism and girl-power fantasy blind you to women's real experience and history. I learned sewing from my grandmother, who learned from her mother, a seamstress. Making my own clothes is a proud working-class legacy.

Yes, the backlash scolds women. But so do you. You cherry-pick grievances, first faulting a character's 'silent suffering', then branding the *Housewives* as 'self-indulgent'. Which is it? Neither. They're cartoon characters. This is high camp, which Sontag calls a multilayered 'mode of enjoyment, of appreciation – not judgment'.

You're still welcome to come over for *Desperate* night – I'll teach you to sew (during commercials). We'll start simple: maybe an apron.

Yours in stitches,
Jessica
Originally appeared in *Ms.* magazine Spring 2005:
http://www.msmagazine.com/spring2005/desperatehousewives.as.

EPISODE GUIDE

Season One: (2004): US premiere 3 October 2004

1: 1 'Pilot'
    w: Marc Cherry
    d: Charles McDougall

1: 2 'Ah, But Underneath'
    w: Marc Cherry
    d: Larry Shaw

1: 3 'Pretty Little Picture'
    w: Oliver Goldstick
    d: Arlene Sanford

1: 4 'Who's That Woman?'
    w: Marc Cherry and Tom Spezialy
    d: Jeffrey Melman

1: 5 'Come In Stranger'
    w: Alexandra Cunningham
    d: Arlene Sanford

1: 6 'Running To Stand Still'
    w: Tracey Stern
    d: Fred Gerber

1: 7 'Anything You Can Do'
    w: John Pardee and Joey Murphy
    d: Larry Shaw

1: 8 'Guilty'
    w: Kevin Murphy
    d: Fred Gerber

1: 9 'Suspicious Minds'
    w: Jenna Bans
    d: Larry Shaw

1: 10 'Come Back to Me'
w: Patty Lin
d: Fred Gerber

1: 11 'Move On'
w: David Schulner
d: John David Coles

1: 12 'Every Day a Little Death'
w: Chris Black
d: David Grossman

1: 13 'Your Fault'
w: Kevin Etten
d: Arlene Sanford

1: 14 'Love Is in the Air'
w: Tom Spezialy
d: Jeffrey Melman

1: 15 'Impossible'
w: Marc Cherry and Tom Spezialy
d: Larry Shaw

1: 16 'The Ladies Who Lunch'
w: Alexandra Cunningham
d: Arlene Sanford

1: 17 'There Won't Be Trumpets'
w: Joey Murphy and John Pardee
d: Jeffrey Melman

1: 18 'Children Will Listen'
w: Kevin Murphy
d: Larry Shaw

1: 19 'Live Alone and Like It (aka. An Unexpected Song)'
w: Arlene Sanford and Jenna Bans
d: Arlene Sanford

1: 20 'Fear No More'
w: Adam Barr
d: Jeffrey Melman

1: 21 'Sunday in the Park With George'
w: Katie Ford
d: Larry Shaw

1: 22 'Goodbye For Now'

w: Joshua Senter
d: David Grossman
1: 23 'One Wonderful Day'
w: Marc Cherry, Kevin Murphy, Joey Murphy, John
Pardee and Tom Spezialy
d: Larry Shaw

Season Two: (2005): US premiere 2 October 2005

2: 1 'Next'
w: Jenna Bans and Kevin Murphy
d: Larry Shaw
2: 2 'You Could Drive a Person Crazy'
w: Alexandra Cunningham and Chris Black
d: David Grossman
2: 3 'You'll Never Get Away From Me'
w: Tom Spezialy and Ellen Herman
d: Arlene Sanford
2: 4 'My Heart Belongs To Daddy'
w: Joey Murphy and John Pardee
d: Robert Duncan McNeill
2: 5 'They Asked Me Why I Believe in You'
w: Alan Cross
d: David Grossman
2: 6 'I Wish I Could Forget You'
w: Kevin Etten
d: Larry Shaw
2: 7 'Color and Light (aka. I Must Be Dreaming)'
w: Marc Cherry
d: David Grossman
2: 8 'The Sun Won't Set'
w: Jenna Bans
d: Stephen Cragg
2: 9 'That's Good, That's Bad'
w: Kevin Murphy
d: Larry Shaw
2: 10 'Coming Home (aka. I've Got You Under My Skin)'

w: Chris Black
d: Arlene Sanford
2: 11 'One More Kiss'
   w: Joey Murphy and John Pardee
   d: Wendey Stanzler
2: 12 'We're Gonna Be All Right'
   w: Alexandra Cunningham
   d: David Grossman
2: 13 'There's Something About a War'
   w: Kevin Etten
   d: Larry Shaw
2: 14 'Silly People'
   w: Tom Spezialy
   d: Robert Duncan McNeill
2: 15 'Thank You so Much'
   w: Dahvi Waller
   d: David Grossman
2: 16 'There Is No Other Way'
   w: Marc Cherry and Bruce Zimmerman
   d: Randall Zisk
2: 17 'Could I Leave You?'
   w: Marc Cherry and Scott Sanlord Tobis
   d: Pam Thomas
2: 18 'Everybody Says Don't'
   w: Jenna Bans and Alexandra Cunningham
   d: Tom Cherones
2: 19 'Don't Look at Me'
   w: Joshua Senter
   d: David Grossman
2: 20 'It Wasn't Meant to Happen'
   w: Marc Cherry and Tom Spezialy
   d: Larry Shaw
2: 21 'I Know Things Now'
   w: Kevin Etten and Bruce Zimmerman
   d: Wendey Stanzler
2: 22 'No One Is Alone'
   w: Chris Black and Kevin Murphy

d: David Grossman
2: 23 'Remember: Part 1'
   w: Jenna Bans and Marc Cherry
   d: Larry Shaw
2: 24 'Remember: Part 2'
   w: Jenna Bans and Marc Cherry
   d: Larry Shaw

FILM AND TV GUIDE

TV

Adventures of Ozzie and Harriet, The (Stage Five Productions/American Broadcasting Company, 1952–1966)

All In the Family (Norman Lear Productions/CBS Television, 1971–1979)

Ally McBeal (20th Century Fox Television/Fox Network, 1997–2002)

Bewitched (ABC, 1964–1972)

Charmed (Spelling Television/The WB Television Network, 1998–2006)

CSI: Crime Scene Investigation (Jerry Bruckheimer Television/CBS Television, 2000–)

Dallas (Lorimar Television/CBS Television, 1978–1991)

Days of Our Lives (Columbia TriStar Television Inc./National Broadcasting Company, 1965–)

Designing Women (Columbia Pictures Television/CBS Television, 1986–1993)

Dynasty (Aaron Spelling Productions Inc./ABC, 1981–1989)

Everybody Loves Raymond (Talk Productions/HBO, 1996–2005)

Family Law (Columbia TriStar Television Inc./CBS Television, 1999–2002)

Father Knows Best (Screen Gems Television/CBS Television, 1954–1960)

Five Mrs Buchanans, The (Marc Cherry/CBS Television, 1994–1995)

Golden Girls, The (Touchstone Television/NBC, 1985–1992)

Hill Street Blues (MTM Enterprises Inc./20th Century Fox Television, 1981–1987)

Hooperman (ABC, 1987–1989)

How Clean Is Your House? (Fremantle Media North America/Lifetime Television, 2004–)

I Love Lucy (Desilu Productions/CBS Television, 1951–1957)

Judging Amy (Barbara Hall/Joseph Stern Productions/CBS Television, 1999–2005)

Knots Landing (Lorimar Television/Warner Bros Television, 1979–1993)

L Word, The (Viacom Productions/Showtime Networks Inc, 2004–)

Law and Order (NBC Universal Television/NBC, 1990–)

Leave It To Beaver (Revue Studios/ABC, 1957–1963)

Lois & Clark: The New Adventures of Superman (Warner Bros Television/ABC, 1993–1997)

Lost (Touchstone Television, ABC, 2004–)

Maude (Norman Lear/Tandem Productions/CBS Television, 1972–1978)

Melrose Place (Darren Star Productions/Fox Network, 1992–1999)

Moonlighting (ABC, 1985–1989)

Monday Night Football (National Football League (NFL/ABC, 1970–)

Murphy Brown (Warner Bros Television/CBS Television, 1988–1998)

My So-Called Life (Bedford Falls Productions/ABC, 1994–1995)

Nanny 911 (Granada Entertainment USA/Fox Television, 2004–)

Newlyweds (7 Network/Media Arts, 1993–1994)

O.C., The (Warner Brothers Television/Fox Film Corporation, 2003–)

Oprah Winfrey Show, The (Harpo Productions/King World Productions, 1986–)

Queer As Folk (Cowlip Productions/Showtime Networks Inc., 2000–2005)

Roseanne (Carsey-Werner Company/ABC, 1988–1997)

St Elsewhere (MTM Productions/20th Century Fox Television, 1982–1988)

Sex and the City (Darren Star Productions/HBO, 1998–2004)

Six Feet Under (The Greenblatt Janollari Studio/HBO, 2001–2005)

Soccer Moms (Touchstone Pictures/ABC Video, 2005–)

Sopranos, The (Chase Films/HBO, 1999–2007)

Super Nanny (Ricochet Productions (II)/ABC, 2005/I–)

thirtysomething (Bedford Falls Productions/ABC, 1987–1991)

Trading Spouses: Meet Your New Mommy (Rocket Science Laboratories/Fox Television, 2004–)

Twin Peaks (Lynch/Frost Productions/ABC, 1990–1991)
Weeds (Lions Gate Television/Showtime Networks Inc., 2005–)
Who Wants to be a Millionaire? (Celador/ABC, 2002–)
Wife Swap (RDF Media/ABC, 2004–2005)
Will and Grace (KoMut Entertainment/NBC, 1998–2006)
The Wonder Years (ABC, 1988–1993)

Film

A Letter to Three Wives (Joseph L. Manciewicz, 1949)
Aliens (James Cameron, 1986)
American Beauty (Sam Mendes, 1999)
Blade Runner (Ridley Scott, 1982)
Blue Velvet (David Lynch, 1986)
Bridget Jones' Diary (Sharon Maguire, 2001)
Diary of a Mad Housewife (Frank Perry, 1970)
Double Indemnity (Billy Wilder, 1944)
Edward Scissorhands (Tim Burton, 1990)
Far From Heaven (Todd Haynes, 2002)
Fellowship of the Ring, The (Peter Jackson, 2001)
Fried Green Tomatoes (Jon Avnet, 1991)
Mean Girls (Mark Waters, 2004)
Mildred Pierce (Michael Curtiz, 1945)
Out of the Past (Jacques Tourneur, 1947)
Phantom Menace, The (George Lucas, 1999)
Planet of the Apes (Franklin J. Schaffner, 1968)
Pretty Woman (Gary Marshall, 1990)
Rebecca (Alfred Hitchcock, 1940)
Safe (Todd Haynes, 1995)
She Devil (Susan Seidelman, 1989)
Snake Pit, The (Anatole Litvak, 1948)
Stepford Wives, The (Bryan Forbes, 1975)
Sunset Boulevard (Billy Wilder, 1950)
Transamerica (Duncan Tucker, 2005)
Working Girl (Mike Nichols, 1988)

BIBLIOGRAPHY

Anon. 'Desperate Housewives Style Guide'. *Heat.* 4–10 June 2005: 73–74, 76.

Anon. 'Style in the Suburbs'. *Now.* 13 April 2005: 52–53.

Adamson, Rondi. 'Why So Desperate to Parse the Popularity of *Housewives?*' *Christian Science Monitor.* 4 February 2005: 9.

Alexander, Jeff and Tom Bissell. *Speak, Commentary: The Big Little Book of Fake DVD Commentaries, Wherein Well-Known Pundits Make Impassioned Remarks About Classic Science Fiction Films. It's a Gas!* San Francisco: McSweeney's Books, 2003.

Ang, Ien. *Watching Dallas: Soap Opera and the Melodramatic Imagination.* London: Methuen, 1985.

Arthur, Kate. *The New York Times.* 52. 10 April 2005: 4.

Austin, J. L. *How To Do Things With Words.* Oxford: Clarendon Press, 1962.

Babuscio, Jack. 'Camp and the Gay Sensibility'. In *Gays and Film.* Ed. Richard Dyer. London and New York: Zoetrope, 1984: 40–57.

Barthes, Roland. *A Lover's Discourse: Fragments.* London: Vintage Classics, 2002: 126.

Battista, Judy. 'ABC Manages to Put NFL in a "Desperate" Situation'. *New York Times.* 17 November 2004: D1, D4.

Beauvoir, Simone de. *The Second Sex.* 1949. Trans. H.M. Parshley; reprinted London: Vintage, 1997.

Belkin, Lisa. 'Opt-Out Revolution'. *New York Times Magazine.* 26 October 2003: 42.

Benstock, Shari. 'Afterword: The New Woman's Fiction'. In *Chick Lit: The New Woman's Fiction.* Eds. Suzanne Ferris and Mallory Young. London: Routledge, 2005: 253–256.

Bergman, David. Ed. *Camp Grounds: Style and Homosexuality.* Amherst: University of Massachusetts Press, 1993.

Blachford, Gregg. 'Male Dominance and the Gay World'. In *The Making of the Modern Homosexual.* Ed. Kenneth Plummer. London: Hutchinson, 1981: 184–210.

Blum, David. 'Married, With Implants'. *New York Sun.* 1 October 2004a: 19.

Blum, David. 'How HBO Lost Its Groove'. *New York Sun.* 16 November 2004b: 18.

Booth, William. 'A Hot Property: For the Cast, Creator – and Fans – of *Desperate Housewives*, the Suburbs are the Place to be'. *Washington Post.* 14 November 2004: N01.

Bordo, Susan. *Unbearable Weight: Feminism, Western Culture, and The Body.* Berkeley: University of California Press, 2003.

Brehm, Sharon S. *Intimate Relationships.* Third edition. New York: McGraw Hill, 2001.

Brenner, Johanna. 'The Best of Times, The Worst of Times: Feminism in the United States'. In *Mapping the Women's Movement: Feminist Politics and Social Transformation in the North.* Ed. Monica Threlfall. London: Verso, 1996: 17–72.

Brooks, Peter. *Troubling Confessions: Speaking Guilt in Law and Literature.* Chicago: University of Chicago Press, 2000.

Brunsdon, Charlotte. *Screen Tastes: Soap Opera to Satellite Dishes.* London and New York: Routledge, 1997.

Burke, Kenneth. *On Symbols and Society.* Ed. J. R. Gusfield. Chicago: University of Chicago Press, 1989.

Butler, Judith. *Gender Trouble: Feminism and the Subversion of Identity.* London and New York: Routledge, 1990; reprinted 1999.

Butler, Judith. 'Imitation and Gender Insubordination'. In *Inside/Out: Lesbian Theories, Gay Theories.* Ed. Diana Fuss. London and New York: Routledge, 1991: 13–31.

Butler, Judith. *Bodies that Matter: On the Discursive Limits of 'Sex'.* London and New York: Routledge, 1993.

Butler, Judith. 'Contingent Foundations: Feminism and the Question of "Postmodernism"'. In *Feminist Contentions: A Philosophical Exchange.* Eds. Seyla Benhabib, Judith Butler, Drucilla Cornell and Nancy Fraser. New York and London: Routledge, 1995: 35–58.

Butler, Judith. *The Psychic Life of Power: Theories in Subjection.* Stanford: Stanford University Press, 1997.

Butler, Judith. *Antigone's Claim: Kinship Between Life and Death.* New York: Columbia University Press, 2000.

Butler, Judith. *Precarious Life: The Power of Mourning and Violence.* London: Verso, 2004.

Carlson, Tucker. 'Devil May Care'. *Talk Magazine.* September 1999: xxx.

Carter, Bill. 'Desperate Housewives Stirs ABC's Comeback Hopes'. *New York Times.* 5 October 2004: C1, C3.

Caughie, John. *Television Drama: Realism, Modernism, and British Culture.* New York: Oxford University Press, 2000.

Chambers, Samuel A. 'Telepistemology of the Closet; Or, the Queer Politics of *Six Feet Under*'. *Journal of American Culture.* 26. 2003: 24–41.

Chambers, Samuel A. 'Revisiting the Closet: Reading Sexuality in *Six Feet Under*'. In *Reading Six Feet Under: TV To Die For.* Eds. Kim Akass and Janet McCabe. London: I.B. Tauris, 2005: 174–188.

BIBLIOGRAPHY

Chambers, Samuel A. 'Heteronormativity and *The L Word*: From a Politics of Representation to a Politics of Norms'. In *Reading The L Word: Outing Contemporary Television*. Eds. Kim Akass and Janet McCabe. London: I.B. Tauris, 2006: 81–98.

Chodorow, Nancy. *The Reproduction of Mothering*. Berkeley: University of California Press, 1978.

Coates, Jennifer. Ed. *Language and Gender: A Reader*. Oxford: Blackwell, 1998.

Collins, Jim. *Architectures of Excess: Cultural Life in the Information Age*. London: Routledge, 1995.

Connell, R. W. *Masculinities*. Second edition. Cambridge: Polity Press, 2005.

Cook, Pam. 'Duplicity in Mildred Pierce'. In *Women in Film Noir*. Second edition. Ed. E. Ann Kaplan. London: bfi publishing, 1998: 69–80.

Cott, Nancy F. *The Bonds of Womanhood: 'Women's Sphere'. In New England, 1780 – 1835*. Second edition. London: Yale University Press, 1997.

Coward, Rosalind. *Our Treacherous Hearts: Why Women Let Men Get Their Way*. London: Faber and Faber, 1993.

Crook, John. 'The Dirty Laundry Piles Up in Suburban Tale'. *Los Angeles Times*. TV Times. 3–9 October 2004: 3.

Dally, Ann. *Inventing Motherhood: The Consequences of an Ideal*. New York: Shocken Books, 1982.

Dellasega, Cheryl and Charisse Nixon. *Girl Wars: 12 Strategies That Will End Female Bullying*. New York: Simon & Schuster/Fireside, 2003.

Dickerson, John. 'What the President Reads'. *Time*. 17 January 2005: 45.

Doane, Mary Ann. *The Desire to Desire: The Woman's Film of the 1940s*. Basingstoke: Macmillan, 1988.

Douglas, Susan J. *Where The Girls Are: Growing Up Female in the Mass Media*. New York: Random, 1995.

Douglas, Susan J. and Meredith W. Michaels. *The Mommy Myth: The Idealization of Motherhood and How It Has Undermined Women*. New York: Free Press, 2004.

Dow, Bonnie J. *Prime-time Feminism: Television, Media Culture and the Women's Movement Since 1970*. Philadelphia: University of Pennsylvania Press, 1996.

Dowd, Maureen. *Bushworld: Enter at Your Own Risk*. New York: Putnam, 2004.

Dunlap, David W. 'Gay Parents Ease Into Suburbia: For the First Generation, Car Pools and Soccer Games'. *New York Times*. 16 May 1996. SC.

Dyer, Richard. 'It's Being So Camp As Keeps Us Going'. In *The Culture of Queers*. Ed. Richard Dyer. London and New York: Routledge, 2004: 49–62.

Elliott, Michael. 'Men Want Change Too'. *Time*. 22 March 2004: 59.

Elliott, Stuart. 'Advertising'. *New York Times*. 26 November 2004: C2.

Faludi, Susan. *Backlash: The Undeclared War Against American Women*. New York: Crown Publishers, 1991; reprinted London: Vintage, 1992.

Farmer, Brett. *Spectacular Passions: Cinema, Fantasy, Gay Male Spectatorships.* Durham, NC: Duke University Press, 2000.

Fausto-Sterling, A. *Sexing the Body: Gender Politics and the Construction of Sexuality.* New York: Basic Books, 2000.

Fels, Anna. *Necessary Dreams: Ambition in Women's Changing Lives.* New York: Pantheon Books, 2004.

Flint, Joe. 'Angry NFL Slams ABC's Desperate Housewives Promo'. *Wall Street Journal.* 17 November 2004: B1, B2.

Foucault, Michel. *The Will to Knowledge. History of Sexuality. Volume 1.* Trans. Robert Hurley. London: Allen Lane, 1979; reprinted London: Penguin, 1998.

Foucault, Michel. *Discipline and Punish: The Birth of the Prison.* Trans. Alan Sheridan. London: Penguin, 1991.

Friedan, Betty. *The Feminine Mystique.* London: Penguin, 1963; reprinted 1965; reprinted 1992.

Friedman, James. Ed. *Reality Squared: Televisual Discourse on the Real.* New Brunswick, NJ: Rutgers University Press, 2002.

Gammel, Irene. 'Introduction'. In *Confessional Politics: Women's Sexual Self-Representations in Life Writing and Popular Media.* Ed. Irene Gammel. Carbondale: Southern Illinois University Press, 1999: 1–10.

Gammon, Lorraine and Margaret Marshment, Eds. *The Female Gaze: Women as Viewers of Popular Culture.* London: Women's Press, 1988.

Gamson, Joshua. 'Death Becomes Them'. *The American Prospect.* 2 July 2001: 36.

Gerhard, Jane. '*Sex and the City*: Carrie Bradshaw's Queer Postfeminism'. *Feminist Media Studies.* 5. 1. 2005: 37–49.

Gillis, Stacy and Rebecca Munford. *Feminism and Popular Culture: Explorations in Postfeminism.* London: I.B. Tauris, 2007.

Goodale, Gloria, 'What Real Women Think of *Desperate Housewives*'. *Christian Science Monitor.* 29 October 2004: 12.

Goodman, Ellen and Patricia O'Brien. *I Know Just What You Mean: The Power Of Friendship In Women's Lives.* New York: Simon & Schuster/Fireside, 2000.

Gopalan, Nisha. 'Edie: Nicollette Sheridan'. *Entertainment Weekly.* 25 March 2005: 26.

Greer, Germaine. *The Female Eunuch.* St Albans: Granada Publishing, 1971.

Greer, Germaine. *The Whole Woman.* London: Doubleday, 1999.

Guthrie, Marisa. 'Both Funny and Sudsy'. *New York Vue (Daily News).* 5 October 2004: 3.

Halperin, David M. *Saint Foucault: Toward a Gay Hagiography.* Oxford: Oxford University Press, 1995.

Haralovich, Mary Beth. 'Sitcoms and Suburbs: Positioning the 1950s Homemaker'. In *Private Screenings.* Eds. Lynn Spigel and Denise Mann. Minneapolis: University of Minnesota Press, 1992: 111–142.

Haralovich, Mary Beth. 'Positioning the 1950s Homemaker'. In *Critiquing the Sitcom: A Reader*. Ed. Joanne Morreale. New York: Syracuse University Press, 2003: 69–85.

Harbutt, Fraser J. *The Cold War Era*. Oxford: Blackwell, 2002.

Harris, Paul. 'TV Sex is New Battle Battleground of Divided US'. *The Observer*. 14 November 2004: 25.

Hatty, Suzanne E. *Masculinities, Violence, Culture*. Thousand Oaks, CA and London: Sage Publications, 2000.

Henry, Astrid. 'Orgasms and Empowerment: Sex and the City and Third Wave Feminism'. In *Reading Sex and the City: Critical Approaches*. Eds. Kim Akass and Janet McCabe. London: I.B. Tauris, 2004: 65–82.

Herzog, Charlotte. '"Powder Puff" Promotion: The Fashion-Show-in-the-Film'. In *Fabrications: Costume and the Female Body*. Eds. Jane Gaines and Charlotte Herzog. London and New York: Routledge, 1990: 134–159.

Heywood, Leslie and Jennifer Drake. 'Introduction'. In *Third Wave Agenda: Being Feminist, Doing Feminism*. Eds. Heywood and Drake. Minneapolis: University of Minnesota Press, 2003: 1–24.

Heywood, Leslie and Jennifer Drake. 'We Learn America Like a Script: Activism in the Third Wave; or, Enough Phantoms of Nothing'. In *Third Wave Agenda: Being Feminist, Doing Feminism*. Eds. Heywood and Drake. Minneapolis: University of Minnesota Press, 2003: 40–53.

Hollinger, Karen. 'Listening to the Female Voice in the Woman's Film'. *Film Criticism*. 16. 3. 1992: 34–52.

Hollows, Joanne. *Feminism, Femininity and Popular Culture*. Manchester: Manchester University Press, 2000.

Holston, Noel. 'Housewives in Desperate Need of Help'. *Newsday*. 5 December 2004: C22–C24.

hooks, bell. *Ain't I A Woman: Black Women and Feminism*. Boston: South End Press, 1981.

Irigaray, Luce. 'Women-Mothers, The Silent Substratum of the Social Order'. In *The Irigaray Reader*. Ed. Margaret Whitford. Oxford: Blackwell, 1991: 47–52.

Ivins, Molly and Lou Dubose. *Bushwhacked: Life in George W. Bush's America*. New York: Random House, 2003.

Ivy, Diana K. and Phil Backlund. *Genderspeak: Personal Effectiveness In Gender Communication*. Boston: McGraw Hill, 2004.

Jameson, Fredric. *Postmodernism, or, the Cultural Logic of Late Capitalism*. London: Verso, 1991.

Johnson, Fern L. 'Friendships Among Women: Closeness in Dialogue'. In *Gendered Relationships*. Eds. Julia Wood. Mountain View, CA: Mayfield Publishing, 1996: 79–94.

Johnson, Fern L. and Elizabeth J. Aries. 'The Talk of Women Friends'. *Women's Studies International Forum*. 6. 1983: 353–361; reprinted in *Language and Gender: A Reader*. Ed. Jennifer Coates. Oxford: Blackwell, 1998: 215–225.

Kaplan, E. Ann. *Motherhood and Representation: The Mother in Popular Culture and Melodrama*. London and New York: Routledge, 1992.

Kim, L. S. '"Sex and the Single Girl" in Postfeminism: The F Word on Television'. *Television New Media*. 2. 4. 2001: 319–334.

Kitman, Marvin. 'FCC Drops the Ball'. *Newsday*. 28 November 2004: C19 and C20.

Kleinhans, Chuck. 'Taking Out the Trash: Camp and the Politics of Parody'. In *The Politics and Poetics of Camp*. Ed. Moe Meyer. London and New York: Routledge, 1994: 182–201.

Knight, India. 'Happy to be Desperate'. *The Sunday Times*. News Review Section. 5 June 2005: 4.

Kozloff, Sarah. *Invisible Storytellers: Voice-Over Narration in American Fiction Film*. Berkeley and Los Angeles: University of California Press, 1988.

Krum, Sharon. 'America's Mom'. *The Guardian*. 20 January 2005: G2 10–11.

Lawrence, D.H. *Lady Chatterly's Lover*. London: Wordsworth Editions Ltd, 2005.

Lehman, Peter. Ed. *Masculinity: Bodies, Movies, Culture*. London and New York: Routledge, 2001.

Lisotta, Christopher. 'Marc Cherry's Winning Formula'. *Television Week*. 23 December 2004: 14.

Logan, Michael. 'The Moral of the Story?' *TV Guide*. 7 November 2004: 8.

Lotz, Amanda D. 'Postfeminist Television Criticism: Rehabilitating Critical Terms and Identifying Postfeminst Attributes'. *Feminist Media Studies*. 1.1. 2001: 105–121.

Lowry, Brian. 'Dirt and Soap Mix in Steamy 'Wives'. *Variety*. 27 September 2004: 87.

Lynch, Frederick R. 'Nonghetto Gays: An Ethnography of Suburban Homosexuals'. In *Gay Culture in America*. Ed. Gilbert Herdt. Boston: Beacon Press, 1992: 165–201.

Mabry, A. Rochelle. 'About a Girl: Female Subjectivity and Sexuality in Contemporary "Chick" Culture'. In *Chick Lit: The New Woman's Fiction*. Eds. Suzanne Ferris and Mallory Young. London: Routledge, 2005: 191–207.

MacDonald, Myra. *Representing Women: Myths of Femininity in the Popular Media*. London: Arnold, 1995.

MacKinnon, Kenneth, *Representing Men: Maleness and Masculinity in the Media*. London: Arnold, 2003.

Macko, Lia and Kerry Rubin. *Midlife Crisis at 30: How the Stakes Have Changed for a New Generation – And What to Do about It*. USA: Rodale Books, 2004.

Malcom, Shawna. 'Wicked Good'. *TV Guide*. 7 November 2004: 31–32, 34, 36.

Martel, Ned. 'Anxious to See How It Ends? So Are the Writers'. *New York Times*. 14 March 2005: E1, E7.

Marwick, Arthur. *The Sixties: Cultural Transformation in Britain, France, Italy and the United States, 1958–1974*. Oxford: Oxford University Press, 1998.

May, Elaine Tyler. *Homeward Bound: American Families in the Cold War Era*. Second edition. New York: Basic Books, 1988.

McDowell, Linda and Joanne P. Sharp Eds. *Space, Gender, Knowledge: Feminist Readings*. London: Arnold, 1997.

McRobbie, Angela. 'Postfeminism and Popular Culture'. In *Feminist Media Studies*. 4. 3. 2004: 255–264.

Medhurst, Andy. 'That Special Thrill: Brief Encounter, Homosexuality and Authorship'. *Screen*. 32. 2. 1991: 197–208.

Medhurst, Andy. 'Camp'. In *Lesbian and Gay Studies: A Critical Introduction*. Eds. Andy Medhurst and Sally R. Munt. London: Cassell, 1997: 274–293.

Mellencamp, Patricia. 'Situation Comedy, Feminism, and Freud: Discourses of Gracie and Lucy'. In *Feminist Television Criticism*. Eds. Charlotte Brunsdon, Julie D'Acci and Lynn Spigel. Oxford: Oxford University Press, 1997: 60–73.

Mertes, Cara. '"There's No Place Like Home": Women and Domestic Labour', in *Dirt and Domesticity: Constructions of the Feminine: June 12th–August 14th 1992*, Whitney Museum of American Art at Equitable Center. New York, NY: The Museum 1992.

Meyer, Moe. 'Introduction'. In *The Politics and Poetics of Camp*. Ed. Moe Meyer. London and New York: Routledge, 1994: 1–22.

Miller, D.A. 'Sontag's Urbanity'. In *The Lesbian and Gay Studies Reader*. Eds. Henry Abelove, Michele Aina Barale and David M. Halperin. London and New York: Routledge, 1993.

Miller, Mark Crispin. *The Bush Dylexicon: Observations on a National Disorder*. New York: W. W. Norton, 2001.

Miller, Mark Crispin. *Cruel and Unusual: Bush/Cheney's New World Order*. New York: W. W. Norton, 2004.

Millet, Kate. *Sexual Politics*. London: Virago, 1970.

Modleski, Tania. *Feminism Without Women: Culture and Criticism in a 'Postfeminist' Age*. London and New York: Routledge, 1991.

Moorti, Sujata and Karen Ross. 'Reality Television: Fairy Tale or Feminist Nightmare?' *Feminist Media Studies*. 4. 2. 2004: 203–231.

Moseley, Rachel. 'Glamorous Witchcraft: Gender and Magic in Teen Film and Television'. *Screen*. 43. 4. 2002a: 403–422.

Moseley, Rachel and Jacinda Read. 'Having it Ally: Popular Television (Post)Feminism'. In *Feminist Media Studies*. 2. 2. 2002: 231–249.

Mulvey, Laura. 'Visual Pleasure and Narrative Cinema'. *Screen*. 16. 3. 1975: 6–18.

Murray, Susan and Laurie Ouellette. Eds. *Reality TV: Remaking Television Culture*. New York: New York University Press, 2004.

Negra, Diane and Yvonne Tasker. 'In Focus: Postfeminism and Contemporary Media Studies'. *Cinema Journal*. 44. 2. 2005: 107–110.

Nelson, Deborah. *Pursuing Privacy in Cold War America*. New York: Columbia University Press, 2002.

Nelson, Robin. '*Ally McBeal*'. In *The Television Genre Book*. Ed. Glen Creeber. London: bfi publishing, 2001: 45.

Ogden, Annagret S. *The Great American Housewife*. Westport, CT: Greenwood Press, 1986.

Owen, David. 'Work Marriage'. *The Atlantic*. February 1987: 22.

Paglia, Camille. *Vamps and Tramps: New Essays*. London: Penguin, 1995.

Peskowitz, Miriam. *The Truth Behind the Mommy Wars: Who Decides What Makes a Good Mother?* CA: Seal Press, 2005.

Phillips, Kevin. *American Dynasty: Aristocracy, Fortune, and the Politics of Deceit in the House of Bush*. New York: Viking, 2004.

Pipher, Mary. *Reviving Ophelia: Saving The Selves Of Adolescent Girls*. New York: Ballantine Books, 1994.

Place, Janey. 'Women in Film Noir'. In *Women in Film Noir*. Second edition. Ed. E. Ann Kaplan. London: bfi publishing, 1998: 47–68.

Poniewozik, James, 'Desperate Straits: the Days of Our Wives'. *Time*. 164. 4 October 2004: 20.

Powers, John. *Sore Winners (And the Rest of Us) in George Bush's America*. New York: Doubleday, 2004.

Press, Andrea. *Women Watching Television: Gender, Class, and Generation in the American Television Experience*. Philadelphia: University of Pennsylvania Press, 1991.

Press, Joy. 'This Is Your Fall Season on Crack'. *Village Voice*. 13 October 2004: 21.

Probyn, Elspeth. 'New Traditionalism and Post-Feminism: TV Does the Home'. In *Feminist Television Criticism*. Eds. Charlotte Brunsdon, Julie D'Acci and Lynn Spigel. Oxford: Oxford University Press, 1997: 126–137.

Rich, Frank. 'The Great Indecency Hoax'. *New York Times*. Section 2. 28 November 2004: 1, 17.

Roberto, Karen A. and Jean Pearson Scott. 'Friendships of Older Men and Women: Exchange Patterns and Satisfaction'. *Psychology and Aging*. 1. 1986: 103–109.

BIBLIOGRAPHY

Robertson, Pamela. *Guilty Pleasures: Feminist Camp from Mae West to Madonna.* London: I.B. Tauris, 1996.

Robinson, Sally. '"Emotional Constipation" and the Power of Damned Masculinity: Deliverance and the Paradoxes of Male Liberation'. In *Masculinity: Bodies, Movies, Culture.* Ed. Peter Lehman. London and New York: Routledge, 2001: 133–147.

Roiphe, Katie. *The Morning After: Sex, Fear, and Feminism.* Boston: Little, Brown, 1995.

Rosenfeld, Lawrence B. and W. Leslie Kendrick. 'Choosing to be Open: An Empirical Investigation of Subjective Reasons for Self-Disclosing'. *Western Journal of Speech Communication.* 48. 1984: 326–343.

Rowbotham, Sheila, Lynne Segal and Hilary Wainwright. *Beyond the Fragments: Feminism and the Making of Socialism.* London: Merlin Press, 1979.

Rowe, Kathleen. *The Unruly Woman: Gender and the Genres of Laughter.* Austin: University of Texas Press, 1995.

Rutherford, Jonathan. *Men's Silences: Predicaments in Masculinity.* London and New York: Routledge, 1992.

Schneider, Michael. 'Get Me Some Housewives, Dammit!' *Variety.* 18 October 2004: 17.

Schrader, Paul. 'Notes on Film Noir'. In *Film Noir Reader.* Eds. Alain Silver and James Ursini. New York: Limelight Editions, 1996: 53–63.

Sedgwick, Eve Kosofsky. *The Coherence of Gothic Conventions.* New York: Methuen, 1986.

Seltzer, Mark. *Serial Killers: Death and Life in American Wound Culture.* New York and London: Routledge, 1998.

Shearin Karres, Erika V. *Mean Chicks, Cliques And Dirty Tricks: A Real Girl's Guide To Getting Through The Day With Smarts And Style.* Avon, MA: Adams Media Corporation, 2004.

Shorto, Russell. 'What's Their Real Problem With Gay Marriage? (It's the Gay Part)'. *The New York Times.* 19 June 2005: 34–41, 64–67.

Siegel, Deborah L. 'The Legacy of the Personal: Generating Theory in Feminism's Third Wave'. *Hypatia: Special Issue on Third Wave Feminism.* 12. 3 Summer 1997: 46–75.

Silverman, Kaja. *The Acoustic Mirror: The Female Voice in Psychoanalysis and Cinema.* Bloomington: Indiana University Press, 1988.

Simmons, Rachel. *Odd Girl Out: The Hidden Culture Of Aggression In Girls.* New York: Harcourt, 2002.

Sloane, Judy. 'Desperate Housewives'. *TV Zone.* 184. February 2005: 84, 90–91.

Sommers, Christina Hoff. *Who Stole Feminism? How Women Have Betrayed Women.* New York: Simon and Schuster, 1994.

Sontag, Susan. 'Notes on Camp'. In *A Susan Sontag Reader.* Ed. Susan Sontag. London: Penguin, 1982.

Spigel, Lynn. 'From Domestic Space to Outer Space: The 1960s Fantastic Family Sitcom'. In *Close Encounters*. Eds. Constance Penley, Elisabeth Lyon, Lynn Spigel and Janet Bergstrom. Minneapolis: University of Minnesota Press, 1991: 205–235.

Spigel, Lynn. *Welcome To The Dreamhouse: Popular Media and Post-War Suburbs*. Durham, NC: Duke University Press, 2001.

Stacey, Jackie. *Star Gazing: Hollywood Cinema and Female Spectatorship*. London and New York: Routledge, 1994.

Stam, Robert, Robert Burgoyne and Sandy Flitterman-Lewis. *New Vocabularies in Film Semiotics*. London and New York: Routledge, 1992.

Stanley, Alessandra. 'Old-Time Sexism Suffuses New Season'. *New York Times*. 1 October 2004: E1, E24.

Steinem, Gloria. 'Foreword'. In *To Be Real: Telling the Truth and Changing the Face of Feminism*. Ed. Rebecca Walker. New York: Doubleday, 1995: xiii–xxviii.

Tanenbaum, Leora. *Slut! Growing Up Female With A Bad Reputation*. New York: Perennial, 2000.

Thornham, Sue and Tony Purvis. *Television Drama: Theories and Identities*. Basingstoke: Palgrave Macmillan, 2005.

Tincknell, Estella. *Mediating the Family: Gender, Culture and Representation*. New York: Hodder Arnold, 2005.

Vary, Adam. 'Marcia Cross: Desperate Rumors'. *The Advocate*. 15 March 2005: 46–50, 52–53.

Walker, Rebecca. 'Introduction'. In *To Be Real: Telling the Truth and Changing the Face of Feminism*. Ed. Walker. New York: Doubleday, 1995: xxix–xl.

Wallis, Claudia. 'The Case for Staying Home'. *Time*. 22 March 2004: 50–59.

Walters, Susan. *Material Girls: Making Sense of Feminist Cultural Theory*. Berkeley: University of California Press, 1995.

Walters, Suzanna Danuta. *Lives Together, Worlds Apart: Mothers and Daughters in Popular Culture*. Berkeley: University of California Press, 1992.

Warner, Judith. 'The Myth of the Perfect Mother: Why It Drives Real Women Crazy.' *Newsweek*. 21 February 2005: 42–49.

Weinraub, Bernard. 'How Desperate Women Saved Desperate Writer'. *New York Times*. 23 October 2004: B7, B12.

Wheatley, Helen. 'Rooms Within Rooms: *Upstairs Downstairs* and the Studio Costume Drama of the 1970s'. In *ITV Cultures: Independent Television Over Fifty Years*. Eds. Catherine Johnson and Rob Turnock. London: Open University Press, 2005: 143–158.

Whitehead, Stephen M. *Men and Masculinities: Key Themes and Directions*. Cambridge: Polity Press, 2002.

Whitfield, Stephen J. *The Culture of the Cold War*. Second edition. Baltimore: The Johns Hopkins University Press, 1991.

BIBLIOGRAPHY

Williams, Andrew 'What Is...Marcia Cross Made Of?' *Metro*. 8 June 2005: 27.

Williams, Joan. *Unbending Gender: Why Family and Work Conflict and What to do About it*. Oxford: Oxford University Press, 2000.

Williams, Raymond. 'Drama in a Dramatised Society'. In *Raymond Williams on Television: Selected Writings*. Ed. Alan O'Connor. London and New York: Routledge, 1989: 3–13.

Wiseman, Rosalind. *Queen Bees And Wannabees: Helping Your Daughter Survive Cliques, Gossip, Boyfriends And Other Realities Of Adolescence*. New York: Three Rivers Press, 2003.

Wittstock, Melinda. 'Mothers of Suburbia'. *The Observer*. Review Section. 7 November 2004: 7.

Wolf, Naomi. *The Beauty Myth: How Images of Women Are Used Against Women*. London: Vintage, 1991.

Wolf, Naomi. *Fire With Fire: The New Female Power and How it Will Change the 21st Century*. London: Chatto & Windus, 1993.

Wolf, Naomi. *Misconceptions: Truth, Lies, And The Unexpected On The Journey To Motherhood*. New York: Anchor Books, 2001.

Wolfe, Tom. *I Am Charlotte Simmons*. New York: Farrar, Strauss, and Giroux, 2004.

Wollstonecraft, Mary. *Maria, or the Wrongs of a Woman*, New York: W.W. Norton, 1994.

Yalom, Marilyn. *A History of the Wife*. New York: HarperCollins, 2001.

Zeman, Ned. 'Bed, Burbs, and Beyond'. *Vanity Fair* (US). 537. May 2005: 197–205, 264–266.

Zeman, Ned. 'Bed, Burbs and Beyond'. *Vanity Fair* (UK). May 2005: 108–115, 182–184.

Web citations

Anon. 'About the Show': http://www.abc.go.com/primetime/desperate/about.html

Anon. 'And The Plot Thickens'. Zap2It.com. 9 February 2005: http://tvbb.zap2it.com/showflat.php?Cat=&Board=desperate&Number=181864&page=0&view=collapsed&sb=3&o=&fpart=2

Anon. '*Desperate Housewives*: Insulting but Fun'. KATC3. 3 October 2004: http://www.katc.com/Global/story.asp?S=2380431&nav=EyAzRZoq

Anon. '*Desperate Housewives* Marcia Cross Denies Lesbian Slur'. FemaleFirst.co.uk. 10 February 2005: http://femalefirst.co.uk/entertainment/28602004.htm

Anon. 'Housewives, Sellers Lead Emmy Pack'. CNN.com. 30 August 2005: http://www.cnn.com/2005/SHOWBIZ/TV/07/14/emmy.nominations/index.html

Anon. 'Marcia Cross: I'm Not Gay'. Movie/TV News. 10 February 2005: http://www.imdb.com/news/wenn/2005–02–10

Anderson, Jessica. 'The Depravity of *Desperate Housewives*'. Concerned Women for America. 11 August 2005: http://www.cwfa.org/articles/8697/BLI/misc/

Akass, Kim. 'Throwing the Baby Out with the Bath Water: Miranda and the Myth of Maternal Instinct on *Sex and the City*'. Feminist Television Studies: The Case of HBO. Ed. Lisa Johnson. *The Scholar and Feminist Online*. Fall 2004: http://www.barnard.edu/sfonline/hbo/akass_01.htm

Arnold, Abby. 'The Rhetoric of Motherhood'. The Mothers Movement Online. December 2003: http://www.mothersmovement.org/features/rhetoric_motherhood/rhetoric_motherhood.htm

Associate Press. 'Suburbia Sizzles in *Housewives*'. MSNBC.com. 30 September 2004: http://msnbc.msn.com/id/6133690/

Baby Name Wizard: http://babynamewizard.com/namevoyager/lnv0105.html

Blyth, Myrna. 'Move Over, Lifetime'. *The National Review Online*. 17 November 2004: http://www.nationalreview.com/blyth/blyth200411170823.asp

Bozell, Brent. 'Boycotts and Catty Girls'. Townhall.com. 22 October 2004: http://www.townhall.com/opinion/columns/brentbozell/2004/10/22/13419.html

Bush, Laura. 'Laura Bush's Stand-Up Act: White House Correspondents' Dinner Transcript': http://politicalhumor.about.com/od/laurabush/a/laurabushcomedy.htm

Carroll, Larry. 'Hobnobbing with the *Housewives*'. FilmStew.com. 29 September 2004: http://www.filmstew.com/Content/Article.asp?ContentID=9771&Pg=1

Cayse, Allison. 'Feminism on the Small Screen'. Research Communications (Ohio University). 22 June 2005: http://news.research.ohiou.edu/studentresearch/index.php?item=131

Crawford, Krysten. '*Housewives* Loses Some Sponsors'. CNN Money.com. 12 October 2004: http://money.cnn.com/2004/10/19/news/fortune500/desperate

D'Arby, Russell. 'More *Desperate Housewives?* Laura Bush to Guest on Hit Show Next Season'. *The Swift Report*. 23 May 2005: http://swiftreport.blogs.com/news/2005/05/more_desperate_.html

Dougherty, Joseph. www.thirdstory.com/thirtysomething/misc/interview2.htm

Feeney, Matt. 'The Voice of *Desperate Housewives*'. Slate. 23 May 2005: http://www.slate.com/id/2119399/

Fields, Suzanne. 'What do "Desperate Housewives" want?' townhall.com: http://www.townhall.com/opinion/columns/suzannefields/2004/11/29/13797.html

Freydkin, Donna. 'I'm Single and Straight, Cross says'. *USA Today*. 9 February 2005: http://www.usatoday.com/life/people/2005-02-09-cross_x.htm

BIBLIOGRAPHY

Frutkin, A.J. 'Cherry on Top'. *Media Week*. 14. 22 November 2004. Communication and Mass Media Complete. Accessed Rowan University. Glassboro, NJ.

Giantis, K. 'Marcia Cross: Yep, I'm Not Gay'. MSN Entertainment. 9 February 2005: http://entertainment.msn.com/celebs/article.aspx?news=181071 (only accessible through http://www.google.com/)

Gilbert, Matthew. 'With Housewives, Dysfunction is Delightful'. Boston.com. 2 October 2004: http://www.boston.com/ae/tv/articles/2004/10/02/with_housewives_dysfunction_is_delightful/?rss_id=Boston%20Globe%20--%20Living%20/%20Arts%20News

Glaister, Dan. 'Wives or Sluts? US Viewers in Love-Hate Match with TV Hit'. *Guardian Unlimited*. 15 January 2005: http://www.guardian.co.uk/international/story/0,,1390995,00.html

Goldsmith, Janet. 'Lessons from America'. *Guardian Unlimited*. 11 July 2005: http://media.guardian.co.uk/advertising/story/0,,1525520,00.html

Goodman, Ellen. 'The Truths of *Desperate Housewives*'. *Washington Post*. 20 November 2004: A19; available at: http://www.washingtonpost.com/wp-dyn/articles/A64033-2004Nov19.html

Greer, Germaine. 'Haunted by the Ghost of Martha Stewart,' *The Guardian*. 3 January 2005: http://arts.guardian.co.uk/news/story/0,11711,1382666,00.html

Guthrie, Marisa. 'ABC Desperately Loves "Housewives"'. *New York Daily News*. 21 October 2004: http://www.nydailynews.com/entertainment/story/244450p209497c.html

Havrilesky, Heather. 'I Like To Watch'. Salon. 25 October 2004: http://archive.salon.com/ent/tv/review/2004/10/25/i_like/

Jones, Jonathan. 'Arnolfini Portrait: Jan Van Eyck (1434)'. *The Guardian*. 15 April 2000. http://www.nationalgallery.org.uk.

Jones, Wenzel. 'Desperate But Not Serious'. *The Advocate*. 923. 28 September 2004. Database accessed Rowan University. Glassboro, NJ. Academic Search Premier, Accession Number 14585467.

Lo, Malinda. 'Bad Bi Boys and *Desperate Housewives*'. AfterElton.com. 2 May 2005: http://afterelton.com/TV/2005/5/housewives.html

McFadden, Kay. '*Desperate Housewives* is a Wicked Pleasure'. *The Seattle Times*. 1 October 2004: http://seattletimes.nwsource.com/html/artsentertainment/2002050544_kay01.html

Mayhew, Betty. 'The Media and Postmodernism'. Society and Culture Association: http://hsc.csu.edu.au/pta/scansw/media.htm#anchor66244

Negra, Diane. '"Quality Postfeminism?" *Sex and the Single Girl* on HBO'. *Genders Journal*. 39. 2004: http://www.genders.org/g39/g39_negra.html

Noah, Timothy. 'Prexy Sks Wrk Wf: Condoleeza Rice's Promotion Creates a Void'. *Slate*. 17 November 2004: http://slate.msn.com/id/2109876/

Oldenburg, Ann. 'From Domestic to "Desperate"'. *USA Today*. 1 October 2004. E1

Orenstein, Catherine. 'Housewife Wars'. *Ms.* magazine. Spring 2005: http://www.msmagazine.com/spring2005/housewifewars.asp

Peterson, Karla. 'Typing in Stereo: Shows Sound Good to Real Housewives'. *SignOnSanDiego.com*. 18 October 2004: http://www.signonsandiego.com/news/features/peterson/20041018-9999-1c18karla.html

Peyser, Marc and David Jefferson D. 'Sex and the Suburbs'. *Newsweek* 29 November 2004: http://www.msnbc.msn.com/id/6542185/site/newsweek/

Potts, Kimberley. 'Advertisers Not "Desperate"'. E Online. 20 October 2004: http://www.eonline.com/News/Items/0,1,15181,00.html?tnews

Pozner, Jennifer L. and Jennifer Seigel. '*Desperate Housewives*: Do We Hate It or Secretly Love It? The Debate Rages On'. *Ms.* Spring 2005: http://www.msmagazine.com/spring2005/desperatehousewives.asp

Schriefer, Amy. 'We've Only Just Begun: Translating Third Wave Theory into Third Wave Activism'. The Laughing Medusa: http://www.gwu.edu/~medusa/thirdwave.html

Slan, Heidi. 'Publicist's Statement' on Behalf of Marcia Cross'. Advocate.com. 10 February 2005: http://www.advocate.com/news_detail_ektid02779.asp

Stevens, Dana. 'The Good Wife: According to *Desperate Housewives*, Most Women Lead Lives of Quiet Desperation'. Slate. 4 October 2004: http://www.slate.com/id/2107693/

Susman, Gary. 'Cross Words'. *Entertainment Weekly*. 9 February 2005: http://www.ew.com/ew/report/0,6115,1026117_3_0_,00.html

Tapper, Jake. 'A 'Major League Asshole': In an Embarrassing Gaffe, George W. Bush Insults a *New York Times* Reporter'. *Salon*. 4 September 2000: http://archive.salon.com/politics/feature/2000/09/04/cuss_word/

Traister, Rebecca. 'Our Favorite Housewife'. *Salon.com*. 23 April 2005: http://www.salon.com/ent/feature/2005/04/23/huffman/index.html

Tucker, Judith Stadtman. 'The New Future of Motherhood'. The Mothers Movement Online. May 2005: http://www.mothersmovement.org/features/mhoodpapers/new_future/0505_1.htm

Tucker, Judith Stadtman. 'Doing Differance: Motherhood, gender and the stories we live by'. The Mother's Movement Online, September 2005: http://www.mothersmovement.org/features/mhoodpapers/printpages/doing-difference.htm

Vary, Adam B. 'Marcia Cross: Desperate Rumors'. *The Advocate*. 15 March 2005: http://www.findarticles.com/p/articles/mi_m1589/is_2005_March_15/ai_n13610510

Warn, Sarah. 'The Outing of Marcia Cross'. *AfterEllen.com*. 8 February: 2005b: http://www.afterellen.com/People/2005/2/marciacross.html

Warn, Sarah. '*Desperate Housewives* Outs Gay Teen with a Kiss'. *AfterElton.com*. 21 February 2005a: http://www.afterelton.com/TV/2005/2/housewives.html

Weintraub, Joanne. 'Oprah Drops by to Visit Housewives'. *Milwaukee Journal Sentinel*. 3 February 2005: http://www.jsonline.com/enter/tvradio/feb05/298799.asp

Welsch, Edward. WHCA 2005 Annual Award Dinner. 3 May 2005: http://www.whca.net/whcadinner.html

Wikidepdia online encyclopaedia: http://en.wikipedia.org/wiki/Romantic_love

Wright, Joseph. 'He's Here, He's Queer??!! Tune in to it!' [comment thread], *PopPolitics*, 26 February 2005: http://poppolitics.com/archives/000114.html

'yU+ co Opens ABC's *Desperate Housewives*'. 12 November 2004. http://www.animationartist.com.

INDEX